French Social Theory

French Social Theory

Mike Gane

SAGE Publications
London • Thousand Oaks • New Delhi

First published 2003

SAGE Publications Ltd
6 Bonhill Street
London EC2A 4PU

SAGE Publications Inc
2455 Teller Road
Thousand Oaks, California 91320

SAGE Publications India Pvt Ltd
32, M-Block Market
Greater Kailash - I
New Delhi 110 048

British Library Cataloguing in Publication data

A catalogue record for this book is
available from the British Library

ISBN 0 7619 6830 X
0 7619 6831 8

Library of Congress control number available

Typeset by C&M Digital (P) Ltd., Chennai, India
Printed in Great Britain by Athenaeum Press, Gateshead

Contents

Preface

This book presents a new assessment of French social theory as it has developed over the last two hundred years and is an invitation to rethink some of the main concerns that have arisen out of this tradition. It is perhaps this tradition which is associated more than any other with terms like existentialism, structuralism, positivism, postmodernism and many others. And after all it is this tradition which has furnished terms such as altruism, anomie, hypertelia, as well as the word 'sociology'. The challenge of this book is that it suggests that in the longer perspective, those interpretations that relate current concerns of French thought simply and directly to Kant miss the great innovative period of French social thought from 1800–80. As the most acute observers have pointed out, behind modern French social theory stands French Marxist theory, and behind that stands Durkheimian and Maussian anthropology and sociology, and behind these stands Comtean theory and utopian socialism (see for example Dews, 1987: 244). Thus this account is not intended to be exhaustive, rather it has as its objective the aim of discussing social theory thematically and in a longer-term perspective, and in order to do this I have provided here a new reading of the contribution of the earlier cycle of theorising (cf. Ray, 1999; Shilling and Mellor, 2001).

French social theory

The thesis of this book is that the main lines of social theory wherever influenced by Comte and Durkheim, or Marx (and Weber), are variations on a common thematic established by the Saint-Simonians in the years 1815–30. On one side is the Comtean law of the three states with its emphasis on cultural modernity and the rise of science. On the other is the social evolutionary schema of patterns of class exploitation from feudalism to modern industry. The reference of this thematic is the paradoxical triumph and failure of the French Revolution of 1789 and the enigmatic social and political crisis that followed. The question has often been posed: When does the revolutionary period come to an end? And after the recent resurgence of right-wing political movements, the question is still on the table. This is because although the Revolution is famous for its republican Declaration of the Rights of Man and for the call for Equality, Liberty and Fraternity, all forms of radicalisation of these values lead to movements that go beyond democratic political forms to their substantive realisation. These utopian movements were also associated with a conception of liberty which promised to go beyond a metaphysical liberalism: liberty became defined as a freedom to act on the basis of adequate knowledge. There is therefore in the French tradition the possible opening to a radicalism, either of left or right, against democratic forms defined simply as 'bourgeois' or an alien feature of British or American cultures. Just as Comte's sociology and 'sociocracy' has influenced both left and right traditions, Durkheim's sociology inspired both left-wing socialists and social fascism. There are many reasons therefore why a study of the long French tradition is instructive today.

This book arranges the material into three cycles of social theory since 1800. It could well be suggested that the way I have grouped the material reflects a preference for a model of a cycle as ending in a phase of religious excess as a moment of disintegration. Another view would hold that this religious moment is indeed always the sign of an early point of a cycle. Again, yet another view would be that as I have concentrated on such a small sample of theorists, it is quite possible that the dominant social currents impelling theory might have a different appearance. These alternative views can be defended. Here I intend only to offer a reading of the major social theories of three epochs which aligns with two other periodisations. The first is that developed by Comte himself, since the periodisation I present is a continuation of the one he invented in founding sociology. The second is the political periodisation of the history of French society itself: the first period of unstable political forms from 1800–79, that is to the fall of the Second Empire, the second is the period of the Third Republic (1880–1940), and the third covers the period of the Fourth and Fifth Republics, to date. These two periodisations are also open to challenge, most evidently in the second case. It could be argued that the decisive break was the First World War. It could also be argued that there was a particularly turbulent phase in French history which lasted from the mid 1930s to the mid 1970s, and which is quite distinctive. These alternatives are plausible. Some of the conclusions I draw are an effect of the particular narrative structure which reflects the underlying thesis of my analysis. The way the analysis proceeds makes it clear that French theory has been reborn more than once. One of the important contributions of this study is to bring to light the complex ways in which such a tradition is renewed.

But what is *social theory*? In this book I take it to be that rather peculiar range of thought in the zone between literary and cultural theory through to sociology (and the social sciences) at one end and at the other that mode of philosophy which is oriented to social ontology, epistemology and ethics (see Lepenies, 1988). It might be called, in contrast to the two other cultures, a 'third culture' or 'third curriculum' (see Zizek, 2001, ch. 5; Serres and Latour, 1995: 184). I touch on but do not examine extensively adjoining domains of psychoanalysis, history, literature, philosophy and epistemology. Only very indirectly is the question of the relation of theory and practice considered. It is important to note that in France at the moment there is no general acceptance of the idea of 'theory' for a genre of writing as there is in the English-speaking cultures ('"theory" sounds strange to my French understanding' (Leclercle, 2001: 36)), even though French thinkers from Althusser and Baudrillard have written famous texts on 'theory'. Nor is there in France the radical distinction between structuralism and post-structuralism, modernism and postmodernism (see Descombes, in Yamamoto, 1998: 464), even though French theorists such as Lyotard wrote some of the defining texts of 'postmodernism'. Baudrillard, for example, recently suggested that 'if there is no overarching representation of the world which gives it a meaning, then there can't be a science either that would be the key to the whole story' ([1997] 1998a: 34). This book is an examination of a particular tradition which tried to challenge universal history with the wager of a single theoretical narrative.

Thus there is a paradox involved in writing this book. I regard myself, on the one hand, as having largely been formed by close involvement with French social theory and therefore not as a pure outsider. On the other hand, for French theorists today, 'French social theory' does not exist.

Remarks on the text

As I noted, this book does not attempt to provide an exhaustive discussion and this has meant that many important contributions are not assessed. The book discusses sects and schools of thought, but I have refrained from providing lists of their members. There are now many specialist reference works and studies of individual thinkers, but this work is not a synthesis of such materials. I have tried to discuss the main movements in thought through significant representative contributions. I hope to have chosen the least equivocal of them. Where possible I have checked translations against the French original, and in some cases made corrections where a theoretical point is at stake. The bibliography which could have been extremely extensive has been kept to essential references.

Acknowledgements

There are many people I should thank for help in one way or another in relation to this book. My acknowledgements have to be in three parts, for Comte-Littré, Durkheim-Mauss-Bataille and for Sartre-Baudrillard respectively.

I owe a huge debt to members of the Social Sciences Department at Loughborough University, as well as to many students, who have discussed the ideas developed here on French sociology and social theory. I have presented papers on Comte to university departments and at international conferences, and I would like to thank in particular those who contributed to discussions in 1994 at Lancaster University (especially Scott Lash and Larry Ray), a seminar in 1994 on Comte's sociology, at the Durkheim Studies Centre, Oxford, a paper at Leicester University (especially Terry Johnson, Sallie Westwood and David Ashton), a seminar held in 1998 at Sussex University (particularly Andrew Wernick, Charles Turner, Robert Fine and Peter Wagner), a Georges Canguilhem Conference held in London (particularly Paul Rabinow, François Delaporte and Michael Lynch) and an Economy and Society Conference in London (particularly Stephan Feuchwang). I owe a debt to the efficient editor of *Renaissance and Modern Studies*, Colin Heywood, and to many members of the editorial board of *Economy and Society*, the journal that organised the latter two conferences in London, especially Beverley Brown, Maxime Molyneux, Thomas Osborne, Ali Rattansi, Nikolas Rose, Grahame Thompson, Tony Woodiwiss, Frank Pearce, Talal Asad and Sami Zubaida. I also would like to thank some participants at the two Auguste Comte Bicentennial Colloques held in Paris in 1998 and to the participants of the Comte Colloque at Cerisy-la-Salle in 2001 (particularly Jean-Michel Berthelot, Michel Bourdeau, Juliette Grange, Johan Heilbron, Angele Kremer-Marietti, Annie Petit and Mary Pickering). I have drawn on the following papers: 'Comte's Inaugural Sociology', Centre for Critical Social Theory, Sussex University, 1998; 'L'état metaphysique et sa periodisation interne', Comte Colloque, Cerisy-la-Salle, 2001.

Since 1990 there have been a number of seminars and conferences associated with the British Centre for Durkheimian Studies at Oxford University, organised principally by W.F.S. Pickering. The first series of 1990 was published as *Debating Durkheim* (edited by W.F.S. Pickering and H. Martins, Routledge 1994) and this was followed by international conferences on Durkheim's key works. Conferences on the work of the Durkheimian school have included: 'Durkheim and Europe' and 'Le Malaise Social: La Fin de Siècle et Emile Durkheim'. The Centre in Oxford also houses the journal *Durkheim Studies*, published annually from 1995. I have presented a number of papers at the conferences and workshops held at Oxford, and would like to thank Bill Pickering, Herminio Martins, Willie Watts Miller, Josep Llobera, Ken Thompson, Sue Stedman Jones, Mike Hawkins, Nick Allen, Christie Davies, Bob Parkin, Wendy James, Geoffrey Walford, David Garland, Philip Mellor, Chris Shilling, Derek Robbins, Edward Tiryakian, Jack Hayward and Philippe Besnard. I also presented a paper at the International Colloque, organised by Charles-Henri Cuin on Durkheim's *Rules of Sociological Method* held in Bordeaux in 1995 and I would like to thank particularly Jean-Michel Berthelot, Phillipe Steiner, Alexandre Gofman, Jeffrey Alexander, Claude Javeau and Charles-Henri Cuin for their discussions.

With respect to my writing on the work of Sartre, Bataille, Canguilhem, Althusser, Foucault, Lyotard, Jean Baudrillard and other contemporary theorists, I would like to thank Chris Rojek, George Ritzer, Roy Boyne, Chris Turner, David Macey, Gary Genosko, Paul Hegarty, Georges Salemohamed, Simon Critchley, Andrew Wernick, Keith Ansell-Pearson, John Marks, Mariam Fraser, Marcus Doel, David Slater, Richard Smith, David Toews, Andrew Benjamin, Jean-Michel Berthelot, William Pawlett, William Merrin, Peter Gibbon, Nicholas Zurbrugg, Steve Brown and John Armitage.

Finally I would like to thank Monique Arnaud, Andrew Wernick, my nephew Nicholas Gane and readers at Sage, particularly Chris Rojek, for assistance with this project. Everyone mentioned helped me in one way or another to clarify and sharpen my ideas. I am responsible in the last instance for any mistakes of fact or interpretation.

M.G.
May, 2002

The First Cycle, 1800–1879

The Birth of Social Theory: Altruism

The most impressive event in the philosophic history of the nineteenth century was the founding of positive philosophy … aside from Cartesianism, there is nothing more important in the entire history of French philosophy. (Durkheim, 1962: 142)

1

The Post-revolutionary Void

> This permanent anarchy ... in the midst of which mankind is struggling seems to frighten some thinkers ... For us the problem is solved. (Bazard, [1828] 1972: 3)

Many French intellectuals, not all, in 1815 saw a society facing the challenge of reconstruction in a void, without models, without theories. Those who did not reject the aims of the revolution sought to understand it by resort to another revolution: a scientific revolution. They sought to construct a new society, morality and polity on the basis of a new knowledge created by the application of scientific methods. These ideas had their most significant outcome via Marxism which received, modified and disseminated the political vision of Saint-Simonian socialism. Relatively unknown today, a work by Saint-Amand Bazard clearly outlined the main lines of socialist theory. The first feminist journal *La Femme Libre* was produced by a group of Saint-Simonian women in the years 1832–4. The first cycle of social theory I examine in this book is broadly defined by the period from 1800 to 1879, that is by the post-Revolution generations that included Comte and Littré, who confronted French society as facing unprecedented problems of reconstruction from the First Empire to the Third Republic.

Contexts

Modern social theory knows well Hegel's dictum 'what is rational is actual; and what is actual is rational' (1952: 10). According to Althusser, this pronouncement of 1820 is best understood to refer to Europe in 1806, the Europe of Napoleon's Empire, the 'miraculous advent' of the Enlightenment in process of realisation as 'Napoleon spread the Revolution across Europe, transforming the world into a concrete universality' (Althusser, [1947] 1997: 145). Althusser brilliantly describes the dilemmas Hegel faced when the Empire collapsed in 1814–15, in the project which was caught in the dilemma 'to abandon absolute circularity and bow to contemporary reality, or else abandon the contemporary content so as to save, at that price, the system of absolute truth. In Hegel's torn and divided world, it was no longer possible to keep a grip on the two extremes simultaneously' (1997: 147). Althusser shows in a few pages how Marx resolves this dilemma: speaking in the aftermath of the defeat of the Paris Commune (1871), Marx says the proletarians 'have no ideals to realize, but to set free the elements of the new society with which the old collapsing bourgeois society itself is *pregnant*'.

Althusser concludes that Marx was right to solve Hegel's problem by finding that the 'proletariat is this implicit universality; in its present state, it contains the future and the freedom of all mankind. It is, potentially, the circularity of the absolute content' (1997: 150).

Modern social theory, influenced by a German philosophical reading of French historical events, the Empire, the Commune, does not now remember well the French reading of these events, nor understand how the German and the French readings are related.[1] In order to grasp these relations and to understand the main currents of French social theory, it is necessary to start not with Hegel but with Saint-Simon and his disciples, who were trying to face up to and deal with exactly the same content, the nature of the new society as it was emerging in the post-revolutionary period: the birth of the social.

The specific context for this was the France of the First Empire (1804–15) and of Restored Monarchy, later of the Second Republic (1848–51), and the Second Empire (1851–70). In 1799, the year following Comte's birth, Napoleon came to power on the back of the victories of the French army in Egypt and Italy. Comte's life was formed primarily in Napoleonic institutions (Lycée, militarised Polytechnique, Empire and failure of Empire, and conditioned by the newly installed Napoleonic civil code). What is striking in this scenario is the continuation of the modernising tendencies of the Revolution on the basis of a new civil code in unstable political forms occupying the void of an established constitution. The military theatre of Napoleon ranged from Egypt to Moscow, Spain through The Netherlands to Warsaw. After Austerlitz Napoleon wanted to be known as the Emperor of the West – modelling himself not on Louis XIV but on Charlemagne – a status Britain refused to recognise. Paris became the capital of a vast French Empire, which in 1811 embraced 130 departments of 44,000,000 inhabitants, with attached confederate states. By 1814 the revolutionary process, which had begun as a struggle against the hierarchy of estates, had ended in the establishment of a new social hierarchy with a new hereditary estate of 75,000 new notables already in place. As one recent French historian has noted, 'Bonaparte had invaded the whole political theatre, and occupied it entirely on his own … a de facto monarchy, infinitely more powerful and despotic than the old one, since there was no longer any intermediary body to oppose its domination over equal individuals' (Furet, 1992: 234).

All this collapsed like a pack of cards in less than a year. The romance of Paris as Imperial Capital, the new legal frame (the civil code, education) created largely under Napoleon, together with the nostalgia for the ideals of Liberty, Equality and Fraternity, survived the collapse in the new situation void of political and religious institutions (Hont, in Dunn [ed.], 1995: 166–231). Saint-Simon and Comte lived through the drama of the collapse and the re-emergence of Bonapartism in the 100 days (1814–15). Saint-Simon had offered advice to the Emperor:

> I beg Your Majesty to deign to accept the dedication of this study. I have called this first sketch of my plan for the reorganisation of European society *Study on Universal Gravitation* because the new philosophical theory must be based on

> the idea of universal gravitation, and because the new political system of Europe must be a consequence of the new philosophy. (1975: 124–5)

Comte took a direct interest in politics, and involved himself in debates, with one brief exception when he rallied at the beginning of the 100 Days, always hostile to Napoleon. Saint-Simon and Comte founded a social science in order to resolve the social question at the outcome of the Revolution. For Comte this became a quest to know what would be the normal state at the end of such a transition. Mary Pickering notes, for Comte 'Napoleon ultimately failed to end the Revolution because he lacked a genuine political doctrine'(1993: 27) based on a science. But how was the revolution to come to an end? (For a discussion of this question see Hayward, 1991: 299–302.) For those thinkers who refused the path of retrogression, status quo, or imitation of Anglo-American models, the problem itself had to be posed in a new way.

As Durkheim later pointed out, there is a world of difference between Comte and Saint-Simon: 'what differentiates Comte and Saint-Simon is that the former separated science from practice more clearly ... Once given this idea of a positive science of societies, he undertook to realise it, not from the aspect of this or that immediate end' (Durkheim, 1962: 146). The Saint-Simonians founded a particular kind of language (modern social theory), and might be said to form Roland Barthes' Logothete – founder of a new language (Barthes, 1976: 3). Barthes adds, however, 'Were logothesis to stop at setting up a rhetoric, the founder of a language would be no more than the author of a system ... In fact to found a new language *through and through* [another] operation is required: *theatricalisation*' (1976: 5). In fact it is probably more precise to say in the case of the Saint-Simonians – *theatricalisations* (Pickering, 1997).

The vanishing mediator from Saint-Simon to Comte and Marx: Bazard

Just before his death in 1825, Saint-Simon nominated Olinde Rodrigues as his immediate successor as leader of the school which quickly developed into a 'sacred college'. Rodrigues recruited young intellectuals trained in the natural sciences at the Ecole Polytechnique to the movement. They 'were young Jewish intellectuals, sons of assimilated Paris banking families and leaders of the religious community' but facing in the France of the restored Bourbons a new religious test and religious intolerance in the University (Jones et al., 1975: 1102). The organisation of the college adopted the Catholic hierarchical form but with two 'Popes': Prosper Enfantin and Saint-Amand Bazard. The latter presented a course of lectures in 1828–9 since called *The Doctrine of Saint-Simon: an Exposition: First Year 1928–1829* (the English translation fails to indicate the author [Iggers ed., 1972]). The popularity of Saint-Simonian ideas at this moment should not be underestimated; 50,000 copies of the exposition were distributed in 1831 (the extent of support and interest is described by Carlisle, 1987, ch. 8). On reading Bazard it is clear immediately that his lectures figure as a key resource for Marx and Engels – the lecture of 25 February 1829 is called 'The Successive Transformation of Man's Exploitation of Man and of the Rights of Property'. Its first section is on 'Master and slave; patrician and plebeian; lord and serf; idle and worker' – a phraseology which goes through to the *Communist Manifesto* twenty years later when Marx and Engels added a theory of capital to this problematic. The course contains perhaps the first coherent theory of human 'exploitation' (Cunliffe and Reeve, 1996).

Durkheim, amongst French social theorists, became by far the most significant interpreter and critic of Bazard's lectures. By arranging, he says, Saint-Simon's thoughts into 'a logical order, he changed them at more than one point and so gave the system a new aspect ... he carried them to their logical conclusions, and at the same time distinguished more radically the purely rationalist and scientific elements ... [w]ith Bazard it attained its maximum logical consistency and flowering' (Durkheim, 1962: 251), but certainly in a direction towards the religious, quite different from that of Marx. The key historical thesis of the alternation of critical and organic periods, says Durkheim, can be found in Saint-Simon, 'but it is Bazard who developed it into a distinct theory ... and the law so formulated is incontestable' (1962: 258). Bazard's argument is that 'the function of distributing the instruments of production among producers will no longer be surrendered to private individuals' but by a new institution (1962: 266). The solution to the problem of the nature of this institution is to be found in religion, the only force capable of ending a critical period, for religion is 'nothing other than the expression of the collective thinking peculiar to a people or to humanity' (1962: 267). Bazard argues that instead of seeing cultural evolution as a linear procession through religion, metaphysical philosophy to a positive stasis, development goes through cycles: 'it is false to say that religious beliefs are no more than remnants of a past destined to disappear. The truth is that they alternately die and are reborn, without anyone having the right to fix an end to these series ... societies become more and more religious' (1962: 268–7).

Bazard's new religion is one that overcomes the dualism of Christianity which tended to invalidate the material world, and becomes a religion which embraces the world as a whole, 'a rehabilitation of matter' (cited from Year II of the exposition by Durkheim, 1962: 271). The work of industry is to be declared holy, and every political order is 'before all else, a religious order' (1962: 272). At the highest point, he said anticipating Comte, the representative of the spiritual is the priesthood, this stratum will direct society. And the highest priest will 'link industry and science in general and watch over their harmonious development so that theory concerns itself with practical requirements and practice understands its need of theory.' The High Priest 'distributes tasks according to capacity and compensates capacities according to accomplishment. Only in taking a theocratic form does industrial society find equilibrium' (1962: 273). The Saint-Simonian sacred college under Bazard was thus a kind of microcosm of the society to come, an anticipatory cult with its determined hierarchy and rituals. The story of the cult is well known. Very soon after Bazard's lectures, the other Pope, Enfantin, initiated an attempt to rehabilitate not only matter, but also the 'flesh' in what Durkheim called the idiom of 'free love – almost sacred prostitution' (1962: 281). Bazard withdrew from the cult. Enfantin announced that his place would be filled by a woman, yet to be identified by Enfantin, who rejected all the women inside the cult. A 'society for welcoming the mother' was formed. The final episode of the story was the departure for the Middle East of a group calling itself 'Compagnons de la Femme', which set off in search for the new woman messiah (and to engage in massive canal and dam building projects).

But the political damage had been done, as Claire Moses, concludes: 'the sexual libertarianism of Saint-Simonianism besmirched the reputation of French feminism for the entire nineteenth century' (Moses, 1982: 262, and see Moses and Rabine, 1993).

Comte

Auguste Comte was born on 19 January 1798, at Montpellier in the south of France. Briefly outlined, his life seems more than usually productive. Educated at the newly created Lycée at Montpellier, he entered as a prodigy the Polytechnique in Paris at the age of 16. It was still run under Napoleonic military discipline, and not for the first or last time Comte was involved in rebellion. In 1816, under the restored monarchy, the Polytechnique was closed down after student unrest. In 1817 Comte became secretary to Henri de Saint-Simon with whom he spent about seven formative years till he branched out on his own account in 1824, the year before Saint-Simon's death. Comte's main source of income was as a teacher of mathematics and an examiner. In the years 1819–28 he wrote a number of essays on politics and social theory, which have become known as the *Opuscules*, in which he outlined a vast programme of work, and which indeed he spent the rest of his life trying to fulfil.[2] The first of the tasks was to establish a theory of the way the sciences had developed, so as to understand the logic of their emergence and the common methodological features of the system which the sciences were in the process of forming.

After establishing this logic, and its methodological frame, the next task was to organise and complete the system of the sciences: to add first a modern biology and then ultimately to found the scientific study of society itself. He called this 'sociology'. The identification of the positive philosophy and the founding of sociology were achieved in the enormous work which occupied him from 1830 to 1842: published as the six-volume *Course in Positive Philosophy*. The establishment of a sociology was not an end in itself. The goal of the project was to work out a political programme to resolve the crisis in France and western Europe on the basis of the new social science. This project began to be fleshed out in detail from 1844 and his conclusions were published between 1851–4 in the four-volume work known as *Système de Politique Positive*.

Between these two key works Comte had lived through a traumatic personal religious conversion which had revolutionary effects on his project. Instead of working out a secular resolution to the western crisis, he now urged the necessity of creating a new religious organisation based on sociology but realised in a new idiom as a 'religion of humanity'. He thus founded, as the continuation of his initial project, not a new political organisation as anticipated, but a new religious cult. Comte is therefore the founder of positive philosophy, the science of sociology, and a positivist religion. Comte has been judged as having founded these dogmatically and naïvely. But the crucial question today is whether Comte is to be understood differently. As Ernest Gellner has suggested, 'Ideas must be clothed in a proper idiom before their death can be a fertile sacrifice ... A particular merit of positivism, especially in its classical, Comtean form [is] that it perceives how and why this needs to be done' (Gellner, 1985: 55).

The first period of Comte's work is best understood as an attempt to transform the doctrine of Saint-Simon by drawing on the models and ideas of the sciences which dominated Paris in 1800 (Serres, 1995a), and to develop the new scientific idiom of sociology. In the second period of his writings he develops ideas that he had already worked on with Saint-Simon, remodelled from Bazard, in a religious idiom appropriate to the new context of social Catholicism inspired and led by Lamennais in the 1830s and 1840s (see Berenson, 1989). Comte had worked through what he called the 'retrograde' Catholic reaction to the revolution of de Bonald and de Maistre, and tried to solve the problems they raised in their idealisation of the Pope, by returning to the idealisation of the Pope, but with himself as 'The Pontiff' of the Religion of Humanity guided by sociological theory (Comte, 1968; vol. iv: 22). Indeed, Comte claimed de Maistre the only nineteenth-century thinker from whom he had taken a significant idea (see Pickering, 1993: 263).

This contextualisation is important and quite different from those conventionally proposed in relation to Comte's work, which is to see Comte only in relation to the ideals of 1789 or to read Comte as a conservative who 'sided with the forces of law and order ... [where] history ends with the consolidation of middle-class society' (Furedi, 1992: 194). In fact Comte was hostile to all the regimes of his period – absolute monarchy, constitutional monarchy, a bourgeois parliamentary republic, Bonarpartism and communism – certain in the belief that the Revolution was imminent through the joint action of the modern proletariat, a new priesthood and the affective influence of women (the place of Comte's thesis among historians of the French Revolution is located by Gérard, 1970: 57). Saint-Simon, in search of funds, appealed to Napoleon directly to allow him to develop schemes appropriate to a modernising programme. Comte later appealed to the Tsar of Russia, and to Napoleon III in a similar style. He never tired of describing his objective as one of searching for a way to end the Western Revolution, and of claiming to have found the way to do it through social science. The new positive calendar which Comte drew up in the 1840s dates modern time from 1789, thus rejecting both the Revolution's calendar, and

Napoleon's return to the Gregorian calendar in 1804 – a simple fact which is entirely problematic in the conservative reading of Comte's position.

The radical elements of Comte's thought are common to the milieu of Saint-Simonianism in which he was immersed as a young intellectual, and out of which sociology and socialism were established. As Kolakowski points out, Comte's theory 'involves the most extreme anti-individualism' (1972: 87). After all, Comte also coined the word 'altruism' (see Wernick, 2001: 123) in order to define that form of action contrasted with egoism. In the next chapter I examine what was involved in establishing a theoretical social science which would be able to answer the question as to the nature of the polity required to resolve the question posed by the unfinished revolution.

Notes

1 Forgetting this whole first great epoch of sociology that was formed outside the university framework, and which included the names of Saint-Simon, Comte, Mill, Littré, Spencer, was indeed a more complex process than might be supposed. In fact it was the first generation of university-based sociologists, Durkheim, Pareto and Weber, who performed the act of patricide. It was always contested. And now after the general collapse of that other version of Saint-Simonianism, Marxism, there is a new opportunity for a reconsideration of this epoch of sociology. It seems that in the attempts at reconstruction that have recently been put forward, many of the forgotten themes of Comte's sociology have returned unannounced. Today a study of Comte can throw light not only on Marx but also on those forms of synthetic and historical sociology that have unconsciously drawn on Comte's ideas. This new reading may also be able to play a part in the general questioning of sociology as a discipline in the process of profound rethinking, or indeed 'unthinking' (Wallerstein, 1991).

Even if recent surveys of historicism (Hamilton, 1996) have excluded Comte, the major debate which was launched fifty years ago by Karl Popper and F.H. Hayek against Comte's historicism and holism can be reviewed with profit. Sociology survived the attack by appealing to the transformed Comtean forms of thought within the sociological tradition, in writers from Weber to Norbert Elias, and the epistemologists following Bachelard, Canguilhem, Althusser and others, who played a crucial indirect role in rethinking sociology in the 1960s. What is interesting today looking back and assessing that debate is to find among the anti-Comteans both the thesis that there can be no such thing as a three-stage law (Popper, 1960: 117), and that the three-stage law comes from mechanics (Serres, in Comte, 1975, vol. i: 4). What is evident in reviewing the writing on Comte is just how problematic are the well-known refutations of Comte's law in recent literature have been. I have drawn at this point on: 'Engendering the End of European History' in *Renaissance and Modern Studies*, (1996), vol. 39: 15–26.

2 The early essays generally known as the *Opuscules* are available in *The Crisis of Industrial Civilization: the Early Essays of Auguste Comte*, introduced by R. Fletcher (London, 1974), and *Early Political Writings*, edited by H.S. Jones (Cambridge, 1998). These essays are also available in an appendix to A. Comte, *System of Positive Polity*, vol. 4 (London 1877 – reprinted in New York, 1974b).

2

Sacrificial Theory and the Sociology of Modernity

> [Auguste Comte], that great honest Frenchman beside whom, as embracer and conqueror of the strict sciences, the Germans and English of this century can place no rival. (Nietzsche [1881], 1982: 215)

Although the sociology founded by Comte was different from that of the Saint-Simonian school, particularly as represented by Bazard, and also from that of Marx, it has nevertheless rightly been suggested (Kumar, 1978: 59) that they can all be shown to be subtle and complex mirror-image transformations of each other. The idea suggests that the *basic* structures of sociological thought may be far more unified than is commonly supposed. Comte's own input into Saint-Simonianism was already significant before the master's death in 1825. Sociology through Marx, and sociology through Durkheim, draw on unsuspected Comtean ideas. Comte's sociology was certainly the first to give these ideas coherent exposition in the framework of methodological control. It was for this reason Durkheim suggested Comte should be acknowledged as founder of sociology, and went as far as to suggest that 'Comte's law correctly describes the way modern societies have developed from the tenth to the nineteenth century' (Durkheim, 1962: 268) despite his reservations about Comte's method and theory. Comte adopted a complex 'programme' for the construction of foundations. It entailed mutual supporting scaffolding between philosophy, epistemology of the sciences, sociology and political programme. This grand interlocking project of this scope was not quite abandoned by the Durkheim–Weber generation, but was narrowed to the relation between philosophy and the social sciences (in France science became more and more the field of specialist epistemologists). It was as though the initial stage of such a vast enterprise of social theorising needed elaborate underpinnings, whereas later sociologies which developed within the universities were more secure and the role of a specialising sociology could be explained and legitimised on its own terms. The sociology established by Comte vanished into the frames of the new edifice. Once installed, the new science took down the scaffolding which had enabled it to come into existence. Lévi-Strauss was quite right to say that the Durkheim generation were not founders but 'chief engineers' of the new social science disciplines (1967: 8). A considerable process of forgetting occurred: not only of the resort to a scaffolding but so also of the (Napoleonic) theatrical scale in which 'sociology' was the means to answer the question: 'What is the social system required by the condition of European societies on the morrow of the Revolution?' (Durkheim, 1962: 146).

What is the nature of the theoretical imagination in the new science? How was sociology constructed? This question is not quite as straightforward as first appears. The question is an awkward one for a number of reasons, not least because the term 'positivism' has changed so much from its usage in the early nineteenth century. Although Comte's positivism excluded in principle any resort to the notion of causal analysis, it did not exclude theory – indeed, each science is related to the unique 'fundamental theory' of its domain.

Comte's analysis of the sciences

The demonstration of the legitimacy and the necessity of the new social science occupied Comte from the first to the third volume of the *Course* (1830 to 1839). Only in volume four (of six) did he attempt to discuss the foundation of social science, and to define the scope of sociology. In the first three volumes he discussed the formations of the sciences, in their order of appearance and consolidation, and in their interdependences within this order. Comte's discussion is often taken as a kind of summary of the results of the sciences, or even a manual. In the version presented in English in the 1850s by Harriet Martineau, some sections were omitted as being already out of date, an argument which appears again in the introduction to the current French edition in which Michel Serres suggests the work had already been left behind even on its first appearance since the sciences were developing rapidly (in Comte, 1975, vol. i: Introduction). Although these are important criticisms of Comte's analysis, they are not fatal, for, as Heilbron (1995) argues, the work was an attempt at quite a different project: to analyse the order of appearance and interdependencies of the sciences, to analyse the way in which they constituted their domains of investigation, their theoretical programmes and methods, their internal divisions, and to suggest ways in which they could develop out of each other. Above all of course, the aim was to prepare the way for and legitimise the foundation of a new science of society: to present its first methodological rules, and to discuss its first rational findings (which occupied Comte between 1839 and 1842). Before looking at the specific forms of observation – this very specific genre of the scientific gaze – he proposed for sociology, it is necessary to examine the way theory arises in a scientific practice.

Theory and fictions in the sciences

Comte's account of the formation of the sciences has been read in a number of different and sometimes divergent ways. Comte himself stressed repeatedly that 'it is evident that the absence of scientific theory today renders social observation so vague and so incoherent' (Comte, 1975, vol. ii:

140). The question posed here is not whether Comte was the founder of a new history of the sciences, but rather, and more simply, how he presented the analysis of the way theory was essential to the constitution of any science. This question is vital to any adequate appreciation of his attempt to establish a new science within the field of the existing sciences, as most recent comment on Comte's work has recognised (Laudan, 1971: 47–52; Hawkins, 1984: 156–9; Schmaus, 1982; Heilbron, 1990; Pickering, 1993: ch. 15).

First of all it is essential to note (as, for example, Serres does not), that Comte argues that to repeat the empirical historical order of the emergence of the sciences as an explanation of their emergence is a basic error. For 'to pursue a science historically is quite a different thing from learning the history of its progress' (Comte, 1974b: 43; this idea later became a central idea for Althusser's reading of Marx). Indeed the difference in the order of appearance of the sciences and their interior order of dependences, or what he notes as their 'dogmatic order', forces the analysis into a consideration of modes of exposition. Comte claims that his account will in the main follow an order of historical exposition for reasons of accessibility, but he will correct this order where necessary in his account of the emergence of each science as a body of theoretical knowledge. His account thus follows the order: mathematics (vol. i, 1830), astronomy, physics (vol. ii, 1835), chemistry and biology (vol. iii, 1835), an order that was by the 1830s established by all the major philosophies of science from Kant to Hegel.

His own theses are threefold. First, that each of these branches of knowledge passes through a scientific revolution (that is through the metaphysical state). Second, that their growth as a system is cumulative, that is, they develop in a certain well-defined order which reveals their dependence on each other once the sequence is started. Third, that although each science develops a methodology appropriate to its own problems, a reflection on the unity of the scientific method emerges in its own right, and this can be disengaged as a new kind of philosophy – one that marks a decisive break with metaphysical or theological concerns. The basic set of texts which inaugurates modern sociology begins with a genealogy of mathematics, and it cannot be stressed too firmly that for the main strands of French social theory, it is essential to recognise, as Serres emphasises, the proximity of modern theory to the system of the sciences including the natural sciences. Indeed Comte's ideas were as influential in the formation of biology as in sociology, and it is quite erroneous to think that sociology was in any simple sense a meta-epistemological system parasitic in a crude manner on an already set of sciences. Although Comte's sociology was not an empiricism, it was a naïve realism, as Lewisohn has argued: there is no real attempt to 'define the nature of the facts which are to provide the empirical underpinning' (1972: 320). The emphasis was placed on methodological controls based on observation, to control the driving force of the imagination in scientific work. As Laudan notes, Comte recognised a danger: for 'is it even possible, after having adopted a notion which admits of no verification, to use it continually, letting it mingle with real ideas, without involuntarily attributing to it an effective existence?' (in Laudan, 1971: 51). The real problems with Comte's method are quite different therefore from those commonly associated with empiricism: they are those associated with a speculative anti-historicism. Comte wants his resort to the imagination and to speculation to have scientific legitimation.

The order of appearance of systems of objective reasoning

Comte begins his famous account of the sciences with a history of mathematics, or so it seems. He wants to show that this discipline is both a type of reasoning and founded in relation to concrete problems. Comte's definition, following Lagrange, of *mathematics* suggests that it occupies a unique field and that has as its aim to determine 'magnitudes by each other, according to the precise relations which exist between them' (1974b: 54). The impetus of mathematics is the practice of approaching 'all the quantities which any phenomena can present as connected and interwoven with one another, with the view of deducing them from one another' (cited in Fraser, 1990). Mathematics is subdivided into geometry and mechanics on the one hand as observational and concrete practices, while abstract mathematics includes arithmetic, algebra and calculus. For Comte the concrete aspects of mathematics constitute the beginnings of a real natural science, while the abstract aspects are a complex development of natural logic.

Comte's analysis does not suggest that the logic of numerical identification is a primary base for mathematics in any reductionist move to base mathematics on a pre-given reality. It is only through a specific type of abstraction that genuine analytic expressions are established to serve as a basis for investigations into observable relations between phenomena. These analytic expressions use the resources from the concrete division of the object, and supplement them with specific kinds of *fictions*, and mathematical artifices to facilitate not the direct calculation of values, but the equations that determine the relations of the phenomenon. In Fraser's (1990) important discussion of Comte's account, the specific contribution of this analysis is its new approach to reading the calculus. This is seen as a process in which such mathematical artifices are introduced to help analytical thought but which are then eliminated, *sacrificed*, at the point of calculation. Here transcendental analysis is conceived as the calculus of indirect functions.

Thus Comte was able to argue that all accounts that consider mathematics as developing independently of observation were purely metaphysical. Equally metaphysical were all positions in mechanics which endeavoured to find hidden ontological origins for things (as was the case in d'Alembert) rather than working on observations. This is why Comte thought highly of the work of Lagrange, arguing that he took 'the science of abstract mechanics to the highest degree of logical perfection – that is, to a rigorous unity' (1974b: 127). Comte holds that although mechanics was based on observation, it could never be reduced to it. It is only brought into a coherent state of knowledge through the imaginative elaboration of the artifice of '*virtual velocities*', introduced and then cancelled in the analysis of motion (1974b: 117, 127), in a way comparable to the use of fictions in calculus. If Archimedes established the statics and Galileo the dynamics, then Lagrange brought the two sides of mechanics together by interposing the idea of virtual momentum and virtual velocity in the analysis of forces acting on a point. Thus he was able, in the theory of statics, to work out the method of determining an equilibrium. Comte criticised Lagrange's approach to dynamics, however, by arguing that

> a dynamic consideration really consists in conceiving any varied motion as compounded, each moment, of a certain uniform motion and another uniformly varied – likening it to the vertical motion of a heavy body under a first impulsion … [this] removes the limits within which we suppose ourselves to be confined by disclosing to us in an abstract way, a much more perfect measure of all varied motion. (1974b: 125)

It is clear from this, and from other interventions, that Comte's view of the sciences was essentially one combining direct observation with abstract techniques of conjecture, sacrificial rectification, improvement and harmonisation – an approach far removed from one viewing the sciences as collections of purely empirical rules based on increasing the range of observations. Thus if Serres is correct in suggesting that Comte essentially used Lagrange (perhaps via Poinsot), to build an analysis of dynamics from the theory of two vectors, it is important to note that these are not, in Comte's analysis, the equivalent of directly observable empirical entities, but of the theory of uniform and varied motion.

Chemistry, by contrast, is a contested domain in this analysis, which still awaits a rational systematisation. Until that is achieved, there are difficulties in defining its true limits. In crucial respects the idea of an 'organic chemistry' rests on a confusion (Comte, 1974b: 262). Only glimpses of an established domain can be seen here and there in such theories as the principle of definite proportions, or electrochemical theory. Comte takes as an example of a law the theory of saline decomposition – 'two soluble salts, of any kind, mutually decompose each other whenever their reaction may produce an insoluble salt, or one less soluble than the other' (1974b: 272). If Comte were the empiricist he is often assumed to be, we might expect him to be satisfied with a proposition of invariance of this kind. But he remarks that this law is fundamentally without basic explanation, since it is disconnected from any general theory of the domain. For although particular regularities may be established through observation, genuine scientific explanation is possible only in relation to the '*fundamental theory*' which governs all phenomena of the same order; otherwise each particular law is limited to highly specific empirical phenomena and is unable to explain itself. It is essentially only an 'empirical rule'. No *genuine law* can be explanatory other than by showing that 'it enters into another more general than itself' (1974b: 272). The domain of any science will introduce a certain kind of *homogeneity* to its own facts. Comte concludes that chemistry can only become a science when it combines the study of organic and inorganic substances (an extant division with no rational foundation) (1974b: 293).

Comte's remarks here evidently note the emergence of significant power struggles for the possession of a domains:

> The division of chemistry conceals or violates essential analogies, and hinders the extension of dualism into the organic region ... and thus the arbitrary arrangement is the chief obstacle in the way of the entire generalisation of the doctrine of definite proportions ... The confusion is more mischievous, but less felt by chemists, under the other view – the comprehension of biological phenomena among those of organic chemistry. The confusion arose from the need of chemical researches in very many physiological questions, and these chemical researches being usually extensive and difficult, were out of the range of the physiologists, and were taken possession of by the chemists, who annexed them to their own domain. (1974b: 294)

These arguments lead to the Comtean programme in biology: to plea for the liberation of biology from chemistry at essential points (anatomy and physiology). He stresses the biological conception of elements of the organism (Blainville) against its simple products (1974b: 294). Indeed, he insists, it is not really a question of liberating biology but of a true *theoretical subordination* of chemistry to biological theory in this realm. Science in Comtean theory is a kind of political epistemology: it intervenes in the struggles over empires and colonies, in campaigns over the possession of new territories and regions.

The object of *biology* is the analysis of living organisms, or more precisely 'of connecting in both a general and a specific manner, the double idea of organ and medium with that of function', connecting the anatomical and the physiological point of view, the organism in its environment (milieu) (1974b: 308). Unlike chemistry, biology is concerned with organised bodies. Its domain is the study of all possible organisms with the aim of understanding human biology. The methodological procedures of observation peculiar to biology are identified: the creation of special instruments, new forms of experimentation, *comparative analysis, pathological analysis*. Comte draws attention to the introduction of *hypotheses*, especially in the investigation of *hidden as opposed to manifest functions* (1974b: 324). And he also draws attention to the difference between the practice of 'imagining a series of hypothetical cases' in mathematics, and the construction of functional hypotheses: 'in the latter case the solution alone is imaginary; whereas in the former, the problem itself is radically ideal.' Comte suggests that in the 'higher conceptions of comparative biology ... the process would be to intercalate, among known organisms, certain purely *fictitious* organisms ... rendering the biological series more homogeneous and continuous' (1974b: 327, emphasis added).

Comte then reflects on the possibility of constructing a perfect abstract biology as a way of revealing for analysis the obstacles to its actual development. The prospect is opened, he says, for the completion of the theory of *classification*, a true biological hierarchy (1974b: 328), for

> each of the fundamental sciences has ... as we have seen the exclusive property of specially developing one of the great logical procedures of which the whole positive method is composed; and it is thus that the more complex, while dependent on the simpler, react on their superiors by affording them new rational powers and instruments ... (1974b: 330)

Comte's consideration of biology notes the fact that although the discovery of the function of the heart and the law of gravity were achieved at the same time, the subsequent *unevenness* of development (the late development of biology) of the two disciplines is remarkable. For Comte,

> such a difference cannot be attributed wholly to the greater complexity of physiological phenomena, and must have depended much also on the scientific spirit which directed their general study – on the one hand, the supposed organic chemistry, a bastard study ... and, on the other hand, vague, incoherent, and partly metaphysical doctrines ... The barren anarchy which has resulted from so vicious an organisation of scientific labour would be enough of itself to testify to the direct utility of the general, yet positive point of view. (1974b: 368)

Much of Comte's analysis of biology is prescriptive. It is not surprising that historians allow Comte not only a significant role in establishing the very term 'biology' (it came into existence about 1800 but it was Comte, along with Littré and others, who brought it into common usage (Heilbron, 1995: 246)), but also of having played a crucial role in its modern development (Canguilhem, 1983: 61 ff.).

Perhaps ironically, however, Comte's emphasis on theory and theoretical abstraction, and the role of fictions, leads his positivism to legitimise as essential to all scientific and precisely the sociological imagination, the construction of conjectures that invoke unobservable phenomena – subject to their eventual verification of course in relation to that which becomes observable later.

Sociology as a body of knowledge governed by theory

Comte's analysis, therefore, rests on the idea that all sciences are organised around a *fundamental theory* which defines the objects of the domain, and are based on methods of observation appropriate to this domain constituted by unique and homogeneous phenomena established within it. The detailed reading of the sciences in the *Course* aimed to identify the specific theoretical techniques employed and developed in each of the main sciences and to understand their unity and differences. As Heilbron has noted, 'Comte was the first to have developed systematically a historical and differential theory of science' (Heilbron, 1990: 155). Comte's idea is that the sciences have developed unequally because there is a structure of dependency in the order of appearance of these bodies of knowledge and to the extent to which they are rationally organised. Comte's advocacy of a new order of philosophy, *positive philosophy*, is aimed to make this conscious and to begin the process of harmonisation of the sciences into a genuine system. That is to strengthen it, to mould it into a coherent intellectual force. If the sciences are dependent on one another in a certain peculiar way, this peculiarity can be understood in a new philosophical reflection which will function to organise it. The positive philosophy therefore is the heir to the earlier seventeenth-century efforts of Bacon and Descartes, who, after Aristotle's (and then the scholastic's) efforts in this direction, tried to 'reconstruct the system of received ideas from top to bottom' (Comte, 1975, vol. 1: 61) in the first of a new type of philosophy *a philosophia prima* (Comte, 1974b: 39; Comte, 1968, iv: 154–60). The nineteenth century will be like the seventeenth, capable of regenerating the whole body of the sciences by reorganising it in to a second and then a third philosophy (1968, iv: 216). Each one is required so that the sciences themselves as a whole grow out of the old shell and each requires new harmonisation and an organisation appropriate for its new social role. Here sociology is destined to complete the system, to give it its most adequate self-awareness in methodology and social purpose as a new kind of spiritual power.

Comte proposed to begin the construction of the new science of sociology by studying the way that sciences depend on former sciences as both resources and controls. As biology is dependent on chemistry and even mathematics in a certain way, so the new sociology will be dependent on biology and will learn from the way in which the earlier sciences and their methods established themselves. In order to achieve the foundation of the new discipline, sociologists have to be competent in the other sciences, their logics, their methods, and to be competent in the new philosophy which studies the law of their uneven development and the structure of their dependencies. Positive philosophy, thus understood, is not simply the attempt to regulate the system of the sciences (some are still isolated outside the system), but aims to produce the conditions for the emergence of new sciences within a precisely defined set of methodological rules. It regulates the system in order to prevent certain pathologies, those anarchic and dispersive tendencies which would weaken its effectiveness as a body.

If we call the formation of the scientific imagination the development of *theoretical logics* of the sciences, then it is clear that for Comte these are only strictly possible in so far as they are controlled by the limits imposed by method and of course the world, as it is observed either directly or indirectly, in the present or in the future. Thus for Comte the fundamental rule is that imagination is subordinate to observation, hence he embarks on the presentation of the main methods of observation open to a social science. However, Comte also held that the imagination must play a formative role in founding the theory of a science, and that involves imaginative fiction. Fictions are then sacrificed to observation that has become systematic. It is because most accounts of Comte's idea of 'positive method' do not grasp this relation that they are in the main strictly worthless. Clearly sociology could not be a simple application of any one set of methods from an established science; the sciences do not simply imitate each other, but are guided by each other.

The sociology of modernity: the metaphysical state

The key to understanding Comtean sociology therefore lies in the way that the theory, the law of the three states, enables Comte to periodise, to establish the principal signposts (*jalons fondamentaux*) on this new continent of scientific history. These also unite the series, which become the genealogies (lines of 'filiation') of the new organic synthesis. It is abstract since the facts as they are experienced within any situation are complex and interwoven, so a rational reconstruction is essential for any adequate understanding at the scientific level: the construction of such a series is to bring events into the pure and homogeneous new linear space of sociology. As we have seen, the way that Comte proceeds in the case of European history is to present the picture of a coherent social organism, the feudal-Catholic system (the formation of which itself given a long analysis), and the industrial positive system as the other, future pole. In this way the French Revolution of 1789 is located within the Western Revolution as a whole, but so are the very early manifestations of the disarticulation of the Catholic synthesis of the Middle Ages. Of Comte's several versions of the twofold movement (the metaphysical stage) of European history, in 1820, in 1841 and in 1853, by far the most comprehensive is that of 1841. This altered in very significant ways in 1853 and after. The changes reflect his new adherence to the Religion of Humanity and the adoption of the subjective method, which fundamentally alters the way in which the sociological imagination works.

Comte provides, in 1841, an objective analysis once more that cannot, like the subsequent subjective analysis, grasp *at the same time and in one analysis* the inverse processes of the 'dual movement'. What Comte intends to show in his analysis is that the materials from decomposition of the medieval polity do not provide the materials for a new viable polity. Here I present an outline of Comte's main points from the decompositional series, but cross over to problems raised in the parallel series to examine some of the ways Comte deals with some findings which disturb the conclusions he wants to reach. But crucially it must be understood that the theoretical fictions guiding these constructions (particularly the final form of the positive polity) were still to find their full elaboration.

The spontaneous phase of decomposition (1300–1500)

The Catholic synthesis was itself inherently unstable with an attempt by the papal authority to control national churches within a framework of the growing power of the monarchies. There was thus a tendency to dispersion, with national clergies taking refuge from the centre under the protection of temporal powers, and a counter-tendency from the papacy to centralise its authority in a desperate move towards total control. The struggle led to fatal disarticulations in the system. The independence of the temporal powers, dominating the fourteenth century, formed the social basis for the spiritual dispersion which dominated the fifteenth. In the new universities, scholastic doctrines introduced metaphysical debates in an assessment of theology (Comte, 1974b: 646), a tendency which was paralleled with the rise of the legal profession which found a new expansion of employment in the conflicts between kings, national churches and the papal authority (1974b: 647).

The dissolution of the temporal political structures followed a similar pattern with the decline of feudal relations and the installation of standing armies, notably in France, which led eventually to the subordination of the aristocracies to kings. The English case was exceptional in that it retained aristocratic ascendancy over the monarchy (for an analysis of the exception at some length see Comte, 1974b: 650), so that towards the end of the fifteenth century, 'the spiritual power was absorbed by the temporal, and one of the elements of the temporal power thoroughly subordinated to the other: so that the whole of the vast organism was dependent on one active central power – generally royalty – when the disintegration of the whole system was about to become systematic' (1974b: 650). By the end of the fifteenth century the papacy no longer ruled western Europe as a whole,

> the papal power was now merely Italian: it had abdicated its noblest political attributes: and it had lost its social utility, so as to become more and more, a foreign element in the constitution of modern society ... thus it is clear that the first disorganisation was almost accomplished before the advent of Protestantism. (1974b: 648)

The Protestant phase (1500–1685)

Luther's intervention was essentially an attack on the discipline of the church, not its hierarchy or doctrine. Calvinism led to an even greater dependence of the church on the temporal power, and this provoked the response in the Catholic countries of a closer alliance between royalty and clergy there too. But this logic was a 'vicious circle, out of which nothing could issue but ruin both to Catholicism and to royalty' (1974b: 651), for royalty then became associated with discredited doctrines. And these doctrines were systematised by the Jesuits, an 'organised mysticism, in which every person concerned must be at the same time and for the same purpose deceiver and deceived' (1974b: 652). Even so, this order remained the principal force against liberalisation. And after the Council of Trent, the church lost 'not only the power but also the desire to fulfil its old destination' (1974b: 653). And then as soon as the Protestant churches and sects became established, they became intolerant of all other religious forms, revealing a deep hypocrisy in the very nature of Protestantism (1974b: 654).

The rise of the absolute state, whether aristocratic (England) or monarchical (France), broke up the 'feudal equilibrium', but nevertheless saved society from complete dissolution, and Protestantism was proved in the end to be supportive of inequalities, indeed of making royalty into kind of new papacy (1974b: 655). The struggles in France and Britain in the sixteenth and seventeenth centuries therefore are to be explained as follows: in England,

> [Protestantism] grew to an excess which occasioned great political convulsion. An equivalent, but opposite result of Protestantism took place on the continent, and even in Scotland, but especially in France, by the nobility being supplied with fresh means of resistance to the growing ascendancy of royalty: and in this second case it took the Presbyterian or Calvinist form, as best suited to opposition, instead of the Episcopalian or Lutheran form, which is best adapted for government. Hence violent repression or convulsion agitation, as the two powers alternatively struggled to repair their former decline. (1974b: 655–6)

There arose in the seventeenth century the power of the ministerial function which hitherto rested with political and military sovereign authority. Both in England and more especially in France, this signalled a further step in the dissolution of feudal authority. There was a parallel rise of the diplomatic class of the temporal authority – a function which was previously carried by the papacy. First of all it was carried out in a new way by diplomats who were formerly clergy, but after this a new civil class emerged associated with this function which more and more reduced the status of the military arms of the state to a mere instruments. The Treaty of Westphalia (1648), the systematic division of Europe between Catholicism and Protestantism, was the chief monument to the development of this new diplomatic class, a diplomatic solution which was 'very inferior to the old Catholic intervention, for the international organism needs, as much as the national, an intellectual and moral basis, such as the Catholic constitution afforded' (1974b: 659).

The fundamental fact, however, was that the tendency towards temporal concentration of power and the development of the revolutionary demand for liberty of inquiry were at the same time 'inseparable and mutually antagonistic' (1974b: 662). Comte's argument is that the one, the

> temporal dictatorship ... by its blind reverence for the past, was for ever restraining the innovations of the other; while the absolute character of negation, on which the critical doctrine prided itself, gave it its counteracting energy; and thus they had in common the absolute tendencies which belong alike to the theological and metaphysical philosophies ... In sanctioning such a political situation, the revolutionary doctrine has erred only in setting up as a normal and permanent state of things an exceptional and transient phase. (1974b: 662)

And even in the Catholic countries, a series of heresies emerged that were similar in structure to Protestant sects, such as Jensenism, and Quietism. Comte then charts the succession of Protestant sects in terms of their discipline, hierarchy and dogma, through Lutheranism, Calvinism, Socinianism to Quakerism (1974b: 664ff.). His somewhat surprising conclusions are that 'the mental operations of Protestantism were in fact the results and not the causes of the revolutions with which we historically connect them' (1974b: 665). The fundamental political revolutions associated with Protestantism were the Dutch revolution against Spain, the English Puritan Revolution, and the American Revolution (which, although belonging to the next phase, was 'as purely Protestant as the others'), indeed has 'developed to excess the inconveniences of the critical doctrine; it sanctions more emphatically than any other the political supremacy of the metaphysicians and the legists' (1974b: 666). In all these cases the true principle of the independence of the spiritual and temporal powers was abandoned.

At this point it is interesting to cross over to Comte's inverse analysis of the relation of Protestantism in the rising series. Here Comte is interested in the relation between the 'spirit of industry' and Protestantism sixty or more years before Weber analysed its relation to the 'spirit of capitalism'. Comte does not adopt the concept of capitalism, and does not consider the positive movement in terms that included accountancy (in this respect Weber's whole analysis in terms of rationality is more Comtean than Comte [Millbank, 1993]). His concern is the relation between the Protestant polity in Britain in particular contrasted with the Catholic polity in France, in relation to what he calls industrial development. Industrial development within the Protestant cultures came early because the nobility is drawn into productive economic life. But this early lead could not be sustained, since the nobility become preoccupied with detail and narrow national interests sets limits on the degree to which it can lead the transformation of the European polity. With Catholic centralisation, industrial development is better extended and organised. Comte is sure that, compared with Catholicism, in reality the 'spirit of Protestantism ... is not more favourable to industry ... and in the end is much less favourable ... by reason of [the] characteristic lack of all true religious discipline' associated with its doctrine of free, independent individual initiative (Comte, 1975, vol. ii: 519). Comte, rather like Durkheim, gave Catholicism a far greater role in the development of modernity than can be found in Weber's analysis.

The deistic phase (1685–1789)

In this phase the critical philosophy is systematised and it becomes evident that it is little more than a 'prolongation' of the previous phase (Comte, 1974b: 669). In effect the 'negative philosophy was, in fact, systematised about the middle of the seventeenth century, and not in the subsequent century, which was occupied by its universal propagation' (1974b: 671). The philosophical revolution was led by Hobbes, Spinoza and Bayle. The latter two were important but it is Hobbes who is the 'father of the revolutionary philosophy' (1974b: 673). (If we cross over to the discussion in the positive series, Comte makes it clear that the transitional philosophy of Hobbes and Locke was driven by the positive impulse coming from Bacon (Comte, 1975, ii: 574)). In fact, his position was more equivocal, for he 'held a much higher position than this, as one of the chief precursors of the true positive polity' (1974b: 673). Comte suggests that Hobbes was perfectly clear about the apparent contradiction in supporting the monarchy in England: monarchy was more adapted 'to facilitate the decay of the old system, and that appeal to royalist nations would lead to the completion of his doctrine' (1974b: 676). Comte sums up the critical philosophy:

> The negative doctrine, improperly called atheism, is simply a final phase of the ancient philosophy, first theological and then more and more metaphysical,

> while retaining the same qualities, the same absolute spirit, and the same tendency to handle questions which sound philosophy discards, as inaccessible to human reason. It substitutes Nature for the Creator, with much the same character and office, impelling to a very similar worship; so that this supposed atheism amounts to inaugurating a goddess in the place of a god ... Such a transformation [*quoiqu'une telle transformation*] may effect an entire disorganisation of the social system which corresponded to the theological philosophy, but it is altogether inadequate to the formation, social or intellectual, of a genuine new philosophy. (1974b: 674; and 1975, ii: 446)

A crucial statement: 'the positive philosophy therefore can acknowledge no connection with the negative doctrine' (1974b: 673–4). Comte's analysis connects the egoism of this doctrine with the continued reign of the temporal over the spiritual elements of authority. His theory of this couple is a central plank of his critique of modern society, since a bourgeois society with its liberation of the egoistic drives, and ideology of rights of the individual, eventually begins to destroy the social bond. The centre of the revolutionary movement moved now from the Protestant cultures to France. The propagators of the new critical doctrines were men without true scientific or rigorous formation but 'men of letters', an equivocal 'class of "authors", a class like that of lawyers without deep convictions' (1974b: 677). Their defects were favourable to their work, for 'such an intellectual condition would be truly monstrous if it were regarded as permanent' (1974b: 677). Even in Catholic circles, controversy was introduced in a self-contradictory way, as Pascal pointed out. It was the school of Voltaire which took the philosophy of Hobbes to deism. Rousseau proceeded to praise the dissolution of modern society itself. In politics deism was raised to the level of a social utopia as a hope against the drift into total anarchy (1974b: 680). In economics there were the parallel propositions of Adam Smith, who led the movement towards individualism and in politics for the state of 'no-government' at all (1974b: 681).

If we cross over to the inverse, positive series, he briefly mentions Montesquieu, Turgot and Condorcet, yet it is clear in philosophy that Comte is struggling to identify a genuine tradition. Philosophy has, he says, in the third phase fallen into '*la nullité radicale*' (1975, ii: 581). His main interest focuses on the development of the sciences.

The revolutionary phase (1789–)

Comte's analysis of the Revolution follows its political chronology, and is a series of assessments of the achievements and failures of each. The period at the very start of the Revolution is seen as dominated by three variants of the metaphysical doctrine: stemming from either Diderot, Voltaire or Rousseau. There are three different attempts to implant something like a constitutional monarchy with a separation and division of powers, as inspired by Montesquieu. The emergence of a military dictatorship which passes into the hands of Napoleon I, who after a period of continuing the revolutionary project, restores aristocracy and monarchy across the new French Empire.

The process continues with monarchy imposed by the victorious allies in 1815, but this solution again fails. In 1848 there is another brief attempt at a parliamentary republic, again a failure, for in 1851 Bonapartism is restored by a *coup d'état*. Comte concludes that the extreme instability, volatility, is evidence of the incapacity of the old regime to find a mode of permanent restoration, or of the metaphysical politicians to find a genuine solution to contain the problems generated by the Revolution. Only social science, says Comte, will be able to define the permanent solution to the underlying problems of French society.

Conclusions

We have now gone some way towards discovering what Comte has in mind when talking about metaphysical phenomena produced in the struggle between theological and positive forces. And it is now possible to say that although Comte is generally regarded as a sociologist of *consensus*, his analysis of the long period of the Western Revolution reveals this period to be characterised by deep antagonism and conflict. But there are many more interesting and puzzling things in Comte's long consideration of this history.

One of these is the very remarkable comparative analysis of the English against the French experience of this 'transition'. The English case is considered from early on in the analysis as an exceptional one; at certain points in time it is the most progressive while at others the most reactionary. The French case is the normal one, though the Revolution itself goes through abnormal episodes. Comte argues that English institutions like the constitutional monarchy are exceptional forms, developed under conditions of aristocratic hegemony, and cannot in any simple manner be transplanted in France, where the monarchical form was dominant and normal. This is an important observation on the whole of Comte's consideration of the way the law of the three states works as a sociological law which identifies normal and exceptional modes of development (Comte provides interesting analyses of early economic development in Venice, and in the exceptional case of Prussian development (1975, ii: 519)).

A second aspect is the fact that Comte's analysis is certainly not a naïve description of the movement of social and cultural progress. If the object of Comte's law is the progression of human thought, then the social analysis of the metaphysical state is one of a permanent simultaneous combination of progression and decomposition. This leads to the problem of periodisation itself, for it is still a major query as to why Comte begins his periodisation of the metaphysical stage at the early date of 1300. His argument is that the complex structural organism of the feudo-Catholic synthesis is no longer functioning and has already dissolved itself into a society of a new type. But it is clear that the social phenomena he calls metaphysical are not yet clearly formed, let alone socially or politically predominant. The Protestant movements are still in the theological stage of the series. It is not until the subsequent, third, sub-period that the predominance of metaphysical philosophies is evident (they were systematised, propagated, and then applied (1975, ii: 459)). Why did not Comte start the metaphysical period from that date or the more symbolic date of the fall of the *ancien régime* (1789)? We know that when Comte constructed his positivist calendar, he adopted the idea, with modifications, of dating the new epoch from the Revolution (1789 as year 1, in Comte's calendar, rather than 1791), and called this the beginning of the final transition to the *positive and final state*, not the culmination of the revolutionary spirit of the metaphysical epoch at the same time as the system of the sciences came to power. Yet his analysis reveals that even after 1789, the oscillations between types of regimes indicated that even the metaphysical polity was not permanently secured. But the only way in which Comte's theory is intelligible is that his thesis suggests the logic of the social structure in France has already established in place the solidity, the positive infrastructure, of a new post-metaphysical state, accumulated piece by piece since the late Middle Ages.

This produced a situation in France which might be called an unstable combination of metaphysical polity alongside a scientific regime. This crisis was resolved by Napoleon in social hierarchies which included the scientists (not Comte, of course, who remained always marginal). The strangely violent political oscillations of the Revolution are, for Comte, the death-throes of the military-theological regime which finally clears the ground for the new society. From 1789, therefore, the positive polity of the scientists is an immanent potentiality at the very moment the metaphysical polity achieves its ascendancy in the republic (for this term see Hont, in Dunn, 1995). Comte's argument is that it is only by conceiving this immanent potentiality of the positive polity (the real prop and support of the metaphysical forms) that the events of 1789 can be understood in any case.

Emile Littré pointed out that the elements for such a political construction and *conversion* were not completed by Comte in time for the 1848 revolutionary conflicts, let alone earlier in 1789 (Littré, 1879). And at the installation of the Third Republic in France in the 1870s, Littré concluded the hour of the scientists' positive polity had already passed. The French form of the metaphysical polity had indeed been successfully stabilised in France with Littré as a leading politician in it.

What periodisation of European history after Comte is in strict conformity with the principles of his analysis? The principal question is whether the social democratic form of the metaphysical state is a sufficiently chronic form of resolution of its basic antagonisms to have produced its own creative and positive logic beyond its subsequent variations? Another crucial question concerns the analysis of the positive series itself, since it is widely felt that since Comte, the scientific system – that of Paris around the year 1800 – has been through further revolutions (in Comte's numeration this would follow the Aristotelian, Baconian, Comtean, and would be therefore a new philosophical integration (the fourth and then even fifth philosophy)). The post-modern condition (Lyotard, [1979] 1984), can be seen from a Comtean perspective to have begun with modifications in mathematics, physics, etc. with anti-system theories, relativity, and uncertainty theory a revolution which continued into genetics and biology, throwing the concept of species into disarray and heralding the 'end of evolution'. These developments have dramatically induced new and important shifts between metaphysical and positive philosophy. This situation represents everything Comte had tried to prevent.

The question today might be posed in the following terms: has the metaphysical polity become sufficiently stable and systematic that it has against Comte's predictions become a social organism capable of organising itself on a new, even positive basis (as Littré had concluded in the aftermath of the Commune)? Is the metaphysical state still driven, but in new ways, by the internal struggle between two systems resting on opposed principles, but in such a way as to transform the positive sciences themselves?

Comte's concept of the metaphysical stage and the metaphysical polity within it was developed at a time when this polity could still be regarded as an exceptional form, and one that was, in Comte's analysis, unlikely to become general. In effect the motive forces supporting the development of this polity, he argued, depended on the displacement of the intellectual authority of the Christian clergy by an alliance of science and metaphysics. In the Revolution of 1789, these two forces competed for hegemony and out of this struggle the restorations began: empires, monarchies, republics, commune. Comte's speculative use of fictions and utopias led him to construct his abstract comparative analysis in order to identify the correct path to the future state. In effect it allowed him to identify key conflictual processes of French modernity, and the way in which the modern polity in France is derived from theological sources by secular inversion resulting from an opposed external impulse. In the next chapter I examine the fate of this idea as Comte looked at it again from a different point of view and method, and which produced results which split his school and have divided all subsequent scholars.

3

Theory in Crisis: Religion and the Subjective

> In rereading him in detail, I found Auguste Comte to be more profound than his successors ... the first to ask the question about the relations between science and society, and, more important, between the histories of science and religion. In this he remains unequaled; none of his successors, in any language, go as far on this decisive point. (Serres, in Serres with Latour, 1996 : 30)

Comte's own hopes for an immediate take-up of his ideas in 1842 were dashed. It was clear that simply announcing his findings did not bring a swift reaction of support and recognition. Not only did the 1840s bring personal crisis and personal reorientation, but the theoretical crisis which came quickly on the failure of his hopes led to attempts to reconstruct his doctrine and strategy from a political to a religious idiom. This chapter examines the extreme forms this rethinking took, and which led to what has been called the first forms of postmodern sociology. His project became one in which the personal, theoretical and religious elements became closely interwoven as he submitted himself to a religious discipline which would prepare him for a 'sociocratic' mission as the Pontiff of the new sacred college of theorists of the Religion of Humanity.

The second Saint-Simonian Sacred College

After completing the founding study of the law of the three states in 1842, Comte's life and thought were deeply shaken by two events. The first was personal. In 1844 he began an intense emotional affair with Clotilde de Vaux, at her insistence platonic, which lasted until her death in 1846 at the age of 32. The second event was the marked change in the social composition of French society and the experience of the revolution of 1848–51, particularly the emergence of the proletariat as a political factor. In that decade (the 1840s) Comte's method and conceptions went through considerable transformations. He rationalised his emotional life, underwent a salutary purification and spiritualisation, and after her death Clotilde was transfigured into a saintly figure of the new religion, whose image Comte began to worship. In the crisis of the insurrection in Paris in June 1848, Comte wrote *'Sainte Clotilde'*, an address in the increasingly common idiom of commemoration on the anniversary of Clotilde's death. In the address he referred to the 'ill-omened detonations ... of the bloody conflict' going on around him. He said:

> I am indebted to thee for finding some pure satisfaction in a dreadful crisis ... Though mingled with warlike sounds, I already hear indications that the human metropolis is returning to its normal condition. The carnage on both sides may have ceased, at least until the next conflict, which will be still more terrible, unless the working men now in arms shall have discovered their real camp. (Comte, 1910: 349–57)

Whereas the Saint-Simonians had gone to Egypt in search of the female messiah, Comte found his female messiah on his doorstep in Paris. Reassessing his own project on the basis of his brief encounter with Clotilde, he argued that all attempts to solve the western crisis through reason and science alone only serve to exacerbate it. All reason, for him essentially masculine, could be effective in the human context only if guided by the moral and emotional superiority of love and affection, essentially feminine. Comte took his own experience of the sublimation of physical love as a necessary process for all those trying to resolve the social and cultural transition of the three states. He installed the maxims of Clotilde within the new religion of humanity in imitation not of the 'rehabilitation of the flesh' as pronounced by the Saint-Simonians, but in a new idiom of sublimation in what he called sociolatry, the worship of society symbolised by the virgin mother and child (Comte, 1968, I: ix–xxix).

The logic of the subjective method

After this traumatic encounter with Clotilde de Vaux (from 1844–6), Comte radically revised his approach to the law of the three states. The new orientation was clear in the second period from 1848 (*The General View*), through the *System of Positive Polity* (1851–4), and the *Catechism* (1852), the *Appeal to Conservatives* (1855), to the *Subjective Synthesis* (1856). Not only is there an explicit acknowledgement that from now on the exposition develops under the influence not of reason but of feeling, or more accurately a plurality of sentiments, but the aim becomes one that places the highest altruistic sentiments in the service of humanity (Wernick, 2001: 148). But there are important shifts in the content of the laws presented under the subjective method. Politically, the events of 1848–51 also left their mark on the theory of the social actors in the completion of the Revolution. Crucially, Comte began his second cycle of writings on the law of the three states from the point of view of the subjective method, altruistic love, of the sacred college and the inauguration of the 'sacred science'.

It is in volume 2 of *System*, published in 1852, that the scope of the changes to the sociology becomes evident. This volume is devoted to social statics and can be compared directly with the single chapter on this topic in *Course*, mentioned earlier. Here we are by contrast treated to a volume of some 380 pages. Whereas in the earlier consideration, of 1841–2, the main issues concerned the individual, the family and society, with an analysis of the relation between the division of labour and spontaneous forms of government, here the structure is quite different. The volume begins with the general theory of religion. It reorganises the analysis of fetishism as the first stage of a history of religion. This is followed by theologism (divided into polytheism and monotheism), and then – not to the metaphysical state as an increasingly secularised religion – but to revolution and to the emergence of 'humanity' as the object of the new cult.

The analysis of social statics, the social order within each society, is refocused. It now embraces the theory of material property, the family, language, and the social organism which concerns families, but also cities and churches (1968, vol. ii: 250). A final section of the work is given to founding under the category of statics a systematic topic of social pathology (theory of normal limits of social variation). It is in the next volume, volume 3 published in August 1853, that the law of the three states is discussed again under the rubric of social dynamics.

Comte gives a full explanation which is worth citing at some length. In the first, fetishistic, stage of the intellectual development:

> two broad divisions of the Fictitious Synthesis differ radically in their conceptions of the directing Wills. In the first, or more spontaneous state, these are supposed to reside in the bodies whose phenomena they seem to explain. The second and more fictitious does not localise them, but attributes them to Beings each of whom is independent of the bodies he governs … Although necessarily consecutive, these two forms of the Fictitious Synthesis are hardly ever sharply separated. Whichever is preponderant, the presence of the other may generally be detected. Thus the passage from Fetishism to Theologism is everywhere an insensible process, although it is the most profound and decisive of our preliminary revolutions.

Comte's revised analysis suggest that:

> When Theologism supersedes or rather absorbs Fetishism, it takes two forms successively, one Polytheistic, the other Monotheistic, the distinction between them is undeniable, although as a rule undue stress is laid upon it … [T]he divine hierarchy may consist either of gods, each with a province of his own as in Polytheism, or of angels and saints ministering to a supreme being as in Catholicism. The spontaneity of the first mode renders it both more complete and more durable … The second being systematised, and therefore capable of being discussed, can have no solidity, mental or social. Its function dwindles to softening the change from Theologism to Positivism.

Turning to the latter, he says:

> Positivity, having not yet taken shape as a philosophy, its work is provisionally delegated to the Metaphysical spirit, which thus seems to become the essential agent of the transition, whereas it can never be anything but an instrument of it. Now Ontology is not special. In its way it is no less general than the Theology from which it springs. Like Theology, it essays the search for Causes, and in a fashion equally absolute; only for deities, the spontaneous creation of the mind, it substitutes entities, the creation of systematic thought; and these, from the very fact that they are shadowy, are the better adapted to a transition. For each entity may be viewed, either as the spiritualised representation of the deity which it supersedes, or as a name for generalised phenomena, according as the thinker is more disposed to Theologism or Positivism. Thus the

> famous controversy between the Realists and the Nominalists, in whatever department of knowledge it arises, is the turning point in the Metaphysical state.

So it is to the real agent that Comte turns:

> The steady decline of the Theological spirit is really the work of the Positive spirit, and of nothing else. It is to be measured by the substitution of relative for absolute conceptions. In the succession of the three phases belonging to the Fictitious Regime, the unseen but real agent is Positivity, although Metaphysics figure as the ostensible instrument of it, because it is their nature to embrace all departments of thought ... the transition from Fetishism to Theologism was due to the spontaneous birth of the Positive spirit, which was then rising from the concrete observation of existences to the abstract observation of phenomena. Ontology springs from such a revolution rather than directs it. In the substitution of Monotheism for Polytheism its action is distinctly traceable, but not before...
>
> In the monotheistic stage, Ontology becomes incurably subversive, because its dissolving force has nothing to act on but a Theologism already reduced to the lowest point compatible with any social efficacy. Then stands confessed the necessary tendency of all Metaphysical thought to set up scepticism in philosophy, corruption in morals, and disorder in politics ... Divorced from science, from which it borrowed all its force, and from theology which alone gave it something to do, it vainly aspires to absolute domination at the very same moment ordained for its entire extinction. Henceforth it forms the principal obstacle to the advent of the Final Synthesis. (1968, vol. ii: 30–3)

In this passage the shifts of conception are registered. Most striking now is the clarity of Comte's idea that there are, from the beginning, only two effective modes of thinking (fictitious and positive), and it is the radical opposition and struggle between them that drives intellectual and social development. This reconceptualisation still has the shape of three stages, but it is evident that in this account the three stages are now those of spontaneous fetishism, then 'Theologism and Ontology' (polytheism, monotheism and metaphysics), and thirdly positivism. This reformulation is necessary because Comte's account is presented in the form of a narrative of the way thought relates to its object. In this perspective fetishism is based on a *First* Causality, while the polytheistic, monotheistic and metaphysical thought are all based on the *Second* Causality, that is via a strategy which appeals to an indirect and inaccessible realm of wills. It is the force of the positive spirit which determines the evolution of the states, and in which the metaphysical is once again seen as a mere extension of theologism, in entities that embody an arbitrary will.

The propositions developed here become even more complex, since it is argued not only that it is the positive movement which drives the development, but also both polytheism and monotheism are in a sense developments out of a fundamental form, fetishism, which always continues to rest alongside them, at times becoming absorbed, and then reacting on them in important ways. Curiously, at the end of the discussion of the laws of the three states, Comte announces (as Marx did for the passage from primitive to higher communism) that under the guidance of positivism, the peoples still at the state of fetishism may be able to pass from that state directly to the positive state, an 'artificial acceleration' made possible by the structural similarities, the 'fundamental affinity' (1968, ii: 128) between them (neither has recourse to the inaccessible realms of gods and entities). The construction of the religion of humanity indeed is the systematic 'incorporation' of fetishism into positivism: in place of an inaccessible Supreme Being, Comte proposes the trinity: Great Being *grand être* (humanity), *grand milieu* (space), and the *grand fétich* (the earth) (see Wernick, 2001: 177–86). The whole of Comte's consideration of the genealogy of the object of religion is to draw a sharp line of demarcation between *metaphysical* Supreme Being (nature personified as a deity), and Great Being (humanity under the emblem of the virgin) proposed within a new science. The latter has different roots and origins, and its arrival will not continue but break the simple historical chain. The function of Comte's sociology is now seen to reside in the capacity to draw this conclusion in order to draw the new religion under the scientific surveillance and control of the sociocrats. But sociocrats as priests of the religion of Humanity should adopt the subjective method, Comte suggests, and this gives imagination a quite different and even more expanded scope: it is not limited by observation and empirical verification, but by the theory and rules governing the construction of the utopias as a sacred genre of scientific fictions. Its limits are those of love's own dimensions (Wernick, 2001: 125–38). All law becomes scientific law, even that of love.

Prior to the famous *loi* Ferry of 1882, which introduced the Third Republic's educational programme of universal secular state education, there was the *loi* Guizot of 1833, which, elaborating on the law of 1816, made religious instruction the basis of post-revolutionary education. Catholicism had been divided in the revolution after the papal 'brief' from Pious VI to the Archbishop of Aix, demanding Catholics choose between the church and the French nation. The attitude of Rome to the post-revolutionary French culture was by and large one of reaction, leading eventually to 'papal infallibility'. Nevertheless, religion returned, fragmented, with the restoration of the monarchy to Louis XVII and Charles X. Subsequently Guizot made it obligatory for each commune to establish primary education, requiring the schools to teach religion through a daily catechism, and singing, and an image of Jesus in each classroom. Berenson notes that 'it was during these years that France's intellectual life was marked by an explosion of religious theorizing christocentric in orientation but at odds with official Catholic dogma.' It was, he reports, the time when, for example, George Sand called for a 'religious and social truth, one and the same', a truth to reconcile the religious spirit of Ballanche and Lamennais with the social idealism of Saint-Simon' (Berenson, 1989: 553). The writings of Lamennais, who broke with the church after a papal censure, in particular were widely popular, instituting what has been called a 'lyrical version of the Communist Manifesto' (Charlton, 1974: 55). Comte's adoption of the theme of love, of the virgin, of science and the priesthood of humanity was itself an attempt to realise this reconciliation: 'Comte was in love' and 'his love letters are treatises' (Lepenies, 1988: 28), and even his changed relations with George Sand who became an honoured follower (1988: 33). Here, as Wernick points out, 'men learn to love (in the exalted sense) *through* women' (2001: 149). Comte perhaps became a troubadour (Lepenies, 1988: 35: Serres, 1997). Comte sought a way through to an idiosyncretic structure that was a challenge not only to socialism, humanism, agnosticism and atheism, but also to both liberal and social Catholicism. He mistakenly thought that his subjective sacred altruistic scientific religion based on love would appeal to all parties.

When Comte explained the 'history of religion' in his *Catechism of Positivism* ([1851] 1891), he was at pains to show that both Protestantism and deism were deviations from the new genealogy of the spiritual authority established through the subjective method (1891: 285) which he presented as lying through French post-Catholicism (1891: 288). (The British experience was 'isolated', the French experienced 'the ephemeral ascendancy of a bloodthirsty deism' then 'the official restoration of Catholicism under the military tyranny' (1891: 291)). The scientific chain, now beginning with Thales and Pythagoras, and passing through Bichat and Gall, Condorcet leads to the founding of sociology with Comte himself architect of a goddess:

> The human point of view prevailing universally, a subjective synthesis could at length construct a philosophy really proof against all objections, and that led to the foundation of the final religion, as soon as the moral development had completed the regeneration of the intellect ... Humanity definitively substitutes herself for God. (1891: 293–4)

Thus Comte strives to accommodate the construction of the new genealogies to the lineage of the positive polity of the second cycle of writings, which seems to circle around his own experiences, his own regeneration, and to a new soft fetishistic fatalism and universal love (Wernick, 2001: 177–86).

But what neo-subjective reading is appropriate to Comte's recourse to fetishism? Here again Barthes is suggestive. Such a reading might take the form of a spiritualist archaeology, for

> if ... the Text ... contains a subject to love, that subject is dispersed, somewhat like the ashes we strew into the wind after death (the theme of the urn and the stone, strong closed objects, instructors of fate, will be contrasted with the bursts of memory, the erosion that leaves nothing but a few furrows of past life). (Barthes, 1976: 9)

Perhaps this return of the author, and of a particular form of supernatural reading, could be a kind of positivist spiritualism which might create the conditions for a series of subjective conversations, perhaps fragmentary and fugitive, with the first 'priest of Humanity'. As Barthes notes, however, 'the author who returns is not the same one identified by our institutions ... he is not even the biographical hero. The author who leaves his text and comes into our life has no unity; he is a mere plural of "charms"' (1976: 8). Perhaps one way of seducing 'Auguste Comte' would be someone with a knowledge of what Barthes calls 'biographemes' – the minor details of a life: its preferences, inflections, loved fetishes that connect with another order of signifiers. (These objects were called *apports* by the spiritualists. Just like those found at the Maison d'Auguste Comte in Paris as described by Ronald Fletcher: 'his two tall candlesticks ... the small wall blackboard ... visiting cards' (in Comte, 1974a: 5), or Lepenies: 'upon the wall, occupying the entire width of the table, there hangs a mirror. When he sat and wrote, Auguste Comte was always looking at himself' (Lepenies, 1988: 46)).

Comte became more directly conservative and wrote an *Appeal to Conservatives* ([1855] 1889). This opened the space for the development of a right-wing tradition of social theory in France which continues to this day. Here the link, rejected within the earlier period of objective method, between Catholicism and positivism is made firmly in the following observation:

> When all fear of reaction is sufficiently dispelled, the apostles of Humanity will encourage towards Jesuitism the sympathies which are proclaimed by the true philosophy of history and sanctioned in the worship it has already produced. At the same time, the real organs of modern Catholicism, renouncing the official power which perverted their social tendencies, will resume, on a better basis, the admirable attempt of their eminent founder to establish the spiritual independence of a noble priesthood. In this way the special worship of the Virgin may soon be transformed as to prepare the Catholic nations for the universal adoration of Humanity [...] the noble enthusiast [Loyola] who founded Jesuitism made an effort to return to the construction of chivalry ... systematised by the Ignatians under Positivist inspiration, these dispositions will soon have over come the resistance both of Protestants and sceptics ... It follows that Catholicism ought at the present day to constitute, in the evolution of the best preparation for Positivism, of which it was, collectively, the necessary precursor ... Although the Universal Religion could only come into existence as a result of complete emancipation, it will be fully appreciated only by those who have never ceased to cultivate feeling in order to establish unity under the most perfect of the provisional forms. (Comte, 1889: 119–21)

Thus, for Comte the genealogy of positivism, when making his appeal to conservatives, is established through the 'celebrated corporation' (the Jesuit order, suppressed by papal 'brief' in 1773, and re-established by a 'brief' from Pious VII, in 1814) between medieval Catholicism and positivism. Again it is emphasised that for the positive polity: the lineage does *not* pass through Protestantism and deism, but through the lineage of the counter-Reformation. As Serres has pointed out, however, the extraordinary omission from the long lists of saints in Comte's new positive calendar is Jesus (Serres, 1995b: 449). This did not prevent the right-wing thinkers of the Third Republic, Barrés, Maurras and Péguy, and Count Léon de Montesquiou-Fezenac (the first to hold the Auguste Comte chair in Positive Philosophy at the Institut de l'Action Français) from believing that the future of France lay in developing an alliance between Catholicism and positivism – not 'positivism in the narrower sense' (Maurras) but the aestheticised positivism of the later Comte (Lepenies, 1988: 44).

Comte claimed that his later writings resulted from the application of 'cerebral hygiene'. He refrained from reading any new texts. He read the great books of the mystical Christian and poetic tradition, particularly *Imitation of Christ* by Thomas à Kempis, in order to know how to pray, and how to prepare himself to serve not God but humanity. Did Comte acknowledge the instruction in à Kempis to 'abandon desire' (Thomas à Kempis, 1997: 140)? Or was Comte simply preparing himself for his great new mission implied in his remark that unlike Christian submission (1977: 208), a 'worthy individuality' is required in the worship before humanity? Indeed, there was hint of arrogance in his reflection that: 'few men are warranted in thinking themselves indispensable to Humanity: such language is only applicable to the true authors of the principal steps in our progress' (Comte, 1891: 57). Certainly, Comte took refuge from the harsh, ironic and cruel reality of this world as soon as he entered into the purifying discipline of 'hygiene'. In his *Subjective Synthesis* (1856), Comte announced his flight into the utopian future, that his attitude would habitually become a posthumous one, and that he was writing, not by false attribution, but in displaced temporality, in the year 1927. This work is constructed on a strange system of numbers (for sentences, paragraphs, chapters) and acrostically (so that the letters beginning each paragraph, and indeed beginning each set of sentences, are arranged to form the name of a saint in the Comtean system (cf. Baudrillard's writing on anagrams (1993b)). *The Subjective Synthesis* is an attempt to construct a subjective mathematics, as a basic order of fetishistic logic, a founding cabala for a neo-pagan priesthood. In fact the work is conceived as an attempt to supplement his analysis of the law of the three states with an account of the vicissitudes of mathematics since the Greeks, and to attempt to intervene and reverse these development trends in neo-metaphysical mathematics towards such theory as permutations, probabilities etc., by resort to pre-metaphysical, pre-theological numerology. Comte's vision of the Western transition is broadened in scope (no longer from the collapse of the medieval polity). It now occurs between the theocracies of Graeco-Roman antiquity and the sociocracy to come (1856: 713). This provides immense resources for Comte to draw on for both neo-fetishistic fictions derived from the sciences and those based on a subjective logic. Thus all the ideas that have suggested the world was not inert but living should be revived (1856: 9). The earth should be imagined as having been a living body and could, altruistically, have arranged its axes, etc., with the express intent of making the seasons possible for the needs of the Great Being to come (1856: 11). Such ideas are the subjective equivalent of the fictions already generated as hypotheses within the positive sciences in the objective idiom, but now become subject to another, an aesthetic socio-centric discipline. Comte also extended the use of the opposition subjective and objective in the life of humanity, such that the objective (actually living) would always increasingly be dominated by the subjective (the dead). Comte therefore outlined a vast and melancholy system of ancestor worship to cement the elements of the new social formation (Comte, 1968, vol. iv).

The radical differences between the two methods

Comte's sociology thus underwent drastic reformulations over the course of thirty years. Having surveyed these changes, we are in a better position to see how Comte constructed his various sociological genealogies, how they developed a radical opposition, and how they combine together. His early analysis of the modes of construction of scientific theory showed how the sciences form a differential system over an ascending series of domains: the branches of the division of knowledge are revolutionised one by one. At a certain point in its development it becomes possible to establish a reasonable harmonisation of the differential system and to derive new philosophical principles from it. The aim of this intervention is to complete the series and to prepare not only a scientific ethics capable of regulating the modern social order but also to establish the sacred college as a spiritual corporation to develop and to govern it.

Comte wants to show us not that the final positive state is simply 'Catholicism minus Christianity' (Thomas Huxley), or 'Catholicism minus God' (Serres), for Catholicism was already a secondary element in his assessment of the medieval polity. Littré is nearer the mark when he remarked it is a conception of 'religion without theology' (1879: 386). The social structures of the proposed utopia, the final state, are those which Comte derived from Rome (patrician, proletarian, matriarchal) and regulated in a new papal spiritual authority, finding its doctrine in a completion of the scientific series initiated in Egypt and Greece. This is a kind of Caesaro-papism without a Caesar, a French Empire without an Emperor (for the thematic of Caesarism, see Thody, 1989; Baehr, 1998: 284–5). And this, as Debray noted, appears to bring Comte close to certain Marxist polities: 'anyone who wants to understand real socialism should read the *Catéchisme positiviste*' (Debray, 1983: 231; for political catechisms in France see Richter, 1995: 112). But Comte is more idealistic than any communist leader. He insisted that in the new regime 'there will never arise in it a temporal power with a possibility of universal domination, such as the phantom emperor of the Middle Ages, who was therein, for Catholicism, nothing but a disturbing relic, an empirical offshoot of the Roman order' (Comte, 1891: 247). This synthesis reintegrates a fundamental fetishism into popular aestheticised culture from above. Comte's subjective conception of the genealogy of social forms which will be fused together follows a parallel course to that of the sciences. Invention, maturation and transmission occur in these three modes.

The significance of combining the two opposed methods

A number of elements are now in place to allow us to begin to analyse Comte's mode of sociological construction. Comments made at the end of volume 2 and the end of volume 3 of the *System* allow us to see exactly what Comte had in mind. Comte says that the theory of social statics must lead to a determination of the overall trajectory of the course of history:

> When a curve has many asymptotes … we may obtain from the sum of them as a preliminary, valuable indications as to the general figure of the curve … But no use of these right lines will ever supply the place of direct and specific treatment of the orbit described by the curve. (1968, vol. 2: 385)

And when Comte had completed the study of social dynamics in the next volume, he concluded that he had previously noted that 'statics' had

> merely ascertained the general system of asymptotes belonging to the orbit which humanity may be said to describe, but that it did not decide the character of the curve itself: those fundamental data being such that they might be equally satisfied by more than one curve. But social dynamics have now determined the actual curve, for they have explained in detail an arc of sufficient length to enable us to foresee what course the arc must take when continued, with as much accuracy as is suited to the practical aim of a study in which we must never try to forecast too precisely. (1968, vol. 3: 534–5).

In fact this is the heart of what is specific to the language of late Comtean sociology, and it has two principal aspects. The first is the identification of the extreme or polar states, which indeed might be called Comtean *polarities*. The second is the mode of construction of the arc or orbit which connects these states: this is done by an analysis which uses each state Comte asymptotically to construct an estimation of its specific orbit, completed in the dynamic analysis. Taken literally, Comte has persuaded himself that he has discovered the ultimate tendency, which if extrapolated will lead to a forecast. We could call this the Comtean *orbit* of the cycle, which describes the *arc* between the polarities. The subjective method, he concludes, can change the order of analysis from 1 → 3 → 2, to 1 → 2 → 3. This can provide the basis for believing that the utopian scheme for the positive polity is the realisation of a historical tendency identified through objective analysis.

It is essential to note that there are further fundamental differences for Comte between these objective and subjective constructions, since the identification of the two extremes, the polarities, is said to be deduced from the law of human nature, and the orbit is induced from socio-historical calculation. Comte talks about a convergence in their conclusions. How is this determined? In fact there are two quite different operations: the intercalation of necessary elements of theory-fiction based on a deduction from the known laws of human nature (phrenology in this case), and an inductive and fictive extension of the orbit on which humanity is known to travel. Mill was right to suggest that Comte followed a method of 'inverse deduction' but was wrong to think that Comte's extreme states were real historical concrete entities. They are products of theory-fictions, both of deduction (Comte's *polarities*) and induction (Comte's *orbit*). It was Comte's hope that he had got it right and that he had accurately determined these logics converged in the positive polity. We must note, of course, that all these fictions were subject to the fundamental rule of Comtean method, that observation forms the basis of the construction and validation.

Comtean sociology is an immense intellectual construction designed to register one essential conclusion: that the line of social and intellectual progression does not lead towards the triumph of (metaphysical) democratic forms characterised by the sovereignty of the people through a genealogy which traverses Protestantism, deism and revolutionary dictatorship. The progressive line of the historical development of humanity follows quite another orbit. The decisive question perhaps is whether this elaborate system of social science fictions tells Comte something about that which remained non-fictional, and which he did not wish to hear? If he did make real discoveries, perhaps they are to be found not in his theory of the future, but where he least expected, namely in his analysis of the metaphysical state which focused at that very point where perfection met imperfection (it produced its own polity where it met an insurmountable obstacle), at the point where conjectures are sacrificed. But when he applied two methods he discovered that his historical genealogies were not of the same type and did not lead to the same end state.

Did Comte reach out, in his subjective method, for 'inter-cultural reconciliation', as Serres suggested, or was he 'the aged thinker [who] appears to elevate himself above the work of his life, though in reality he ruins it through infusing it with enthusiasms, sweetness, spices, poetic mists and mystic lights' (Nietzsche)? Or was this project a gigantic effort in cultural imperialism?

The period before Comte's death in 1857 was taken up with the theatricalisation of the transition to the final and highest stage of society as a ritual of purification. The key element in this vision was the completion of the sequence of the sciences, with moral science making its entry as the final seventh science. Here the sciences become organised by a new priesthood extending its authority over the process of the withering-away of the state: the European states would be divided into sixty small and relatively weak city-states (Vernon, 1984; Comte, 1968, vol. iv: ch. 5). In order to attain the final polity, the dictatorship of the proletariat would purify the economic life of the commercial spirit. Paris would become the spiritual centre of the new republic, a sacred city, and the remains of the key players in the long formative drama of the 'three states' would be reinterred there in vast memorial ceremonies. Comte proposed that Napoleon's remains should go back to St Helena (1968, vol. iv: 245). The new spiritual authority, based on a complete and harmonised system of scientific knowledge, would guarantee an era of peace and stability in rational time. In effect Comte had created the second of the Saint-Simonian sacred colleges with himself, following in the steps of Bazard and Enfantin, as the third Saint-Simonian Pope. Indeed Littré reports that at one of the last meetings of the Positivist Society he attended, Comte referred to a letter he had written to a member as a 'brief'. For a moment, Littré says, he thought this was metaphorical, but it was a request from Comte issued directly as a papal brief (*bref*). 'From this moment on', says Littré the astonished witness, 'Comte made himself the High Priest of Humanity, Pope, and wrote *briefs*' (Littré, 1864: 631).

In the next chapter I examine the significant but underestimated attempts by Littré to learn from the failures of Comteanism, and to try to save 'sociology'.

4

The End of the First Cycle: Scholasticism

> Of Littré's Dictionary: 'the undertaking of one man, over a period of more than thirty years ... if copied on one column only, would be over twenty miles long' (Aquarone, 1958: 77)

Emile Littré was Comte's most eminent disciple. Born in 1801 into a Protestant family, his education was largely in classical languages, philology and medicine. He broke off his medical education at the age of 26 in order to look after his mother and brother after his father died. He became known as a political activist in the events of 1830, the overthrow of Charles X, and by his subsequent writings in the journal *National* (1830–51) and his many translations. Certainly today he is far more famous than Comte and known throughout France as the author of the *Littré* – the standard French dictionary. Littré, Comte's most important disciple in the 'objective' mode, refused to follow Comte into the Religion of Humanity. Like Mill he remained a rationalist, and committed to the project for a scientific sociology promised in Comte's writings up to 1844. After Comte's death the positivist movement divided into two. On the one hand was the religious tradition of positivism, and on the other the rationalist tradition which had Littré at its head until his death in 1881. It was Littré who kept the writings of the early Comte in the public eye with a second edition of the *Course in Positive Philosophy* in 1864 with a 'Préface d'un Disciple' (Littré, 1864b: v-L). Littré not only composed the monumental French dictionary (*Dictionnaire de la langue française* 1873), but had also constructed a *Dictionnaire de médecine* in 1863, a work which was associated with the Société de Biologie he founded in 1848 with Charles Robin and Claude Bernard. But Littré contributed to the sociological tradition in two very important ways at the end of the first cycle in relation to a Société de Sociologie and the journal *La Philosophie Positive* which he established with a Russian émigré, Wyrouboff. First he tried to reconstruct Comtean sociology in 1872 by reworking its basic concepts, and secondly in the 1870s he revisited all the major predictions of Comteanism of the 1840s to try to assess their accuracy and to learn from the errors he could find. Before examining these, it is important to pose the question: why did Littré reject the subjective method?

Littré's critique of the subjective method

Like Mill, Littré refused to follow Comte from philosophy into the Religion of Humanity, and refused to accept the papal authority that Comte began to claim in issuing *brefs*, on the model of the Catholic Pontiff (Littré 1879). Littré's position rejected the inauguration of a religion that was simply based on a series of fictions, however much they were associated with genuine emotion arising from the death of Clotilde de Vaux. But his objection was more fundamentally concerned with method. He cited Comte's formulation from *System*, 'It is the two methods [objective and subjective] together that found the true religious logic, which regenerates and consecrates the two opposite paths followed by theology and science in preparing, each in its own manner, our definitive state' (cited by Littré, 1879: 536). In fact, Comte had always insisted previously that the two paths were opposite or even 'radically opposed'. But what Littré objected to was that Comte really wanted an 'amalgam' of the two methods, in which the subjective method was misconceived. Instead of it conforming to the rigour of a truly deductive procedure, it worked, he said, by 'the liaison of premises and consequences into an unlimited field, nothing could stop it or give it boundaries, and because of that, it was a metaphysical *construction* which embraces man and the world'. By contrast, the deductive method was one that had to face real obstacles which arose from experience, in order to verify, correct, or reject inadequate theory. Comte entered onto the slippery slope of 'premisses and consequences', the false route in the sciences and 'particularly in sociology' (1879: 534). But what interested Littré was Comte's new use of fictions. He noticed that in the first volume of *System*, Comte had written:

> If life was universal, the existence of any natural law would be impossible ... Those thinkers who put forward the conception that the Earth was an immense animal, could have had no proper idea of what the word animal implied: or they would have felt that such an hypothesis was utterly incoherent ... Prevision of future event, whether founded on reason or experience, would be alike impossible. (Littré 1879: 575; Comte, 1968, vol. i: 357).

Comte is quite naïve, says Littré, to think that any cult would develop in relation to beliefs that are known to be invented fictions. Comte's construction is simply a transformation of his adolescent Catholic belief in the Trinity, now become the positive trinity: space, earth, humanity – 'grand-milieu', 'grand-fétiche', 'grand-être' (1864: 576).

Littré's attempt to resolve the crisis of sociology in the 1870s

In a paper to the first sociological society, Littré attempted to reconstruct the basic features of Comte's objective sociology. The paper was called 'Plan for a Treatise in Sociology' (the paper was read to the Société de Sociologie on 23 May 1872). This reconstruction was not however an attempt to draw out the lessons from the mistakes of sociology, but was developed at an entirely conceptual level. The short text of seven pages is one of the most scholastic essays ever conceived. The paper is labyrinthine, and bristling with neologisms of such complexity that no discourse using them could ever realistically have taken place. Littré takes essential ideas from Comte and ingeniously reworks them, taking as his main organising principle the distinction between social statics and social dynamics. He introduces new conceptual divisions in an avalanche of neologisms. Statics becomes *sociomérie*; dynamics is divided into two: *sociergie* (the study of social reproduction) and *sociauxie* (the term for progress and the site of the law of the three states).

The important conceptual innovation in this paper is the general reorganisation of social dynamics. The concept of *sociergie* relates to what Littré calls the dynamics of social maintenance, and this dynamic is to be found in five social functions, each of which has its own new concept: *socioporie* (production and consumption), *sociagathie* (ethics), *sociocalie* (aesthetics), *socialéthie* (science) and *socioarchie* (government and law). These are seen to be reproductive or maintenance of the basic population (demography) and human family which is the core of social statics (*sociomérie*). The larger field of social dynamics is *sociauxie* – is it here that Littré establishes the order of theological, metaphysical and positive states. His proposed treatise aims to discuss *sociauxie* in eight chapters (from the accumulation of culture, to milieux and races). But this discussion of dynamic processes is used as a way of returning to statics (*sociomérie*) to examine the social orders themselves: tribe, clan, city and commune, nation, groups of nations, civilisation and humanity. Finally, Littré proposes to replace the notion of pathology with that of *sociotaraxie* in four main instances: demographic decline, crises of production, fortuitous calamities in history, and the case of revolutions (where opinion becomes incompatible with social institutions). Littré gives the derivation for each Greek part of the nine new terms.

The effort of solving theoretical problems by reconceptualisation is evidently an important element of reconstructing a discipline, especially when terms have become dated and imprecise. However, in this case the effect is quite ludicrous. This riot of neologisms is done largely for its own sake and makes discourse quite impossible: the reaction of the sociological society is not recorded. But the main defect is that any new idea is drowned with unnecessary change. There was no call for production to become *socioporie*, or pathology to become *sociotaraxie*. But the reconceptualisation of dynamics into *sociergie* and *sociauxie* has merit, though the terms are not elegant. The basic theoretical change which Littré sought to introduce was to make social statics more focused on the human population and family, on which the larger structures, cities, and nations were developed, and then to envisage production and government etc. as dynamic functions, seen from the '*point de vue sociergique*'. This text, then, is an object lesson in purely scholastic reconstruction, an attempt to resolve a crisis in sociology through the conjuration of new terminology.

Littré's sociological 'confessions'

Littré's attempt to examine the validity of Comtean predictions was published in the second edition of his book *Conservation, revolution et positivisme* in 1879. It is worth noting that Emile Durkheim by that time was already 21. The first edition of the work had been published in 1852 as a collection of articles published in the journal *National* from July 1849 to October 1851. Each article is followed by an appraisal written in 1878. This set of self-criticisms Littré calls his 'confessions' (1879: 480). The judgement is harsh against the notion of the imminence of the positive polity, the emergence of the spiritual power in the form of a priesthood modelled on feudal faith and homage, the role of the proletariat, the scope of positive philosophy in governing the sciences, and the future of the Religion of Humanity and much else. The main plank of Comteanism, viz. the positive polity, 'appears to me today' as an impossible 'utopia', he wrote (1879: 65). Littré had by this time rejected the revolutionary tradition of 1848 and the Commune, and had thrown his lot in with the reconstruction of France and the compromises of the Third Republic. In the field of education, for example, he noted that the discipline was still divided between the state (intellectual and scientific education) and the clergy (moral education), but a compromise had been reached whereby the state was strong enough to resist any attempts by the church to change the situation (1879: 219).

A new form of legitimacy through consent had become established, Littré argued. This form was based on universal male suffrage and he embraced it enthusiastically in the 1870s. 'Consent is the social axiom which has replaced the theological axiom' (1879: 65). This is not, he insisted, any absolute sovereignty of the people, but a social form subject to law. This was a dramatic change of position, for Littré had written a report for the Société Positiviste in August 1848 on the form that the new revolutionary republic should take, and it was a resumé of this which was published in *National* in October 1849 (1879: 246). One of the key proposals of that report was to shift power to 'eminent proletarians' who would lead society through the 'revolutionary transition' to the new society (1879: 241). The purely parliamentary organs were to be avoided, since they are simply governed by rhetoric and elocution. The economic management should be organised at a local level in Departments, and should be in the hands of experienced, self-financing, rich administrators and limited to purely budgetary affairs. The central power should be elected only from Paris and the great cities and should take the form of a triumvirate (1879: 243). Littré argued that the modern revolution had been led first by the kings, then the bourgeoisie. It was now the moment of the proletariat to seize the initiative, since proletarians were free from all metaphysical prejudices and possessed the 'sentiment of sociability' necessary for this role (1879: 242–3).

He reviewed this in 1878, noting that during the Commune of 1871 someone had quoted it against him and accused him of furnishing arms for the Commune. But as he had already retracted his position publicly in 1863, the accusation was withdrawn (1879: 247). He noted that Comte's own manifesto for 1848 came too late (1879: 157). But Littré's reappraisal suggests in fact that there had been no real possibility of a revolutionary transitional government in 1848: the provinces were against Paris, the bourgeoisie had a preponderance over the proletariat and the peasants were against socialist systems (1879: 248). Had Comte lived to see the Commune of 1871, he would not have recognised the proletariat at all, for Paris had become 'ultra-revolutionary' (1879: 249). The Commune was a failure since it had lost touch with the country, so that 'neither the Government nor the provinces accepted its authority'. In 1878 universal male suffrage had been re-established and a new polity was becoming stabilised. Did this realise Comte's idea of transition? 'In no way', said Littré (1879: 250): Comte's view was that the parliamentary regime would be quickly replaced by 'something like industrial feudalism, where captains of industry would submit to the new spiritual power' (1879: 250). In fact the parliamentary regime, whether monarchical or republican, had become more general through Europe than ever: 'These regimes give sufficient guarantees for order, also for liberty … and are open to reform.' The new regime does not yet have an ideal, and this is where Comte's analysis may be useful, said Littré: the direction of the republic should be towards greater and greater influence of positive knowledge in society and over its government, a growth accompanied always by greater humanity and justice; the goal is to give the positive conception of the world a definitive ascendancy, thus stamping its character on the new regime' (1879: 253). But this will not come, he stressed, as a result of socialism now become too metaphysical, too revolutionary, too much the enemy of the laws of history and civilisation (1879: 454).[1]

Not only is there reflection on politics and philosophy, but Littré also reflected on religion. In 1878, he said that religion can be defined as 'an ensemble of doctrines and practices which constitute the relation of man with the divine power. It expresses therefore an idea of the supernatural, and even deism admits a personal god which is not part of nature.' But Comte's version is that 'religion is an ensemble of doctrines and practices which constitute the relation of man with an ideal' (1879: 385). Positive knowledge acts as an irresistible dissolving force on all major religions, and this very fact makes a new situation come into existence, the possibility of a universal religion in which humanity will be a new ideal, and this will be a 'religion without a theology' (1879: 386). Littré even talks of the collective idealisation of humanity (1879: 397), but since the 1840s, this ideal which was embraced so warmly had gone cold (1879: 410). Comte wanted a demonstrated not a revealed religion. But the problem for Littré is that in defining religion through its philosophy, there remains the problem of defining the social state that corresponds to the definition. Comte had attempted to reflect and revise the law of the three states to accommodate the fact that it was only within the tradition of Western Catholicism and Protestantism that the evolution to the positive polity had occurred. The three monotheisms – Judaism, Christianity and Islam – for Littré show this stage is 'susceptible to many different solutions'. New religions cannot control the outcome of their own development (1879: 412), and so Littré leaves the law of religious evolution in ruins.

As for the nature of science, he draws forthright conclusions. The more the science is 'simple' in the Comtean sense, the easier it is to make predictions, as in astronomy, Littré concluded. The more it is 'complex', the more difficult it is to make them. His predictions of more and more peaceful order in Europe had been utterly refuted by wars in Russia, Italy and then in France itself. Comteans did not foresee either the growth of nationalist movements and how they would become a threat to international peace (1879: 479). Thus there are different types of prediction: prevision and conjecture. The first can only be made at an advanced state of any complex discipline, the second can be made in the light of theory and experience (1879: 484). The process of learning was to be a protracted one requiring systematic rectifications of theoretical assumptions.

Conclusions

Littré was near the end of his intellectual career when he wrote these 'Confessions' in 1878. But neither his positivist journal (and the sociology society), nor the Religion of Humanity organised in the various positivist churches across France and the world, served to regenerate sociology. Heilbron has analysed the membership of the Société de Sociologie from details of the 25 members given in its journal and elsewhere: 17 out of 25 had been to university and some held university positions; 16 had political functions; 3 were writers; 5 were officials; 5 were members of parliament; 3 were ministers. In 1872 their average age was 48. Littré did not impose any intellectual discipline so it could not function as a sect or a school or indeed a college (Simon, 1963: 38). In 1883 the journal debated whether to change its format and become a wider general philosophical journal. It chose to cease publication in the face of 'general indifference for general questions' and lack of interest in 'scientific synthesis' (see Aquarone, 1958: 156–8).

The orthodox positivists followed Pierre Lafitte in the Société Positiviste – in 1857 there were 43 members, these were either intellectuals (10 of whom were physicians) or skilled workers (15). Lafitte was a mathematics teacher, who was elected to a newly created chair in the history of science at the Collège de France in 1892. But the journal of this society, *Revue Occidentale* published no new material on sociology at all, as if all there was to be done had been done. Heilbron succinctly sums up the situation in the latter part of the century. He notes that in both the Lafitte and the Littré groups

> the most striking fact was perhaps the absence of university philosophers. In neither of the positivist networks was there anyone with a position at the Faculty of Letters ... In the decades after 1870 most sociologists were graduates of the Ecole normale supérieure who sought careers in the Faculty of Letters. They were the ones who turned sociology into a university subject. (Heilbron, 1995: 257)

A new cycle was about to commence.

Note

1 The prospect of a positive polity in the sense of a political structure guided by a social science was picked up by French communism as it appropriated the revolutionary tradition of the Commune. As Furet notes, 'The Commune represents a major date in the history of the exile of the working-class movement in French democracy: only Jaurès, at the end of the century, would try to bring it to a close, but without success, because after the First World War the communists would, on the contrary, turn it into the principle of their influence' (Furet, 1992: 506).

The Second Cycle, 1880–1939

The First Rebirth of Social Theory: Anomie

A state of *anomie* is impossible wherever organs solidly linked to one another are in sufficient contact … But … if some opaque environment is interposed, then only stimuli of a certain intensity can be communicated from one organ to another. Relations, being rare, are not repeated enough to be determined … The lines of passage taken by the streams of movement cannot deepen because the streams are too intermittent. If some rules come to constitute them, they are, however, general and vague, for under these conditions it is only the most general contours of the phenomena that can be fixed […] if the division of labour does not produce solidarity … it is because the organs are not regulated; it is because they are in a state of *anomie*. (Durkheim, [1893] 1964: 368, 1984: 304–5)

5

Social Theory Reborn

> Alone in Bordeaux, Durkheim was painfully aware of the vastness of his task and his relative powerlessness. (Mauss, 1983: 140)

Before a large group standing on the pavement in front of 92 Boulevard Roosevelt, Bordeaux, on Thursday 18 May 1995, a plaque was unveiled to Emile Durkheim, 'founder of French sociology'. A number of speeches were made by local dignatories and academics attending the Colloque International being held at Bordeaux in celebration of the 100th anniversary of Durkheim's famous *Rules of Sociological Method*. Charles-Henri Cuin, who had organised the conference, emphasised in an interview for the local newspaper that the fame of Durkheim had had to be reinstated in Bordeaux where Durkheim had written his founding works after decades of neglect when students had been instructed to 'forget Durkheim'. But this very act of remembering Emile Durkheim only served to contradict Durkheim's own careful judgement that sociology had been founded by Auguste Comte: 'It is only with Auguste Comte that the great project conceived by Saint-Simon began to become a reality ... It is Comte who is the father ... It was also Comte who gave it the name sociology' (Durkheim [1915], 1975, vol. 1: 110–11; see also Heilbron, in Besnard, 1993: 59–66) and Gane, in Cuin (1997: 31–8). But if Comte founded sociology in his *Course in Positive Philosophy* (1830–42), Durkheim was not even a second-generation sociologist.

It should be remembered that even the recognition now accorded to Durkheim is recent and hard won. Indeed, the centenary of Durkheim's birth (1958), as Lévi-Strauss was to point out, 'passed almost unnoticed', although a belated commemoration was held at the Sorbonne in January 1960 (Lévi-Strauss, 1967: 8). Today French sociology likes to think of itself as beginning with Durkheim. This is to place the beginnings of sociology with its inauguration as an institutionalised, university discipline. None of the Littré generation of sociologists was educated at the Ecole Normale Supérieure, however Durkheim's generation were principally educated there (Heilbron, 1995: 257). But sociology did not begin in a university, it began outside the academy, two-thirds of a century earlier. It was already known throughout the world in the works of Comte, Mill, and above all Herbert Spencer, well before Durkheim was appointed to teach at the crucial strategic intersection of the Third Republic: 'social science with pedagogy' in Bordeaux in 1887, where the Rector at Bordeaux noted '*Il entend son enseignement comme une sorte d'apostolat*' (in Clarke, 1973: 183). With Durkheim, sociology receives its first genuine renaissance.

Durkheim and the rebirth of sociology

Durkheim did not claim to be the founder of sociology, rather he claimed to have made a decisive modification to the intellectual tradition that originates from Saint-Simon and Comte. In so doing he broke with the 'orthodox' Comtean traditions following either Littré or Lafitte, or the rival right-wing Comteans of the Institut de l'Action Français – those 'royalists and republicans, socialists and reactionaries, atheists and Catholics [who] persisted in their assertion that there existed a legitimate sociology serving the national interests of France: the sociology of Comte' (Lepenies, 1988: 46). The project for a new sociology was led by young philosophers trained at the Ecole Normale Supérieure; as Heilbron rightly emphasises, 'Comte's followers did not play any role in this process' (Heilbron, 1995: 257).[1]

Although Durkheim's sociology belongs to a tradition that was evolutionist and holistic, and refused to acknowledge a break between anthropology and sociology, it was within the Durkheim school that this separation occurred, with important effects on theory. Durkheim's holistic approach continued Comte's belief that the role of social science was to provide guidance for specific kinds of social intervention to restore societies to normal states. Crucial to the success of this project was the need for sociology to align itself with other, more established sciences within the institutions of the higher educational system, the universities. These were seen as a relatively autonomous haven for research which could remain free from direct political partisanship. As part of this endeavour, the concept of social pathology was given considerable importance, thereby revealing the extent to which Durkheim's sociology, like that of Comte, was consciously modelled on the medical ideal of therapeutic intervention. There was no fundamental philosophical reason why sociology could not define and legitimate, in its own special way, social and moral norms. An essential part of Durkheim's project was to work out new rules for determining the distinction between normal and pathological social phenomena. In this respect Durkheim went much further in a direction outlined in principle by Comte.

Although Durkheim secured a position teaching social sciences at the University of Bordeaux from 1887, his initial formation was in philosophy which he taught at various Lycées (Sens, Saint-Quentin and Troyes). His position at Bordeaux and later in Paris (from 1902) required that he teach courses in education as well as in sociology. The corpus of Durkheim's work consists of major books (*The Division of Labour in Society, The Rules of Sociological Method, Suicide*, and *The Elementary Forms of the Religious Life*), one or two minor books (on Montesquieu, Primitive Classification [with Mauss], Moral Education), but also important lecture courses that were published posthumously (*Socialism, Professional Ethics, The Evolution of Educational Thought in France*) and courses which are based on notes taken by students (*Pragmatism*). In addition there are a large number of journal articles (some gathered into collections), verbatim reports of debates, book reviews, and letters (letters to Marcel Mauss, for example, published for the first time in 1998). But Durkheim did not work in isolation, he founded a school of sociology organised around the journal *L'Année Sociologique*. The aim of the project was to ensure the implantation of sociology within the universities as a reputable discipline with a vital role to play in the identification of the normal forms of the emerging institutional structures of modern societies, for French society in the 1890s was in turmoil (Kaplan, 1995).

There are two notable features of Durkheim's sociological writings. The first is the commitment to rationalist idioms. This is particularly clear in his methodological requirements with their demand for clear and precise conceptual definition, rigorous formulation of problems, careful consideration for quality of evidence, canons of proof: sociology should break with ideological methods and establish a scientific rigour that could facilitate the discovery of the basic social laws governing social development and the formation of different modes of social solidarity. The second feature is Durkheim's disavowal of the central role of cognition in social processes. If Durkheim follows in general the aims outlined in Comte's *Course*, (1830–42), yet he criticised the specific forms of Comte's analyses and their results in detail. It is striking, for example, that Durkheim from the first focused on what he called 'moral facts', as against the emphasis on cognition in Comte's law of the three states. Indeed, Durkheim's studies reveal something missing in Comte: a serious absence of any sociological consideration of morals, laws, norms, sanctions, as well as what might be called 'social causation' in the treatment of religion, culture and social development. For Comte, progression revolves around revelation, conversion, demonstration, as a progression of reason.

Durkheim's emphasis seems to reflect a new awareness both of the importance of Kant's work in the writing of Renouvier and others, the problem of the relation between the individual and society, and the fact that religions do not arise from cognitive reflection but are born in social effervescence. The irruption of religious fervour in the French Revolution stemmed not as an intellectual legacy from Rousseau but as the effect of a social cause: the surge of new social energies (Durkheim, 1975b: 331). This new project can be seen as an attempt to unify within the field of the sociological project the perspectives, transformed no doubt, of Kant and Comte (and Spencer). In Durkheim, work on the social categories, the sociology of knowledge, and sociology of religion is situated in a broader concern to deal with the philosophical problems raised by these earlier writers and to place their ideas, suitably reconstructed, into a single analytical frame. The image of the social organism was thus considerably modified by Durkheim – a change evident in the importance he gave to the concept of the action of the *conscience collective*.

Durkheim repeated several times that he was 'following the path opened up' by Comte (Durkheim, [1907] 1980: 77), but was doing so in a new way. He remained highly critical of Comtean epistemology and the way Comte's law of the three states was formulated: 'If, as Comte thought, historical development is unilinear, if it is constituted by a single and unique series which begins with humanity itself and continues without end, it is evident that, since all terms of comparison are lacking, it cannot be reduced to laws' ([1906] 1980: 73). The law of the three social states – theological, metaphysical and positive – did not for Durkheim establish an adequate conceptualisation of social species: it was essentially arbitrary – for why should evolution stop at the third state? Yet if Durkheim was hostile to the general form of Comte's sociology, he affirmed very specifically Comte's analysis of European history since the Middle Ages: 'Comte's law correctly describes the way modern societies have developed from the tenth to the nineteenth century – but it does not apply to the entire course of human evolution' (Durkheim, 1962: 268). And rather than adopt Comte's terminology of the three states, he opted for a modified version of the morphological classification developed by Herbert Spencer, a classification by mode and degree of complexity of social composition, from segmental to organised societal forms. Durkheim was at pains to insist the form was not unilinear, but involved genuine non-teleological diversity: 'the genealogical tree of organized beings, instead of having the form of a geometric line, resembles more nearly a very bushy tree whose branches, issuing haphazardly all along the trunk, shoot out capriciously in all directions' ([1888] 1978: 53). Thus Durkheim made a fine distinction between the genealogical analysis within a single real continuous society (historical sequence), a comparative analysis within a single society and societies of the same type, and a much more abstract, comparative cross-cultural analysis leading to the construction of a theoretical evolutionary typologies.

It is important to specify what is involved in these distinctions. There is a convincing argument that Durkheim's evolutionary conception at the beginning of his career was a six-stage model: the elementary horde, simple clan-based tribe, tribal confederation, ancient city-state, medieval society, modern industrial nation (Wallwork, 1984). Durkheim divides these societies into two basic types, and in this respect he departs from Spencer: the societies that are 'mechanical' accretions of elements (kinship groups) as 'compound' or 'doubly compound' in Spencer's terms, as against those societies that are organised on the basis of an 'organic' division of labour and interdependent specialisation of function (comprising medieval society, and the modern nation). The idea of basing a classification on what is called social morphology, or what has become known since Spencer as social structure, is quite different from one based on cultural configuration such as can be found in Comte's sociology.[2]

There are notable differences therefore between the models of Marx and Comte on the one hand, and Spencer and Durkheim on the other. In the first place, for Marx and Comte, the final stage is a messianic logical construction of a future utopia; for Spencer and Durkheim the sequence contains no reference to the future. This remains in principle open and unknowable. The Spencer–Durkheim scheme is descriptively and empirically holistic: it does not depend on a presumed part–whole form of causal theory. Moreover, when theory is introduced, both Spencer and Durkheim reject the idea that there is a simple development of forms of social inequality through the sequence. Such stratification is affected not only by degree of social complexity, but by the degree of concentration of power in society and this is decisively determined by the condition and form of social mobilisation: for war, external or civil, or peace and industry. In other words, Spencer and Durkheim reorganised the Comtean evolutionary thesis that society moves from warlike to industrial occupations, to one in which these can be found as modal states at any stage of development.

The new sociological method

Following in Comte's footsteps, Durkheim attempted to specify the unique domain of sociological phenomena within the branches of the scientific division of labour. It is tempting to suggest that this is an attempt to align sociology within the rationalist tradition stemming from Bacon and Descartes. But Durkheim insists that rules of method strictly parallel other ethical and moral rules: 'methodological rules are for science what rules of law and custom are for conduct' and whereas the natural sciences appear to have some form of common ground, the 'moral and social sciences' are in a state of anomie: 'the jurist, the psychologist, the anthropologist, the economist, the statistician, the linguist, the historian, proceed with their investigations as if the different orders of fact they study constituted so many different worlds' (Durkheim, [1893] 1964: 368). Rules of method are far more than rules for gathering information. They organise and regulate the field and identify the ground for scientific strategies and legitimate the way these strategies should be assessed. Durkheim's writings on methodology, not surprisingly, have given rise to important controversies. These are of two kinds. The first concerns the orientation and content of some of *The Rules of Sociological Method*. The second concerns the apparent conflict between certain rules.

The methodological orientation is from the start one that strives for maximal objectivity of investigation. As if traumatised by a surfeit of individual and subjective introspection, even the primary definition of the terrain of sociology itself, the very object of social analysis, Durkheim formulated as 'any way of acting, whether fixed or not, capable of exerting over the individual an external constraint' (1982: 59). In this argument, *Rules* (Durkheim, [1895] 1982) seems intent on correcting an apparent weakness in previous sociological practice, for the emphasis is insistent: all preconceptions must be discarded; never assume the voluntary character of a social institution; always study social phenomena that are detached from individual forms. The fundamental rule for observing social phenomena is 'to consider social facts as things' (1982: 60). It is evident that Durkheim considered the common ideological formation of the sociologist as modern citizen in a sense, and paradoxically, both a support and a fundamental obstacle to social research. His critical judgement is that 'instead of observing, describing and comparing things, we ... reflect on our ideas ... Instead of a science which deals with realities, we carry out no more than an ideological analysis' (1982: 60). It is no wonder that this particular text has been read as a revolutionary manifesto in sociology, for it essentially demands that each sociologist reverse habitual and everyday forms of thought. In this sense it is a fundamental text in a tradition which starts with Comte, but Durkheim clearly radicalises it: social science comes into being in a revolutionary epistemological break with ideological methods. This idea is certainly latent in Comte, but Comte's own presentation of it maintained the continuity of science with other forms of social consciousness.

The very specific character of Durkheim's method is that it carries the idea of radical objectivity into the very conceptualisation of its object, the social itself. The terms social exteriority, constraint, collective form, are transcendent as against individual manifestation, and are clearly conceived as decisive indications for the investigator and for social research in general: the most objective of objects are the fixed social forms and these are to be given priority because they offer a privileged route for investigative analysis. Durkheim is, however, explicit: these terms are provisional. They are to be adopted in the first instance because they offer the best chance of avoiding significant obstacles to social science. It is clear that as a manifesto, this system of rules calls for a revolutionary transformation in the mode of practice of sociologists, and calls for commitment to sociology as a vocation. This vision is concerned not with the isolated and lonely genius, but with a collective practice, organised and disciplined within the modern educational system. Sociological research is a collective procedure, subject to rational rules of evidence and verification that are unique to sociology. These rules mark out and define a legitimate territory for study against competing claims: the domain of social facts.

It is clear, however, that these rules are also closely bound up with Durkheim's own ideas about the content of social analysis, and indeed his own changing and developing research priorities. What seems at first to be an attempt to produce a definitive text on methodology, the *Rules*, is more complex than its appears. Many of the major formulations of this text had already appeared as the first Introduction to *The Division of Labour in Society*, edition of 1893.[3] The first formulation of the field of study is developed in terms not of social but moral facts: 'moral facts consist in a rule of sanctioned conduct' (1964: 425). Durkheim adopts this definition since the study of moral evolution not longer depends on the study of norms but also of sanctions which he conceives as 'an external fact reflecting [an] internal state' (1964: 425). His aim remains consistent. The development of the 'positive science of morality is a branch of sociology, for every sanction is principally a social thing' (1964: 428). In this first Introduction there is a very clear separation between those forms of action that are moral obligations and other 'gratuitous acts' that are the free choice of the individual and which Durkheim assigns to the domain of aesthetics and art (1964: 430–1).

What happens between this first Introduction to *The Division of Labour* and the appearance of the essays called *The Rules of Sociological Method* which were published separately as articles in 1894 (before appearing, slightly modified, in book form in 1895), is that all the characteristics of the moral fact are displaced and incorporated into the category of the social fact. It is significant to note, for instance, that Durkheim in 1893 referred to a group of acts as a 'gratuitous' and outside morals:

> The refinements of worldly urbanity, the ingenuities of politeness ... the gifts, affectionate words or caresses between friends or relatives, up to the heroic sacrifices that no duty demands ... The father of a family risks his life for a stranger; who would dare to say that was useful?' (1964: 430–1)

In *Rules*, however, Durkheim specifies a whole new range of ways in which external constraint occurs, from informal sanctions of ridicule and social ostracism to technical and organisational necessities. Moral obligation and sanction form the first object of Durkheim's methodological reflection, but constraint and circumstantial necessity broaden this into the essential characteristics of social facts in general. In these 1894 formulations it is made clear that the sociologist must give primacy to the study of facts from 'a viewpoint where they present a sufficient degree of consolidation' (in Berthelot, 1988: 138). By the time the book version of *Rules* was published in 1895 with a large number of revisions, this particular injunction was changed to the rule that the sociologist 'must strive to consider [social facts] from a viewpoint where they present themselves in isolation from their individual manifestations' (1982: 82–3). It seems clear that Durkheim had altered his research priorities and was edging towards the full-scale study of suicide statistics, published in 1897 not long after the appearance of *Rules*. Towards the end of *Rules*, Durkheim gives suicide as an example of a problematic social fact: 'if suicide depends on more than one cause it is because in reality there are several kinds of suicide' (1982: 150). The existence of suicide statistics makes it possible for sociologists to study social currents as phenomena that are 'independent of their individual manifestations'. In social rates of suicide there is something more to the phenomena than random 'gratuitous acts'. It is apparent then that far from being a fixed and unique definition of the object of sociology, Durkheim has a number of options which are refocused and specified according to the task at hand. He does not seem to be worried if he does not follow to the letter his own hastily conceived prescriptive rules, as long as he remains consistent at a higher level of epistemological theory.

There was a strong injunction throughout the methodological writings to this text (1895) that the sociologist must start from things not ideas; indeed the sociologist must start from 'a group of phenomena defined beforehand by certain common external characteristics' (1982: 75). Strategy demands that analysis must work from these external features towards an understanding of their internal causal relationships. When investigating suicide statistics, Durkheim seems to have started in this way as prescribed by his rules. The procedure required that he group together those suicides with the same external features (e.g. how suicides were committed) and 'would admit as many suicide currents as there were distinct types, then seek to determine their causes' (Durkheim, 1970: 146). In the analysis published as *Suicide* ([1897] 1970), Durkheim says this procedure could not be used, rather he was 'able to determine the social types of suicide by classifying them not directly by their preliminarily described characteristics, but by the causes which produce them' (1970: 147). Durkheim uses what he calls 'this reverse method'. Instead of proceeding from the characteristics in the facts themselves, he says 'once the nature of the causes is known we shall try to deduce that nature of the effects ... Thus we shall descend from causes to effects and our aetiological classification will be completed by a morphological one' (1970: 147). It comes as something of a surprise to learn that the social causes of suicides (anomic, egoistic, altruistic) are already known, since the concept of altruism (of Comtean origin of course) has hardly figured in Durkheim's sociology up to this point. It is also surprising that Durkheim could reverse the order of analysis, prescribed so insistently in his recent writings (particularly *Rules*), with such apparent ease and assurance. In the study of suicide rates, Durkheim does not group suicides according to an external characteristic of the act of suicide as his previous rules required: he classifies them according to his theory of the major types of solidarity. I examine this reversal in detail in Chapter 7.

Apart from the problems of orientation and inconsistency of usage, there is also a profound problem concerning the relation of theory to method: are the two independent or dependent? Clearly Durkheim did not think method completely separate from theory but developed alongside the progress of substantive sociology itself. At least in one crucial instance a conflict between a substantive thesis and methodological principle can be identified. This conflict arises in the central Chapter 3 of *Rules*, in a discussion which deals with the problem of determining the difference between normal and pathological social facts. It is clear from the social analysis presented in *The Division*, and especially its famous second Introduction to the edition of 1902, that Durkheim considered French society to be in a grave condition of malaise, due to a social structural abnormality: with the abolition of the guild system in the eighteenth century, a severe structural imbalance had been introduced into French society. The severe political oscillations which had occurred since then were ultimately a result of this social structural imbalance: only by re-introducing some modern equivalent of the guilds, towards a pattern he called an 'institutional socialism', could the normal system of counterweights be restored (thus Durkheim's political thought takes Comteanism into the left versions politics of corporatism, as opposed to rightward direction of the l'Action Française [Elbow, 1953; Hawkins, 1994]).

The methodological problem posed at the heart of the Durkheimian project was to be able to define unambiguously the way such a question could be resolved. His primary rule is clear: if the social fact is general in the average form of the social species under consideration, the fact is to be judged normal. But he introduced another much more theoretical consideration, requiring a demonstration for a normal fact 'that the general character of the phenomenon is related to the general conditions of collective life in the social type under consideration' and this 'verification is necessary when this fact relates to a social species which has not yet gone through its complete evolution' (Durkheim, 1982: 97). These two rules contradict each other in the case under discussion. The state of deregulation identified by Comte, Durkheim calls 'anomie'. If the lack of regulation characteristic of segmental societies is continued, 'we shall be forced to conclude that this now constitutes a morbid state, however universal it may be' (1982: 95). In other words, the theoretical analysis of the forms and functions of regulation suggests that economic anomie is pathological even if it is general; the principal rule would suggest its generality indicates normality. This problem goes to the heart of modern Durkheimian scholarship. On the one hand those Durkheimians who follow the primary empirical rule would be forced to conclude that the modern democratic state with its absence of economic solidarity has proven to be a normal social type. On the other, those Durkheimians who follow more strictly his theoretical analysis of modern societies with their lack of integration see a proliferation of many kinds of social pathological phenomena.

The impact of research on social theory

Durkheim's basic theory developed and changed over the course of his career, as did his methodological reflections. In the earlier writings he held that primitive societies were characterised by similitudes and passions whereas the advanced societies were characterised by individualism and calm restraint. He later revised this view completely. An example of this can be seen in his writing on education. In his early lectures on moral education (Durkheim, 1973) he argued that there was a plague of violent punishment in the schools of the Middle Ages, and the lash remained in constant use up until the eighteenth century. After researching his lectures on educational thought in France (Durkheim, 1977), he describes the idea of the violent medieval colleges as simply 'a legend'. The reason for this, he argues, was that the educational communities remained essentially democratic and these forms 'never have very harsh disciplinary regimes' because 'he who is today judged may tomorrow become the judge' (1977: 155–7). The new analysis suggests that the turn towards a more oppressive disciplinary regime began at the end of the sixteenth century, at the moment when the schools and colleges in France became centralised and cut off from the outside community. In these circumstances, he says, the whip became a regular feature of college life.

In his lectures to teachers, Durkheim discussed the problem of how to arrive at a rational approach to discipline and punishment in school. Between the offence and the punishment, he observed, there is a hidden continuity, for they are not 'two heterogeneous things coupled artificially' (Durkheim, 1973: 179). Because the mediating term is obscure, a series of misleading theories of punishment arise. One such misleading theory sees punishment as expiation or atonement; another sees it primarily as a way of intimidating or inhibiting further offences. From a pedagogical point of view, the problem concerns the capacity to neutralise the demoralising effects of an infringement of group norms. The true object of punishment, he argues, is a moral one. Its effectiveness should be judged by how far it contributes to the solidarity of group as a whole. The problem is that certain kinds of punishment can contribute to the creation of further immoral acts (1973: 199), and once applied, punishment seems to lose something of its power. A reign of terror is, in the end, a very weak system of sanctions even driven to extremes by its own ineffectiveness. The recourse to corporal punishment seems to involve a counter-productive attack on the dignity of the individual, a dignity valued and fostered in modern societies.

The central theoretical issue here was addressed once again in his attempt to reconstruct the theses of *The Division of Labour in Society*, in an article of 1900 called 'Two Laws of Penal Evolution' (Durkheim, 1978: 153–80). Durkheim criticises Spencer for thinking that the degree of absoluteness of governmental power is related to the number of functions it undertakes, but he works towards a very Spencerian formulation: 'the more or less absolute character of the government is not an inherent characteristic of any given social type' (1978: 157). It is here that Durkheim presents an account of French society that can be seen to be diametrically opposed to that of Marx, yet aligned in a very subtle way with Comte: 'seventeenth-century France and nineteenth-century France belong to the same type', he says. To think there has been a change of type is to mistake a conjunctural feature of the society with its fundamental structure, for governmental absolutism arises, not from the constituent features of a social form, but from 'individual, transitory and contingent conditions' in social evolution (1978: 157). It is this very complication which, taken together with the specific form of governmental power, makes analysis of social type extremely complex, since transitory forms of power can neutralise long-run social organisation.

Durkheim's argument suggests that social theory, especially its anarchist and Marxist variants, is often mistaken in thinking the state is either a purely repressive machine, or that the purely political division of powers can deliver political and social liberty in the fullest sense. For Durkheim the thesis that freedom is freedom from the state ignores the fact that it is the state 'that has rescued the child from family tyranny [and] the citizen from feudal groups and later from communal groups.' Indeed Durkheim argues the state must not limit itself to the administration of 'prohibitive justice … [It] must deploy energies equal to those for which it has to provide a counterbalance'. Against the political illusion of power, for example as found in Montesquieu's theory of the separation of powers, Durkheim tries to show that liberty is based on a particular form of the total social division of power: the state 'must even permeate all those secondary groups of family, trade and professional association, Church, regional areas, and so on' (Durkheim, 1992: 64) if the full potentialities of human development are to be realised.

But the state can become too strong and develop its own pathological dimensions and capacities. In his pamphlet '"Germany Above All": German mentality and war' (1915), he presented a critique of the ideas of the German political philosopher Heinrich Treitschke, which he took to be representative of the mentality which brought war not just to France and Europe in 1914. He was careful to say that he was not analysing the causes of war, but only one of the manifestations of a condition of social pathology (1915: 46). Durkheim contrasts the democratic idea in which there is a continuity between government and people with Treitschke's thesis that there is a radical antagonism between state and civil society. This latter idea requires a state power capable of enforcing a mechanical obedience from its citizens (their first duty is to obey its dictates) and leaders who are possessed of enormous ambition, unwavering determination, with personalities characterised by aspects which have 'something harsh, caustic, and more or less detestable' about them (1915: 30–4). In practice these states flout international law and conventions, and their idea of war pushes the development of military technology which is almost 'exempt from the laws of gravity ... They seem to transport us into an unreal world, where nothing can any longer resist the will of man' (1915: 46).

This analysis of the German war mentality draws on Durkheim's crucial concept of anomie, developed most clearly with respect to anomic forms of the division of labour (Durkheim, 1964: 353–73) and anomic suicides (Durkheim, 1970: 241–76). It is evident from Durkheim's first formulations of this idea that it is derived from Comte's analysis of the unregulated division of the modern sciences. Durkheim also follows Comte's conception (itself derived, as we have seen, from Broussais) of pathological facts as exceptional phenomena, that is exhibiting exceptionally high or low intensities. Thus crime, for example, is not in itself an abnormal feature of human societies: the sociologist has to determine normal and abnormal rates of crime. Changing intensities of social facts in Durkheimian theory are determined in relation to modifications in the power dynamics of social systems. Where there is a shift towards the concentration of power in the state, as occurs in wartime, the structures protecting individual values are weakened. In wartime there is to be expected not only an increase in altruistic suicide, most commonly associated with military organisation (1970: 228ff.), but also an increase in civil homicides since the individual is less protected in moral value (Durkheim, 1992: 110–20).

It seems clear that there is a long-term continuity in Durkheim's interest in moral statistics from the early essay on variations in birth rates through a range of studies of family, divorce, to political statistics (Turner, 1993). This aspect of his sociology has attracted attention as installing an experimental rationalism as a founding moment in the modern discipline (see Berthelot, 1995: 75–105). Whereas Comte focused on a single line of evolution unifying the historical experience of humanity as a whole, Durkheim investigated the dispersive branchings of social evolution and this strategy may have legitimised a more experimental and comparative methodological inventiveness. There is also a marked difference in the conception of the role of theory in sociology between Durkheim and Comte. For the latter, the aim of analysis is to be able to construct a hierarchical system of laws of co-variation: with sacrificial theory no reference to causal explanation is required. For Durkheim, the role of theory is paramount in the search for causes, and is essential for a complete sociological explanation of social laws. Durkheim, it must be stressed, still embraced the aim of discovering basic social laws, and many of these are formulated in his early works. These are always related to a causal or aetiological analysis which even becomes, as against morphological analysis, the explicit organising principle, as is the case in *Suicide*.

Durkheim's theoretical frame did not remain static, as has already been indicated. The most evident development of theory in Durkheim's work can be found by comparing the depiction of early societies in the two studies at each end of his career: *Division of Labour in Society* ([1893] 1964) and *The Elementary Forms of the Religious Life* ([1912] 1995). In the first study the fundamental fact of the early societies is that they are held together by 'bonds of similitude' and characterised by intense and violent reactions to infringements of the highly uniform 'collective consciousness'. There is little in the way of social differentiation: even the gender division of labour is so slight that there is no contractual regulation between the sexes. The era of 'mechanical solidarity' was one of sexual promiscuity (Durkheim, 1964: 57–8). Durkheim's investigations into Australian tribal society led him to change this view fundamentally. He came to see kinship organisation as complex, and based on deeply embedded forms of sexual and age divisions. He came to see social structure as the complex outcome of symbolic practices, particularly those crystallised in ritual traditions. He established the thesis that ritual beliefs were structured on knowledge categories, which were socially produced and reproduced. Fundamental to such systems of religious categories were concepts of the sacred and profane, good and evil, which were involved both in organising such rituals and being at the same time produced by them. Instead of elaborating or criticising Comte's theory of early societies as being characterised by forms of fetishism (worship organised in relation to charged objects), Durkheim suggested that the earliest form of religion was totemistic (group kinship and religious practices were organised in relation to a hierarchy of objects: the totemic emblem, the totemic group, the totemic species). The practices of the group produced widely different forms of experience, for example religious effervescent, high-energy ceremonials contrasted with low-energy, utilitarian food gathering. These socially produced distinctions formed the material basis for category differentiation. In this way Durkheim thought he could arrive at a definitive sociological critique of Kantian *a priorism* on the one hand, and Spencerian individualism on the other. Durkheim tried to identify those groups that could draw moral strength from the solidarities produced by sacred rituals, and those with weaker solidarity who would then be vulnerable to the process of scapegoating, for example misfortunes befalling the group were blamed on women (Durkheim, 1995: 404).

Durkheim developed a theory of sacred categories, of good and evil, on top of the distinction between the sacred and profane social spheres, a distinction which he showed was produced in ritual practice. This investigation also tried to show that the idea of the individual soul was intimately linked to the structure of social groups and their internal differentiation (in some groups, for example, women did not have souls). Because Durkheim's attention had shifted to these symbolic processes and practices of intervention in and reproduction of such symbolic materials, it has been assumed in some interpretations that his whole sociology had itself become a subjective exercise in symbolic interactionism (Stone and Farberman, 1967) . It seems clear though from the text of *The Elementary Forms*, that there was no break in continuity of methodological reflection and prescription. The focus of analysis was no longer on the transcendent external modes of sanctioned conduct (moral facts), but had moved to social epistemology, or what he called 'the sociology of knowledge and religion', which examined the way immanent infrastructures imposed their exigencies on action and the way that religious consciousness, the sacred language (Gane, 1992), arose not through intellectual reflection but in the effervescence of social ritual. In other words, Durkheim had moved to a large and empirically based study of the cognitive structures of the earliest societies: Comtean terrain, but Durkheim locates his discussion almost entirely with respect to post-Comtean theory. A very different theoretical strategy, but one which, as I discuss in the next chapter, still retains a significant place for the problematic category of social pathology.

Notes

1 There is today considerable interest in the precise balance of influences on Durkheim's thought, against the trends in sociology (Mucchielli, 1998) and in philosophy (Brooks, 1998) in this period. Discoveries of more texts from all periods of his career have opened up more lines of enquiry (e.g. Durkheim, 1996, 1997). These new materials are likely to be influential in making interpretation of Durkheim's intellectual career more sensitive to the way Durkheim's sociology intervened in the currents of French thought and politics in the period of the Third Republic, as they show the emergence of a sophisticated confrontation with the positivist tradition on the one hand, and idealist, neo-Kantian schools on the other (Gross, 1996). In this chapter I have drawn on 'Durkheim's Project for a Sociological Science' in G. Ritzer and B. Smart (eds) *Handbook of Social Theory* (Sage, 2001).

2 For Comte, rather as for Marx, it was essentially one decisive element in society, its determining element, the method of knowing, which should form the basis of classification. Comte's classification, in effect, followed a parallel five-stage model: fetishist, polytheist, monotheist, metaphysical, and positive societal types, in a single logical sequence explained by the struggle of positive reason against theological reason. Marx, of course, also had a five-stage model: primitive communism, slave, feudal, capitalist, and higher communist societies, a sequence determined by the economic mode of production and class struggle.

3 This Introduction was replaced in second edition of 1902, but can be found, as an appendix, in the English translation of 1964 (but not in the second translation of 1984).

6

French Society: Vanguard without a Norm

> If … we find an objective criterion, inherent in the facts themselves, to allow us to distinguish scientifically health from sickness in the various orders of social phenomena, science will be in a position to throw light on practical matters while remaining true to its own method. (Durkheim [1895] 1982: 86)

Many serious misconceptions have arisen in relation to the importance of the concept of social pathology in Durkheim's work.[1] Problems also arise from the fact that while in psychology the concept of pathology survives, in sociology, with notable exceptions (Bataille, Caillois, Baudrillard, Maffesoli etc.), the whole field has been abandoned, except for the 'sociology of deviance', which has in fact developed as a different problematic. As we have seen, it was Comte who first established the terrain of social pathology and provided Durkheim with the essential means for thinking about it as a way of relating theory to practice. Of course, some of these resources Durkheim neglected, while others were invented and added by Durkheim himself, or were drawn from other sources. Durkheim's sociology is largely situated within a restructured Comtean framework, a framework Durkheim sought in important respects to make less extreme and less unpalatable to late nineteenth-century social and political opinion (partly by trying to show that there were other sources for his sociology apart from Comte).[2]

There can be little risk of error in emphasising the importance of the field of pathology for Durkheim. A long third part of *De la division du travail social* is devoted to it. Durkheim was struggling to understand the nature of the continuing turbulence of French society. And certainly there were peculiarities confronting him. Durkheim followed closely the changes in birth and death rates in France, because they had taken on a strategic importance for France. During the period 1891–95, deaths in France exceeded births and there were some years (1890, 1892, 1895) when there was an absolute decline in the French population (Nye, 1982: 107). This was in great contrast with population changes in Britain and Germany, and therefore became a concern in French political and military circles. Durkheim had long been interested in the relation of birth rate and suicide rates and had shown in 1888 that countries with a strong birth rate had low suicide rates. France had a suicide rate that was increasing faster than any other in Europe (Durkheim, 1975: ii, 216ff.). His rules here were designed to answer this question: 'Only according to certain characteristics of the structure and functions is it possible scientifically to distinguish old age from infancy, or maturity … for example, for a society, regular lowering of the birth rate may be used as proof that the limits of maturity have been reached or passed' (Durkheim, [1893] 1964: 433). Durkheim's conclusion in fact was not that France had reached a state of maturity, but that French society was afflicted with structural imbalances which could be understood sociologically (through a study of social pathology) as having resulted from the unique trajectory of French history.

In this chapter I discuss the basic orientation to the question of social pathology adopted by Durkheim and then the famous Chapter 3 of *Rules* and the rhetorical order it adopts where he claims to have made new discoveries by applying his functional method.

Social pathology

Before entering into a discussion of Durkheim's definitions of pathology, I shall begin with a consideration of a central idea that relates Durkheim to Comte's doctrine, and thus to Comte's own sources, particularly Broussais (Pickering, M. 1993: 406–12) Durkheim rarely refers to Broussais directly but it is clear, even for example in the Latin thesis on Montesquieu, that he regarded the transition to the modern notion of pathology as decisive. Durkheim argues that Montesquieu was still trapped within the Aristotelian view that held disease to be a violation of nature and therefore outside normal causation, consequently outside of science. Revealingly Durkheim says: 'Political science could not free itself of the error all at once, especially since disease has a greater place in human societies than anywhere else and the normal state is more uncertain and difficult to define' (Durkheim, [1892] 1997: 56e).

It is essential, says Durkheim (following Comte's appropriation of Broussais), to define the normal, indeed the whole terrain of normal phenomena, as located in the average (*la moyenne*) of the societies, as the living individuals of a given species (*espèce*). And from this established norm one should work to a definition of pathological phenomena as those social facts that deviate from the normal limits of the forms developed in the species (Kremer-Marietti, 1982: 111–42). The importance of the idea of species is different from that found in Comte, and even has philosophical value, for it allowed Durkheim to find a middle ground between nominalism and realism (1982: 108). Indeed Durkheim used this idea to distance himself from Comte's historical method: 'If … social types exist which are qualitatively distinct from one another … one cannot join them together exactly like the homogeneous segments that constitute a geometrical straight line' (1982: 109). However, there are essential elements of Comte's thought that are carried through into Durkheim's new sociology.

From Comte to Durkheim

Difficulties are foreseen by Durkheim in coming to terms with this principle in sociology right from the beginning, especially when the object of study is a society in 'transition' or 'passing crisis'. This remark refers to Durkheim's theses developed in *Division*, concerning the problems of societies developing on the basis of an organic solidarity arising from the process of the social division of labour. It also points to the original matrix of that theory which is Comte's law of the three states. In Comte's law, the second state, 'metaphysical', is defined as a transitional state between the first (the theological state) and the third (the positive state). In fact Comte's own conception of nineteenth-century France was of an '*âge de transition révolutionnaire*' which had reached the crucial and imminent threshold to the positive polity (Comte, 1975, vol. ii: 380–4). The instability of the metaphysical stage is determined by the 'heterogeneous' action of two competing systems: the declining theocratic order (its '*decomposition croissant*'), and the organic growth of the positive order ('*l'essor graduel des éléments correspondants du nouveau systéme*'). In effect the triumph of the metaphysical over the theological spirit is really the transitional effect of the growth of a 'new system' which props up yet transcends the metaphysical state. Durkheim's theory in *Division* in effect rewrites Comte's law in recognition of this latent fundamental dichotomy. It becomes for Durkheim a law of two social states (mechanical and organised).

The problem of the notion of the transitional form lies at the heart of the difficulties of definition in chapter 3 of the *Rules*. Durkheim's formulation is that in a period of transition:

> the only normal type extant at the time and grounded in the facts is the one that relates to the past but no longer corresponds to the new conditions of existence. A fact can therefore persist through a whole species but no longer correspond to the requirements of the situation. (Durkheim, [1895] 1982: 153–4)

This is the intellectual problem common to Durkheim and to Comte, a problem of the first magnitude. Durkheim illustrates it in the following way:

> To know whether the present state of the peoples of Europe, with the lack of organisation that characterises it, is normal or not, we must investigate what in the past gave rise to it. If the conditions are still those pertaining to our societies, it is because the situation is normal, despite the protest that it stirs up. If, on the other hand, it is linked to that old social structure which elsewhere we have called segmentary ... is increasingly dying out, we shall be forced to conclude that this now constitutes a morbid state, however universal it may be. (1982: 95)

This example goes to the heart of the problem: how to distinguish the normal growth of the new system when elements from the previous system now in decay are still widely active? Comte defined the metaphysical state as essentially unstable, as the passing from the predominant influence of the theological to that of the positive elements, to found its own adequate internal principle. The way the problem arose in Comte then, was to pose the question of the relative abnormality of the features of the metaphysical state, the aberrations of the revolution, and the new forms of social deregulation and egoism characteristic of post-revolutionary France. There were specific problems arising from the fact that the transition from the metaphysical to the positive seemed to lead to the emergence of extreme forms. While Durkheim still uses the idea of transition yet does not elaborate it into a specific 'state' as Comte did, there is still the same concern about the abnormality of social facts in the situation when the developmental process is incomplete or blocked. It is not sufficiently recognised that Comte did admit the possibility that the transition to the positive stage might never occur, and that the metaphysical state might degenerate into an interminably chronic and incurable condition.

Durkheim refers to the proposition he has demonstrated in *Division* that the normal tendency of social development is towards a weakening of religious belief, and a concomitant weakening of strong 'collective sentiments towards collective objects' (Durkheim, 1982: 106). This sounds very anti-Comtean; at least it is very much contrary to the pronouncement of the late Comte that humanity becomes more and more religious. But, as we know from the Conclusion to the *Elementary Forms*, Durkheim modified his own position in the course of time and came to predict the refashioning of religion in line with the requirements of the organic division of labour. Nevertheless in the mid 1890s Durkheim had developed a theory of the decline of strongly marked states of the collective conscience, and promoted the view that new structures had not been sufficiently developed to replace them. This is the theoretical basis of analysis of anomie (in *Division*, Part 3). When Durkheim gave his famous lectures on Saint-Simonianism in 1896, it was Saint-Amand Bazard and not Comte whom he credited as having formulated the basic law of the alternation of critical and organic periods, and he added, 'the law so formulated is incontestable' (Durkheim, 1962: 258). Yet he says, in a formulation that leans towards and then away from Comte:

> What escaped Bazard is that the further one advances in history, the more one sees the traits of the critical period prolonged in the midst of the organic period … Reflection, criticism, exist next to faith, pierce that very faith without destroying it, and occupy an always larger place in it … Saint-Simon, much more than his disciples, considered this rationalism to be increasing under the influence of collective beliefs. (1962: 258)

Durkheim, by implication, claims to be more Saint-Simonian than Comtean. And Durkheim points, in *Suicide*, to the inevitable and normal development of anomie in the higher societies, an idea which Comte could only admit was a feature of the transitional state, not the final positive polity. In *Division* Durkheim says:

> Although Comte recognised that the division of labour is a source of solidarity, it seems that he did not perceive that this solidarity is *sui generis* and is little by little substituted for that which social similitudes gives rise to. That is why … he considered [the obliteration of the strong collective conscience] a morbid phenomenon. But we cannot consider it as the cause of the abnormal phenomena that we are studying … [these occur] because all the conditions for the existence of organic solidarity have not been realised. (Durkheim, [1893] 1964: 364–5, trans. modified)

The change from Comte's to Durkheim's framework is here made perfectly clear: problems arise because of an incomplete development of the 'higher' social type, or in other terms used by Durkheim, because the 'transition' within the higher type is incomplete.

It is important to note that Durkheim adopts the same European historical frame as Comte but points to different social structural conditions as decisive for social development, extending it only to include greater complexity of Comte's 'theological' state (the new Australian materials being the most significant). Because the time scheme is the same, that is both Comte and Durkheim refer to the crucial dissolution of the medieval polity as the point of departure of the transition, Durkheim's theories can be seen to be a modification, a variation of Bazard's and Comte's idea. Durkheim looks for social determinants of Comte's analysis of the metaphysical period; or, more accurately, Durkheim overturns the dominance of ideational elements of the Comtean scheme just as he did of these elements in his critique of Kant. Yet Comte, from the beginning of his writings, insisted that alongside the series Theology → Metaphysics → Positivism, there existed a parallel series relating to activity: first an aggressive militarism and slavery, evolving in the early Middle Ages into defensive militarism and serfdom, and this transition followed by the development of industrialism and proletarianisation. Durkheim takes up Comte's formula that with the division of labour, the growth of industry (and its natural alliance with the scientific movement) becomes the prime mover of the dissolution of the theological polity of the European Middle Ages. Durkheim's analysis of the specificity of this evolution pointed to the destruction of the social solidarity of the corporations, the occupational guilds, the 'professional' structures of the medieval period, as the root cause of widespread problems, pathologies, of social structures (see Durkheim, 1964: 218–19). Actually this thesis can be found in a form in Comte's works: his consistent opposition to the commercial bourgeoisie, which he called the corrupted class, and which he considered to be the main social support of egoism. This class, replaced by the patrician estate, had no future in Comte's positive utopia.

The *Division* represents Durkheim's analysis of the organic composition of the new state previously defined by Comte as the metaphysical state. For Comte, the positive state may never be completed or may never finally triumph over the metaphysical state. Such a blocked evolution would then see a great proliferation of pathological features. Durkheim abandons these terms altogether and erects a theory of the formal structures of the balanced organic social totality. And for Durkheim it is this formal social not political or religious balance which takes precedence: i.e. Durkheim specifies the degree of breakdown and replacement of segmentalism by new organic dependencies and solidarities. In this way Durkheim escapes the need for an elaborate utopian vision; he only has to identify a society which can function as a model of balance of an organic kind, a type which can be taken as a norm. Durkheim can then analyse the evolution of Western societies, and France in particular, as a moving and evolving balance of elements where the structure of relations remains stable as a feature of each social type (Lacroix, 1981: ch. 3).

Again, to emphasise the difference between Comte and Durkheim: this type of analysis is not a possible option for Comte since for him the metaphysical stage is one of permanent conflict between the theological and the positive principles. Comte's analyses of this stage (*état*) follow the decline and growth of the two opposed systems in a dynamic regressive and progressive analyses. Durkheim in effect replaces this with a series of static, synchronic analyses without having to pose any transcendent end state. Crucially in Durkheim, abnormalities arise within the line of static analyses. It is with the abolition and not replacement of the occupational corporations, that the new system becomes unbalanced. Even so, it is important to note that even this opposition between Durkheim and Comte is relative, since when Durkheim adopts the idea of 'transitional' states, and he does just that when he refers to the period of transition between segmental and organised structures, the latter are still in the process of formation (an idea that exactly corresponds to the content of Comte's idea of the positive series of the metaphysical state).

Durkheim's discussion in the *Rules* is now clarified because although he wants to be able to arrive at an unambiguous rule specifying the normal as that which is found in the average constitution of the social species under consideration. However the generalised 'lack of organisation' at the economic level would then count as a normal feature of modern societies, which is something Durkheim will not admit. Indeed, once the idea of 'transitional' forms is allowed, all kinds of difficulties arise in relation to the identification of survivals and anticipations if such a purely statistical method is adopted.[3] Durkheim, however, presents his rule in this way: 'A social fact is normal for a determinate social type, considered at a determinate phase of development, when it occurs in the average of societies of this species, considered at a corresponding phase of their evolution' (Durkheim, 1982: 97 trans. modified).

If this rule were applied to European societies, then the absence of guilds or professional corporations would appear quite normal. Durkheim refused to accept the proposition that unregulated capitalism was simply unnatural, brought about by force or trickery. He thought it a clear abnormality of structure. Exactly the same problem arose in the consideration of crime, religious belief, state power, etc. In conditions of transition, or 'passing crisis' (Durkheim, 1964: 434, a phrase he often uses) normality could not be determined by generality despite the preference stated in his primary rule.

Durkheim was thus constrained to develop an alternative, or auxiliary, rule which seeks to establish normality indirectly. It seeks to establish the generality of the phenomenon to the 'general conditions of the collective life under consideration' (Durkheim, 1982: 97). This is the rule which must be applied in periods of transition, or as Durkheim says, must be applied when the relevant social species under investigation has not been fully established. This formulation is significant, since Durkheim now notes the necessity to consider whether there has been a complete formation of the organised type;

previously he talked simply of 'periods of transition'. The expression now changes. The problem is seen as one relating to the incomplete evolution of the species, in fact 'a social species which has not yet gone through its complete evolution' (1982: 97). There is then in the *Rules* a fundamental oscillation between the idea that 'economic anarchy' is a survival of a condition originating in segmentalism (that is, it is a problem arising in an 'incomplete transition'), and the second idea that this anarchy has been introduced by the inappropriate abolition of a range of institutions – a specific crisis of French history (Durkheim, 1964: 218–19). In this latter case it is not a question of a transition between segmentation and organisation, but of the adjustment to conditions within the species itself. He says of the corporations that: 'it is legitimate to presume *a priori* that the changes through which they have passed demand less a radical destruction of this type of organization than a transformation' (1964: 218–19). In fact, Durkheim's rule could be adjusted in the light of this observation. The theoretical problem is to define the correspondence of the institution to the 'general conditions of collective life' without falling into the need to elaborate a utopian norm as Comte had done.

But further problems arise when we turn to Durkheim's explanation in the text of the *Rules*. For Durkheim expressly says that if such anarchy is linked to the condition of segmentalism, and if segmentalism is 'dying out', then this is a normal fact since presumably death, the final state of the life cycle of segmental society, is normal.[4] It can really only become abnormal if this state detaches itself from segmentalism and inhibits or blocks the development of new institutional forms. These images really only apply to the theory of transition, not to what might be called the theory of equilibration. This confusion does not arise in the presentation in the first edition of *Division*, since there Durkheim points out that sickness in old age is not a normal part of old age (1964: 433). But Durkheim here in the *Rules* has introduced a fatal conflation which resonates in this text.

In *Division*, Durkheim wrote: 'there are cases where, to distinguish the healthy state from the sick, it is not enough to refer to the normal type. This is so when all of the traits have not been formed; when, disturbed in certain peculiars by a passing crisis, it is itself in process of becoming' (1964: 434). And yet Durkheim quickly reaches the conclusion that: 'the method remains the same. One must begin by fixing the normal type; and towards that the only means is to compare it with itself' (1964: 434). Durkheim seems unable to find a way out of this dilemma. Again in 1906 he took up the same problem. Here he reiterates the problem:

> The consciousness which society may have of itself which is expressed in general opinion may be an inadequate view of the underlying reality. It is possible that opinion, weighed down by survivals, lags behind the real condition of the society ... under the effect of passing circumstances, certain principles, even though essential to the existing morality, may for a time be relegated to the unconscious and so appear not to exist. (Durkheim, 1953: 38)

Thus, for Durkheim, the Catholic church itself was such a survival, and 'from the sociological point of view is a monster' (Durkheim, 1975b: 331).

Durkheim's discussion here provides a very un-Comtean example:

> [L]et us suppose that at a given time the society as a whole tends to lose sight of the sacro-sanctity of individual rights. Could we not correct it with authority by reminding it that the rights of the individual are so closely bound to the structure of the Great European societies and our whole mentality that to deny them, under the pretext of social interests, is to deny the most essential interests of society itself ? (1953: 60)

Durkheim does not envisage, as Comte does, the withering away of rights leaving only duties. As one commentator has noted, it is in 'striking constrast with … Saint-Simon and Comte [that] Durkheim reintegrated … "metaphysical" law (after transforming it) … within "objective" sociology' (Hayward, 1960: 20). In fact the central struggle of the Third Republic, like that over the 'Dreyfus Affair', is for Durkheim a struggle for human rights: it 'is possible to believe that *individualism* necessarily resulted from *individual* and thus egoistic sentiments. In reality, the religion of the individual is a social institution like all known religions' (see Durkheim's essay in Lukes, 1969: 14–30). Thus Durkheim makes a connection with Comtean theory through the idea of secular civic religions.

In the *Rules* he deepens the discussion of the health of the organism by posing the problem in relation to the way social facts are generated and become linked together. In one form they appear as an inevitable, even 'mechanical' effect of general social conditions. Pain felt in childbirth: this, in the light of the rule, is normal and bound up with the human condition of reproduction. But a different form is the development of institutions which allows the organism to adapt to conditions (Durkheim, 1982: 94). This second type suggests relations of utility and function. Now an organism that is sick may require a remedy and is useful. If theory is not alerted to this possibility, this secondary structure may be confused with an effect which is directly beneficial, just as something which is painful may be defined as simply abnormal and harmful. Normality thus cannot be defined directly in relation to pleasure or use because 'the notion of utility goes beyond that of the normal' (1982: 96). The only way to define these relations is to be able to define in a fundamental way the normal condition of the healthy organism. In opening up this possibility, Durkheim has daringly hinted that the widespread adoption of a useful 'remedy' to a symptom of a social illness may come to be misrecognised as a normal fact of the society. It leaves the pathological cause untreated and may render it untreatable. All these qualifications discussed by Durkheim lead at this point to the conclusion that 'generality' cannot be taken as a guide to normality when considering a society in transition.

Durkheim's Rule

At this point in Chapter 3 of the *Rules*, Durkheim operates a complete rhetorical *volte-face* in the exposition. He abandons completely the problematic of 'transitional states' and that of equilibration. He now seeks to prove by the application of his primary rule that a decisive discovery can be made immediately in relation to crime and criminal statistics. Some of these arguments were developed in *Division* but here, in the *Rules*, Durkheim pushes the conclusions as far as possible. He suggests that, as crime can be found in all known societies, in all known social species, it must therefore be regarded, against all prejudices to the contrary, as a fact normally found in human society. His ideas were so radical they were immediately misread by writers like Tarde, and Durkheim was immediately drawn into clarification and a crucial debate on causality (Gane, 1988: 76–81).

Durkheim's rhetorical strategy has therefore shifted: instead of concentrating on trying to solve the problems of politics and religion, he dramatically and surprisingly reverses the nature of the discussion into an attack on the commonsense notion of the pathological – for crime is something generally considered as a prime example of pathology and abnormality. Durkheim wishes to show that, on the contrary, 'there is no phenomenon which represents more incontrovertibly all the symptoms of normality, since it appears to be closely bound up with the conditions of collective life' (1982: 90). Durkheim even goes so far (and again against Comte) as to describe crime as a basic 'factor of public health' (1982: 90). As he has demonstrated in *Division*, there are different structures of sanction: now, he concludes crime itself is universal. It must therefore, he argues, have something beneficial to contribute to society in some way. Durkheim now produces one of his most surprising observations, which hints at a real 'abnormal' side of crime: 'Far from being cause for congratulations when it [the crime rate] drops too noticeably below the normal level, this apparent progress assuredly coincides with and is linked to some social disturbance' (1982: 102). Thus the function of punishment is not to 'cure' society of crime, its function is quite different (1982: 103). Note here the fact that Durkheim uses the Comtean term 'perturbation' to point up the target of his attack.

Durkheim discusses the necessity of different kinds of crime, but immediately returns, in spite of all the qualification in his discussion of transitions, to his first definition of normality: 'the generality of phenomena must be taken as the criterion of their normality' (1982: 104). The constant aim of practice is, he concludes, returning also to his equilibration theory, to 'maintain the normal state, to re-establish it if it is disturbed, and to rediscover the conditions of normality if they happen to change (1982: 104).

It is thus striking that the last third of this chapter of *Rules* deals almost exclusively with the purely logical discovery of the functional nature of crime looked at from the newly emerging sociological point of view. Durkheim no more than hints at the possible implication that for France there might be abnormal aspects of crime. Yet it is clear that this exists and is conceived in the style of Broussais and Comte: 'It can certainly happen that crime itself has abnormal forms; this is what happens when it reaches an excessively high level' (1982: 98). He emphasises the fact that 'what is normal is simply that criminality exists, provided that for each social type it does not reach or go beyond a certain level' (1982: 98). At the very end of the chapter in *Rules*, he added a footnote (to the 1901 edition), commenting on the general upward surge of crime in France in the nineteenth century. In his opinion 'this development has been in general, pathological' (1982: 107). Once again Durkheim insists that all these facts have to be considered as relative to specific social species: for each species there are normal rates of crime, and therefore the possibility exists that the rates may be abnormally low or high.

This is Durkheim's very specific solution to the question raised in Comte of the normal limits of variation of social types (effects of climate, geography, race, etc.). His preference, against the spirit of Comte, is to seek a statistical solution. But for many different reasons this is not always possible to achieve. Durkheim, faced with this difficulty, again turns to the theory of the 'general conditions of collective life' of the species under consideration. When we search out the meaning of this concept in relation to the discussion of crime (in Chapter 3 of the *Rules*), we find that Durkheim has again changed focus. His discussion now relates not to the conditions of collective life in relation to a specific social species but, surprisingly, more generally to the conditions of collective life of all social species. His discussion at this juncture becomes extremely abstract. He ventures to discuss what would happen in an imaginary 'community of saints'. Instead of the disappearance of crime in the 'perfect monastery', minor faults would tend to become more important. The basic condition which gives rise to this is the fact that perfect uniformity and homogeneity of individuals are impossible. Differences arising from time and place mean that diversity will always exist. From a functional point of view this is essential, since these divergences are the basic materials of social change. In order to change and develop, a certain minimum basis of plasticity must exist, allowing scope for the formation of the rationally and morally autonomous individual. Thus some crimes represent ways of thinking that are clearly anticipations of future moralities (e.g. Socrates; Durkheim refers to this example several times in his work; see Durkheim, 1982: 102). This example is the nearest Durkheim comes to considering any other specific examples, but refers to general issues: 'not only do law and morality change from one social type to another, they even change within the same type if the conditions of collective existence are modified' (1982: 101). The discussion of crime seems to take Durkheim some way from Comte, especially with reference to the importance of 'individual originality'.

The Third Chapter of *Rules*

The chapter as a whole thus charts a strange trajectory. It began with the emphasis on the need to define the normal through generality. The second part of the chapter questioned whether this was strictly possible in periods of transition: in this case, says Durkheim, the normal has to be considered in relation to the basic conditions of collective life of the relevant social species. The third part of the chapter returns to the necessity in social development of the emergence of individual differences which appear ambivalent but in fact play a crucial role in the formation of new ideals.

Curiously, Durkheim could not avoid referring, once again, to a case of social transition in his example of Socrates. At the time of Socrates, the old faith 'no longer corresponded to their conditions of their existence' (1982: 102); even general, moral traditions were out of step with the basic conditions of social life. The crime of Socrates is therefore symptomatic of social disjunctures. Here at least is the basis of a theory of abnormalities arising in transitions: or where the old traditions are too strong and inflexible, or the new moralities are too weak and lacking sufficient strength to triumph over the old ones. Here the fundamental rule, the one that must, according to Durkheim, always be applied first, and which is statistical and relies on comparison, must be overruled by the second rule of a different order of theoretical significance which relies on abstract deductive reasoning.

It is clear the latter rule is decisive since it is related to the definition of the social genus and analysis here cannot proceed statistically. The problem of the definition of social species is not given by Durkheim in this chapter (it is deferred to the next, *Rules*, Chapter 4). Yet obviously much of the discussion of pathology is predicated on Durkheim's own solution to this fundamental theoretical task. When we reach the definition of social species, it is clear that Durkheim wants two things: a very tight and clear division between segmental and organised types, viewed in fact (apparently against Comte). Within these types, different species are developed according to the degree of complexity and organisation they possess. Classification must specify type: both social component, and the kind of combination of these component elements. These do not give 'historical phases'. Within each genus there are very many sub-types (Durkheim had a problem over the term, opting in the end for 'varieties' [1983: 115]).[5] Superficially, it seems that Durkheim rejects Comte's classification and adopts one that is much closer to that of Spencer. Indeed Durkheim goes out of his way to criticise at length Comte's law of the three states. This seems confirmed by the difference, say, between Comte's and Durkheim's treatment of the Roman Empire. For the latter it was a unique formation and the only case of its type (Durkheim, 1982: 117). We know for Comte that it was not unique but a principal example of a military polytheistic regime. But in the large perhaps these are not incompatible definitions. It is possible to regard the theological form as a superstructure of such segmentalism.

On the basis of these observations it is clear just how relatively unimportant, compared with social structure, the economic mode of production is for Durkheim. Indeed it becomes clear that neither Comte nor Durkheim has a theory of the division of labour as part of an economic system, capitalism, which is subject to its own laws. Japan, he says, can adopt Western industrialism but it remains a different social species. England also remains a separate type even though industrialised: 'It may well happen that in a particular society a certain division of labour, and notably the division of economic labour, may be greatly developed, although the segmental type may be strongly pronounced there. This seems to be the case of England' (1982: 282). Far from the economic division of labour forming the basic social infrastructure, for Durkheim in sociological analysis the division of labour 'passes on the surface of social life'. The division of labour can even occur 'without the social structure sensibly changing' (Durkheim, 1964: 282), as a kind of external addition. This kind of analysis is much more in line with the Comtean vision of the specific importance of French development in its European context. This is continued in Durkheim's sociology against the example of England (where economic development is superficially connected to the survival of 'the segmental type' (1964: 282)).

It is also important here to refer to Durkheim's discussion of the formation of the medieval framework of French society in his second Introduction to *Division* (written in 1902). There he discusses the way in which the occupational guilds were added on to existing Roman institutions in antiquity, but in France they 'served as the elementary framework of our present societies' and must be 'the essential element of our social structure' (1964: 21, 29). They were, he insists, even the 'normal' form of the economic organisation of the bourgeoisie (1964: 20), even of political representation (1964: 28), a theme developed in lectures on *Professional Ethics* given throughout the 1890s. Durkheim refers to the guilds as the earliest structural form of the bourgeoisie (1992: 34); that is, they are not simple external additions but constitutive of a new social system. In his lectures on Education in France (1977), he points to the significant development of the University of Paris, its corporative form with its offshoots in England and elsewhere. Paris was the first genuinely European city. In these lectures Durkheim constantly draws up balance sheets in terms of what was gained and lost at each epoch since the middle ages. For instance, he longs for a return to the relaxed democratic atmosphere of the Middle Ages in educational institutions without extravagent stimulants and punishments. But it is clear that the university as a corporation is a basic form; the word *universitas* even means, he notes, a corporation (1977: 90).

In these lectures on education in France, Durkheim does not follow a Comtean mode of exposition, that is one in terms of the 'heterogeneous' tendencies at work. The 'basic structural form' is established very early on, and we follow its visissitudes. Particularly noticeable, however, are the latent Comtean themes in Durkheim's search for created elements, crucial innovations that have been destroyed in counter-revolutionary changes. This is an emphasis which is quite anti-Comtean, since Comte's method simply precludes this appreciation as it is governed entirely by a 'filiation' to the vision of the imminent third, positive state and its constitutive elements. Durkheim's vision for French education as he formulated, was for a realisation of the tendencies which had already been expressed in the course of French history: 'the academic history of the nineteenth century was not very rich in innovations; it was a slow, gradual recovery of ideas which were already well known to the eighteenth century' (1977: 305). In these lectures Durkheim does not resort to his notions of pathology, but it is clear that his analysis is based on his concept of 'period of transition' outlined in *Rules*.

Conclusions

Durkheim came close to fulfilling one of Comte's wishes, namely that the time would come for a considered treatment of the problem of pathology (Comte, 1968, vol. ii: 360). In one sense Durkheim did not have recourse to all the materials suggested by Comte (he rarely used the idea of perturbations of orbits, etc.). But in another sense the importance he gave to the thematic of pathology was much deeper. Comte thought of pathology mainly in terms of excess, of transgression of the fundamental 'limits of variation'. Durkheim, however, rejected Comte's abandonment of causal analysis and found a way to circumvent the features of Comte's sociology that had fallen into disrepute: its obsession with future states, its naïve religion of humanity. In place of this Durkheim substituted a civic religion of the individual, which he found already well developed in the Third Republic, but under attack. As I discuss in the next chapter, Durkheim tried to define the effects of the structural abnormalities of this society in his study of rising suicide rates.

Notes

1 My own early publications on Durkheim seriously underestimated the importance of the dependence of Durkheim on Comte's sociological ideas and methods, especially with respect to the notion of pathology. I have drawn at this point on my papers 'La Distinction du normal et du pathologique' in: Borlandi et al. (eds) *Les Règles de la méthode sociologique*, (Paris: L'Harmattan), 1995, pp. 185–205; and 'Durkheim contre Comte' in: H. Cuin (ed.) *La Méthode Durkheimienne d'un siècle a l'autre*, (Paris: Presses Universitaires de France), 1997, pp. 31–8.

2 Some recent writers, for example Jacques Michel, have argued that the basic problematic of Durkheim's *Rules* is taken from Claude Bernard (Michel, 1991: 233ff.), and it is true that Durkheim adopted the term *milieu intérieur*. Two observations are possible. First that Bernard read Comte very closely, as Canguilhem points out. But as Kremer-Marietti points out, Comte's influence is greatly underestimated by Canguilhem, since the notion of the *milieu intérieur* was well established in Comte's theoretical writings and could have influenced Bernard and Durkheim independently (Kremer-Marietti, 1982: 143–57).

3 Canguilhem draws attention to the difference between the tradition which emphasised statistical notions (e.g. J. Brown) and the tradition from Bichat to Broussais, Comte, and Bernard which tended to reject a statistical formalisation (Canguilhem, 1989: ch. 2). Hacking has indicated another polarity, that between Durkheim and Galton (Hacking, 1990: ch. 20).

4 It is not at all clear that Durkheim read Mill closely. For example, Mill wrote on 'false analogies' that 'bodies politic' can die of old age (*System of Logic*, 1974: 796).

5 Durkheim's control of the terminology of genus and species was far from secure. See, for example, the change of the formula of the rule for determining species in the versions of the *Rules* from 1894 to 1895 (this is not picked up in 1988: 179, where Durkheim changed the term *espèces* to *variétés* in the rules concerning classification).

7

The Crisis in Method and the Resort to Theory in *Suicide*

> Let us reverse the order of study… instead of being morphological, our classification will from the start be aetiological. (Durkheim, [1897] 1970: 146–7)

The status of 'theory' as such in Durkheim's work is not evident from his methodological writings. In fact there is a widespread view that his proximity to positivist methods precludes the active role of theory in his sociological analyses. This is problematic for two quite different reasons. The first is that, as we have seen, Comte's sociology accorded a crucial role to theory. The second is that when confronted with the real problems of his social analysis, Durkheim was forced to concede that he could not use his chosen method of working through 'morphological' features of the relevant social fact, but had to introduce theoretical definitions directly.

Durkheim says in *Suicide* that the 'chief methodological problems elsewhere stated and examined' (i.e. in *Rules* [1895]) arise again in a new context in the study of *Suicide* (Durkheim, 1970: 37). In the Preface to *Suicide* [1897], he emphasises that these methodological problems are above all those relating to the definition of the 'social fact' – a phenomenon conceived by Durkheim as being external to individuals: 'any way of acting, whether fixed or not, capable of exerting over the individual an external constraint' (Durkheim, 1982: 59). This definition in its simplicity does not prepare us for the complexity of the relation between theory and method we encounter in this study.[1]

What was Durkheim's strategy?

The drama that appears in *Suicide* is the fact that here Durkheim claimed to have applied the order of analysis prescribed in *Rules* in reverse. If this has occasionally been noted by commentators, it has rarely if ever been the subject of serious and critical reflection. On the one hand, there are those who see in it nothing of any great significance, following Durkheim's own comments in *Suicide* itself (see Schmaus, 1994: 8, 150–84; Berthelot, 1995). On the other hand, other writers have begun to read the reversal as a significant event in Durkheim's development. As yet however the real significance of the issue remains ill-defined. In this chapter I hope to clarify what is at stake in this debate. My argument is that in trying to work with suicide statistics,

Durkheim was forced to override the principles he laid out so brilliantly in 1895; and this very fact reveals a great deal about Durkheim's conception of the inventive, flexible, undogmatic role of methodology. But it also led him to face more radically the possibility that his position in *Rules* had been, in part, misconceived – a possibility that would have important and wide ramifications for his sociology.

In this chapter I examine and discuss the following problems: first, the method prescribed in *Rules*; secondly, how (if Durkheim had been consistent), the method should have been applied to suicide; thirdly, what Durkheim actually did in *Suicide*; fourthly, to what 'discovery' his 'reversal' of methodological practice corresponds; and to discuss an alternative way of looking at the significance of this issue, particularly the relation of theory and method to the substantive content of Durkheim's sociology.

The Method of *Rules* [1895]

Although Durkheim tried to crystallise his method in the book called *Rules of Sociological Method*, his writings on method are not limited to the formulations in this work. Indeed, it is possible to argue that even this work exists in two, three, even four different versions. Many writers have argued that Durkheim changed his methods, and some have argued that his real method was different from his stated or 'official' method (e.g. Lukes, 1969, 1973). It seems clear that he redrafted his manuscript on key points between 1894 and 1895 (Berthelot's 1988 edition gives only some of the changes) following a decision to study not consolidated social facts, but ones that were identifiable as independent from their individual manifestations (Durkheim, 1988: 138). *Rules* is clearly very ambitious, seeking to define not only procedures, but also strategic priorities.

The steps prescribed in Durkheim's work are as follows. The book demands that sociologists first define the kind of social facts that form the object of investigation. These facts are to be treated 'as things' – that is, they are external to individuals and have the force of a collective phenomenon. They are to be defined by characteristics observed to belong to the order of facts themselves, not by commonly held presuppositions or previously conceived judgements. The sociologist must follow rules for treating the reliability of data. Third, the sociologist must follow rules for distinguishing between normal and pathological forms. This is done by determining the character of normal features of the social species. Social types are, fourth, to be classified – morphologically – at this stage. The social facts under study are to be interpreted through an understanding of the inner social milieux of societies (moral volume and density) concerned in order to discover social causes, since they suggest possible invariant relations. The proofs, finally, concerning these relations are to be administered by comparative analysis of a sufficient number and quality of comparative series, and aim to establish laws of co-variation.

This brief outline of Durkheim's procedure shows just how systematic and comprehensive the sociological method is. It is certainly not restricted to techniques of investigation and gathering of evidence. The general character of the method is to present the elements of rationalism, objectivism, and experimental reason (Berthelot, 1995: 140). A key feature is the application of the division between normal and pathological facts which Durkheim uses to link his method with practical intervention. Essential to the method is the specific requirement that observation take precedence over imagination, in Comtean fashion, but without Comte's insistence on the development of analysis under the aegis of a fundamental theory of the domain. Durkheim insists on a different point throughout *Rules*: scientific sociology is only possible if the order of analysis begins with the work of objective observation and rational classification of objects in its domain defined in advance by specific characteristics. Durkheim argues that there are a number of facts in society which are observed to have the character of being necessary, determined and determining, independent of the subjective or objective will of individuals. It is to this body of phenomena that sociologists must attend, and without ideological prejudgement. However, he does make room for a second order of analysis which might be applied as a 'verification' of the first. An example of this is his set of famous rules for determining the division between normal and pathological facts. The preferred method is one that identifies 'some immediately perceptible outward sign, but an objective one, to enable us to distinguish these two orders' (Durkheim, 1982: 91). In cases where this is difficult, or in periods of transition, a second method is required to verify the first (1982: 94). The rule for determining the normal in the second method is as follows: the results of the first method 'can be verified by demonstrating that the general character of the phenomenon is related to the general conditions of collective life in the social type under consideration' (1982: 97). He says of this second and more theoretical procedure that it 'should in no case be substituted for the previous one, nor even be the first one employed' (1982: 96). This is reiterated time and time again: analysis must begin with observation, never in a way which 'presupposes that either causes or functions' are already known (1982: 96).

How should the study have been conducted?

Suicide was not studied according to this set of rules. How should it have been studied if it had followed these rules? There are some remarks in *Suicide* that help answer this question. Durkheim says that the preferred method would be to group together suicides by specific characteristics that they have in common, to sub-divide them by these resemblances and differences, for there are 'as many suicidal currents as distinct types'; the sociologist should 'then seek to determine their causes and respective importance' (Durkheim, 1970: 145–6). He says at this point, 'we have pursued some such method in our brief study of suicide and insanity' (*C'est à peu près la méthode que nous avons suivie dans notre examen sommaire au suicide vesanique*' (1960: 140)). Let's turn to this study in chapter 1 (part 3) of *Suicide*.

Here Durkheim reports a remarkable attempt to classify suicides of the mentally ill by their morphological characteristics. Four different types are found from the detailed investigation (manic, melancholic, obsessive, automatic). What Durkheim does is to examine the evidence with a view to establishing social causation. He subjects the evidence to comparative analysis with respect to sex, religion, age, more general social suicide rates, and to time sequences. He notes a rule *en passant*:

> To estimate the possible effect of psychopathic states one must eliminate cases where they vary in proportion to the social condition ... They must be considered only where they are in inverse proportion to one another; only when a sort of conflict exists can one learn which is decisive' (1970: 70)

His conclusion is that 'the social suicide rate ... bears no definite relation to the tendency to insanity' (1970: 76). He says these particular psychopathological types lie outside the influence of social forces, and outside the field of sociology. His method is instructive: the suicides are classified morphologically in the first instance as 'insane suicide', and these groups are then analysed with reference to other known social phenomena in order to discover the pattern of agreements or differences.

Thus what Durkheim should have done, if he had been following his rules throughout his study, is the following. The analysis would commence with the obligatory definition of suicide. In fact this is done of course in the Introduction:

> The term 'suicide' is applied to all cases of death resulting directly or indirectly from a positive or negative act of the victim himself, which he knows will produce this result. (1970: 44)

Interestingly, Durkheim notes that in the case of the mentally ill, the suicides are 'either devoid of any motive or determined by purely imaginary causes' (1970: 66). These suicides are included as a definite category since the question of motive is not part of Durkheim's definition. But the crucial point is that if Durkheim had followed this method throughout his study, suicide statistics would then be classified by the whole character of the act itself, that is as a voluntary 'passive or active' act based on a real knowledge of its consequences. We could say this would involve an idea of the context and resolve, and the way the suicide was committed but not its motive. Durkheim's methodological imperative is based on the thesis that the rational definition of suicide, identification of the objective character of the act, is the specific, empirical and only route to a scientific analysis of the facts themselves: this is because the unknown causes are *expressed* in these objective manifestations (their special mark). Grouped by these characteristics (positive, negative, etc.) these facts would be subject to comparative analysis to discover the causes of the different types of suicide expressed in them. In Durkheim's own words, the order of research is the following: 'one would admit as many suicide currents as there were distinct types, then seek to determine their causes' (1970: 145). But, as noted, given the possibility of a second kind of analysis which seeks to explain these facts by relating the phenomena to 'the general conditions of collective life in the social type under consideration' (1982: 97), Durkheim might also be expected to follow through his analysis by relating suicide rates to the conditions of collective life. He would then present his proofs by testing the evidence in search of 'inverse' co-variation.

How was the study conducted?

Durkheim is disarmingly open (at the beginning of the second part of *Suicide*) about the fact that the study was based on a quite different principle: 'we shall be able to determine the social types of *Suicide* not directly by their previously described characteristics but by the causes which produce them' (1970: 147). He is quite prepared to identify the presumed costs of such a move: it assumes there are different types without being able to identify them at the start, it may indeed prove the existence of types but not their characteristic forms. Durkheim is very insistent at this point that *because the cause is expressed in the effect,* it is possible to 'deduce' these morphological characteristics from the causes he identifies. The method 'in reverse' therefore also depends on the unbroken link between cause and effect (1970: 147).

Durkheim does offer an important clarificatory comment here, at the moment he discusses motives. He says that on inspection, the similarity of suicide motives given in statistics across very different occupational groups (rural and urban) suggests that motives are only 'apparent causes' – an effect of 'moral casuistry' (1970: 151). He announces at this point that because of this immediately evident problem, 'we shall try to determine the productive causes of suicide directly, without concerning ourselves with the forms they can assume in particular individuals' (1970: 151). The famous chapters which follow examine three types of suicide: egoistic, altruistic and anomic. After determining and analysing these types, the final chapter of Book 2 returns to examine 'Individual forms of the different types of suicide'. Now it is precisely this order of enquiry which is at issue. The key methodological problem here is why should this order of investigation stand? How did Durkheim come to establish his aetiological classification?

If we examine Durkheim's analysis of egoistic, altruistic and anomic types of suicide, we can see that it certainly does not proceed from the characteristics of each type of suicide considered as an act. His analysis of *egoistic* suicides proceeds via an analysis of suicide rates relative to religion, sex, eductions, etc. Crucially, it does not work *directly* with comparisons of sex, age, region, etc. (see Baudelot and Establet, 1984: 101). It concludes that this particular type is revealed to vary inversely with the degree of social integration of these milieux (the famous formulation is given on in Durkheim, 1970: 208). He explains this law at two levels: first individualism simply produces insufficient social cohesion (1970: 210), but more profoundly he suggests since man is essentially *homo duplex,* absent here are essential transcendent objects to provide a necessary level of symbolic solidarities. Durkheim's proof was that society expresses its own disintegration at certain periods in waves of sadness and despair (1970: 213–14).

The discussion of *altruism* is different in structure. It begins more theoretically and works by comparison to and contrast with the established egoistic form (1970: 221). Durkheim notes that this type is chronic in the military milieu: here there is a coefficient of aggravation of suicide, identified as the intensity of the spirit of abnegation (1970: 237). He adds, 'the facts prove that the causes of military suicide are not only different from, but are in inverse proportion to most determining causes of civilian suicide' (1970: 236).

His discussion of the third type of suicide, the *anomic,* begins with an analysis of economic crises (1970: 241). He argues that this concerns patterns of deregulation, and declassification, and works towards a definition (1970: 258). With the decline of religion and the absence of strong moral codes and of secondary institutions, a certain anomie had become chronic in modern civilised cultures. There is also a type of anomic suicide which varies with intensities of solidarity in the family, a conjugal anomie which is associated with the strength of the marriage bond and the type of conjugal relation.

Durkheim has presented in these key central chapters a mixture of statistical analysis and theoretical investigation. His discussion is organised around the identification of three quite different suicide types which he concludes are produced by three distinct social causes, and three suicide currents. He sums than up as follows: 'Egoist suicide results from man's no longer finding a basis for existence in life; altruistic suicide, because this basis for existence appears to man situated beyond life itself. The third sort of suicide … [anomic] results from man's activity's lacking regulation and his consequent sufferings' (1970: 258). His method is circular in the sense that because he has grouped his material by the category of each suicide, he comes to discover a proof that there are indeed such groups, a circularity his method was supposed to avoid.

In the final chapter of the second part of *Suicide,* he therefore returns to the question of individual forms of morphology. He notes, in its first section, that this 'morphological classification, which was hardly possible at the commencement of this study, may be undertaken now that an aetiological classification forms its basis' (1970: 277). He again emphasises that what is required is 'to see the characteristics of special suicides grouped in distinct classes corresponding to the types just distinguished' (1970: 277). The explanation for this, he make clear, is to follow the work of expressive causation in reverse, to follow the way that these causes go 'from their social origins to their individual manifestations' (1970: 277), for each type has a 'special mark' carried from its cause to its effect. The analysis here proceeds 'deductively' (1970: 278). Durkheim gives a warning at this point that this procedure involves making purely 'logical' implications, and that these 'may not be able to receive experimental confirmation' (1970: 278). This procedure is always open to question, for it may seem that what is achieved is merely a presentation of illustrative material to give a 'concrete character' for results attained by other means. The following brief account concerns clear examples of first, egoistic suicide (Lamartine's Raphael) as a 'lofty' form, the epicurean as a contrasting form (1970: 278–83); second, altruistic suicide contrasting violent and emotional with calm and dutiful forms (1970: 283–4); and finally, the anomic form, associated with disappointment (1970: 284–5). He then presents a sketch of combined types 'ego-anomic' 'anomic-altruistic' and 'egoistic-altruistic', the stoic type (1970: 288, 289).

This brief analysis provides us with a good idea of what Durkheim meant by 'individual manifestations' or key 'special marks' of the way suicides were committed. However, the second section of this chapter introduces a complete bombshell. It is at this moment Durkheim chooses to explain the real reasons for his very drastic change of mind on methodology. It is worth quoting the passage in full:

> One might think a priori that some relation existed between the nature of suicide and the kind of death chosen by the one who commits it. It seems quite natural that the means he uses to carry out his resolve should depend on the feelings urging him on and thus express these feelings. We might therefore be tempted to use the data concerning this matter supplied us by statistics to describe the various sorts of *suicides* more closely, by their external form. But our research into this matter has given only negative results. (1970: 290)

This is a devastating statement with important implications and ramifications for all of Durkheim's methodological pronouncements. To repeat, the study discovers the expected continuity of social causation into the 'external form' of the act has not been confirmed. As the whole procedure outlined in *Rules* is based on this 'a priori' assumption, *this discovery, even if a negative one, ranks as a central finding of the study*. It has long been overlooked, one suspects, because it is negative on the one hand, and because it intervenes at the level not of empirical finding but of methodology itself. Methodology is revealed here (in a way not fully exposed before) to be closely bound up with substantive sociological assumptions and presuppositions. One might say that Durkheim discovered that one of his own crucial ideological prejudgements – the concept of the 'act' and 'ways of acting' as prenotions, *idola* – had not been removed.

Durkheim immediately announces a curious aspect of the new finding: 'social causes certainly determine the choice of these means; for the relative frequency of the various ways of committing suicide is invariable for long periods in a given society' (1970: 290). Durkheim presents his statistics for the different ways suicides are committed in four different countries in the 1870s. It is clear that his investigation into the 'external form' of the suicide was not prevented for lack of evidence. What the figures reveal, says Durkheim, is that '[t]he social causes on which suicides in general depend … differ from those which determine the way they are committed; *for no relation can be discovered between the types of* suicides *which we have distinguished and the most common methods of performance*' (1970: 291, my emphasis). Curiously, the modes of committing suicide are more stable than suicide rates (1970: 291).

Durkheim provides a consolation: a set of hypotheses about the ways certain of his types might have been expected to concern the mode of performance and which therefore would have confirmed his methodological assumption. Altruism might show a link through death by firearms, but this is not confirmed. Egoism might have its 'natural expression' through hanging, but again this is not confirmed. Durkheim interprets these figures to show that the motives for suicide are quite different from motives for choice of means. The latter is influenced by available technology ('under trains'), and by the very prestige of certain means. He concludes with the unexpected but typically extreme formulation 'the form of death chosen is therefore *something entirely foreign to the very nature of* suicide' (1970: 293, my emphasis). And consequently, 'the first has nothing to teach us about the second; it was discovered by a wholly different study' (1970: 291).

The final third part of *Suicide* concerns suicide as a 'social problem'. But its first chapter is again highly theoretical, concerning in the main a long critique of Quetelet's conception of the average (1970: 300–6). Durkheim uses this topic as a vehicle to develop a detailed exposition of his conception of the difference between his idea of social facts as collective causes and any kind of averaging from individual forms. When he discusses methodology it is to stress that his findings in this study confirm the proposition that social facts are objective and external to individuals: the principles set out in *Rules* (1970: 310, 313). What is striking about this recapitulation of themes from *Rules* is that it reiterates many of the formulas which contain the thesis of expressive causality relating internal and external characteristics. For example,

> We start from the exterior because it alone is immediately given, but only to reach the interior. Doubtless the procedure is complicated; but there is no other unless one would risk having his research apply to his personal feeling concerning the order of facts ... instead of to this factual order itself. (1970: 315)

This is Durkheimian myth-making. This return to the *Rules* – its emphasis on the objectivity and externality of social facts at the end of *Suicide* – effectively closes off an appreciation of what Durkheim has actually just discovered. But he wants to end the chapter with an investigation into the theory of social life as a process of equilibration of the three currents (egoistic, altruistic and anomic) and in particular the idea that 'no moral idea exists which does not combine in proportions varying with the society involved, egoism, altruism, and a certain anomie' (1970: 321). In this discussion it is striking that Durkheim again resorts to a notion of expressive causation. The causes of the tendency to egoism and anomie also affect the mental constitution of individuals at a deep level, for 'they are expressive of the same cause: this makes them combine and become mutually adapted' (1970: 323). But then Durkheim recoils. He concludes with the more subtle observation that '[t]he productive cause of the phenomenon naturally escapes the observer of individuals only; for it lies outside individuals' (1970: 324). Thus the effect on mental constitution is not a cause of suicide but of certain effects which might lead to predispositions to suicide in certain groups, depending on the intensity and direction of suicide currents (1970: 324).

In the final two chapters of *Suicide*, Durkheim attempts a quite impossible task, to complete other requirements demanded by his method outlined in the *Rules*. This comprises (a) a wide comparative analysis over historical time, across different social species, a diachronic analysis from antiquity to the present (1970: 326–38); (b) a synchronic analysis, varying suicide with other social criminal and moral facts in contemporary society (1970: 358–60); and (c) the question of normal and pathological suicide rates and what might be done practically about the rise in the reported rates of suicide (1970: 361–92). The first and second problems deal, according to Durkheim, with the question of whether suicide should be considered an immoral or criminal act; the third problem concerns the question of the state of modern society itself. Durkheim reaches complex conclusions: first the tendency towards thinking suicide might become entirely a matter of individual volition is an error. Second, there is no simple connection between suicide and other criminal forms, so no formula can be used to determine the solution to forms of sanction against them. Finally, Durkheim works systematically to a conclusion that the current rates of suicide in France and modern Europe are rising in an abnormally rapid way. His remedy, as is well known, is the reintroduction of secondary occupational groups between the state and the individual: *institutional socialism*. In Durkheim's words, 'we may believe that this aggravation springs not from the intrinsic nature of progress but from the special conditions under which it occurs in our day' (1970: 368). This modern crisis is not part of a 'regular evolution' since completely abnormal causes are at work (1970: 370). Durkheim's solution is spelt out: it involves a complete restructuring of the state – even its forms of democratic representation (1970: 390). Durkheim's analysis is really only intelligible in the context of this theoretical envelope established elsewhere.

How important is the reversal of method? Could the study simply have been presented differently?

I now want to examine the question of the importance of Durkheim's decision to change his method. What difference does it make in the analysis? Is it fundamental and does it arise from a discovery concerning the nature of suicide itself?

This study would have been largely a presentation of statistics but not a purely empirical study. It might have resembled Comte's own prescription of a positive method, one devoted to establishing (but of course never achieving) laws of con-commitance and co-variation with the addition of causal analysis (see Schmaus, 1994; Cherkaoui, in Cuin, 1997: 153ff.). If this is one alternative to the present form, it is also important to note that *Suicide* is clearly not the empiricist study it is sometimes mistaken to be.

What Durkheim achieves in his study is quite different. Ironically, the empirical 'discovery' that the mode of the suicidal act is quite external to the cause of suicide is the basis on which Durkheim very suddenly and dramatically renounces the logic of 'expressive causality'. He was thus provoked into the theory of complex social mal-integration in a way which he could not handle with any degree of assurance. It seems that the theory presented through a method of 'deduction' (see Gane, 1988: 49–51) remains radically incomplete, for this does not provide us with a good statement of what Durkheim actually did in *Suicide* from a methodological point of view. Nor does it genuinely reflect the sociological discovery of the complexity of certain kinds of human 'acts' like suicide (and the domain of sociology is made up of such acts: religious, political, cultural etc.).

Unlike the route to an analysis of action which some argue Durkheim secretly followed, Durkheim's analysis led in quite the opposite direction, to an unexpected but specific kind of *deconstruction* of action. He analyses suicides as the meeting of at least two heterogeneous currents: the suicidogenic current giving rise to the resolve itself, and the different current which furnishes the means. Both are outside the immediate rationalisation of action by the agent and the immediate triggers of such phenomena. Such 'ways of acting' (if we return to the definition of a social fact) are complex, made up of elements that come together but do not mutually express or cause each other, for they are 'foreign' to each other. The implication for methodology is that sociology should not assume that by following the natural logic of action it is following a privileged linear causal chain. Importantly, the presupposition that sociology can work from the external features of a given social fact directly to its internal cause is thrown into doubt.

One could say that the delayed explanation of the full complexity of the suicide act, the bombshell thesis that the mode of committing the act is foreign to the nature of suicide itself, leads to the greatest surprise of all, the greatest ruse of *Suicide, namely that he did not use his method in reverse*. Because the causal chain is broken, Durkheim could not work back from the causally determined types to the 'external manifestations' as effects in any completely continuous analytic sequence (the method of deduction).

If the reverse method is impossible, what was his method?

What he did in the famous Book 2 was the following: first he grouped the facts relating to egoistic suicide in such a way that he was able to discover the condition of egoism (a completely circular manoeuvre). He then found, ingeniously, contrasting forms of altruism and anomie (and fatalism). He followed, in effect, the method he called in *Rules* an analysis of the relation of the phenomenon 'to the general conditions of collective life'. The injunction he broke was that '*this method should in no case be substituted for the previous one, nor even be the first one employed*' (1982: 96). From these aetiologically determined types, he argued that the phenomenological emotional moods which expressed crisis states resembled the proposed 'manifestations' of these crises and their 'rationalisations'.

However, this means that there is, in *Suicide*, no analysis of any suicide act, no analysis of *any* suicidal process. Indeed, as one analyst has noted,

> nowhere is evidence presented to demonstrate that some or all of the suicides of a particular sociological type actually experience the subjective states attributed to them. Although Durkheim characterised the egoistic suicide as apathetic and anomic as angry, there is no evidence for rejecting the reverse possibility. Durkheim offered virtually no empirical evidence to link his etiological classification with his morphological one. (Pope, 1976: 198)

There is no attempt at all to analyse the complex interaction or overdetermined meeting of the suicidal causal chain and that which determines the means to achieve it. Durkheim provides first a *theory* of differential forms of social integration and social regulation; second he presents evidence on inverse co-variation of social integration and suicide rates; and third he provides a brief and very imaginative evocation (which is essentially synthetic fiction-theory) of what might be expected of the subjective mood under which the act is committed and its associated 'co-enaesthetic' forms.

Conclusions

Durkheim had many reasons for writing his study on suicide. Sociologists in the main have seen it as an attempt to undertake an empirical study of a subject that appears at first sight to fall only within the purview of individual, or the psychological. He is seen, wrongly, as choosing this subject to demonstrate his new methodology. But the strategic reason, which is rarely discussed, is that he wanted another proof of the fact that France was in a perilous moral state because of its institutional imbalances. As he noted in his new Preface to the second edition of *The Division of Labour in Society* ([1902] 1964), many commentators judged that Durkheim's proposal to restore the professional groups or corporations, could not be justified by his account of the evil. Durkheim replied that he had not changed his mind: 'we lack a whole system of organs necessary to the normal functioning of social life'. As he did not have sufficient data to attempt to prove this empirically, he was forced, *faute de mieux*, into theory.

Note

1 This chapter draws on 'The deconstruction of social action: the "reversal" of Durkheimian methodology from *The Rules* to *Suicide*' in W.S.F. Pickering and Geoffrey Walford (eds) *Durkheim's Suicide: A Century of Research and Debate*. (London, Routledge), 2000, pp. 22–35.

8

End of the Second Cycle: Anthropology and Religion

> La crise, c'est le 'dégel', c'est le départ des molécules de la gelée de viande sur le macaroni … c'est l'état moléculaire'. (Mauss [1942] 1997: 772)

Durkheim's death left a void in French sociology. Although Marcel Mauss took over the leadership of the school, or what remained of it after the decimation of the war years, he devoted himself principally and most effectively to anthropological themes ('I have never been a militant of sociology', he said), and to editing and publishing Durkheim's lectures (on socialism, education, professional ethics, etc.) as well as the works of Hubert and Hertz (1983: 141–2) (For a wide survey of Durkheimianism in this period see Marcel, 2001.) One of the consequences of this imbalance was that Durkheimian or what was referred to as 'French' sociology took on a character which was marked by anthropological themes and terms. In the inter-war period the framework established by Comte and Durkheim began to face the challenged posed by Marxist theory given great impetus by the 1917 revolution in Russia. Mauss himself wrote an 'assessment' of Bolshevism (Mauss, 1992), but by the end of the 1930s imaginative attempts were being made to combine Marx and Durkheim together with other themes from Hegel, Nietzsche and aesthetic influences such as surrealism in a theoretical frame polarised towards anthropological perspectives.

Mauss: anthropology versus sociology?

Mauss's career, intellectual orientations and contribution to social theory were quite different from those of Durkheim, even though they were both leaders of the 'French sociological and anthropological school'. Mauss's very large corpus of writings does not include a single book. Those works, like the famous essay on 'The Gift', were originally published as journal articles, even the very long text jointly written with Durkheim on social classification. In fact a large proportion of Mauss's output was co-authored. He also had a leaning against the theoretical in favour of a close proximity to social facts, and was against what he called 'the pretentious search for originality' (Mauss, 1983: 139). He was an original thinker, and has had a much greater effect on post Second World War theory than Durkheim, but not as often perceived. For example, the theory of the 'total social fact', which Lévi-Strauss and many others took as his greatest contribution, was in fact coined initially by Durkheim (Dubar, 1969: 519). Mauss did attempt to reconstruct the main categories of sociological theory after Durkheim died, in essays in the second series of the *Année Sociologique* for which he took overall responsibility. Indeed he was sometimes accused of emphasising the sociological dimensions too strongly. But essentially his main contribution was in establishing the field of anthropology. Mauss, however, claimed that the most important characteristic of his approach was not simply that he was a 'positivist' and thus not interested in 'the lofty realms of ... metaphysical ideas' but that he was essentially a member of a school, a team, a workshop – in fact he had been Durkheim's 'recruiting agent' (Mauss, 1983: 140). Before the First World War, Mauss had become famous for a series of exemplary studies in anthropology which included, with Hubert, 'Sacrifice: its Nature and Function' (1899), and 'A General Theory of Magic' ([1902] 2001); with Henri Beuchat, 'Seasonal Variations of the Eskimo' ([1906] 1979), and many others. These studies were given Durkheim's own synthesis in his 1912 study *Elementary Forms*. But Mauss admitted in 1930 that Durkheim's argument about the nature of the sacred remained open: 'We were never sure that he was correct and I still continue to speak of the magico-religious' (Mauss, 1983: 149).

'The Gift' however, was published in the first issue of the second series of the *Année* in 1925, and all commentators have agreed that it marks a considerable shift away from the problematic of the earlier essays. Some suggest that it is the real beginning of structuralism (Lévi-Strauss, 1987), some that it marks the beginning of the analysis of power (Baudrillard, 1993b), perhaps the 'foundation of ethnology' (Fournier, 1994: 501ff.), others that it marks the 'invention of the symbolic' (Tarot, 1999). Talcott Parsons likened the analysis to Mendel's discoveries in genetics (in Dillon, 1968: 6). In any event there is a seismic shift from Durkheim's remark that the gift is of no moral interest because it is merely a gratuitous act, to Mauss's discovery that it forms an obligatory form of exchange in all societies, but a central one in the societies falling under the view of the new anthropology. It forms the basis of a quite new problematic, that was to be made famous in Mauss's lectures at the Collège de France after his appointment there in 1931–40. For the appointment Mauss drew up an 'intellectual self portrait'. This provides a statement of his new theoretical position. From the facts, he says, he

> drew out that at once religious, mythical and contractual idea of the gift. I also brought out the idea of total prestation between clans, between generations (usually staggered), between sexes and between descent groups (see Malinowski): I established the collective nature of archaic forms (see Davy) and, above all, this notion of 'total facts' which set the entire economic, moral, religious, aesthetic and mythical (see Granet) social whole in motion. Superimposed on reciprocity and conflict, a system of purely sumptuary, military, athletic etc., rivalries developed within these societies ... [T]he previous ways of posing questions have been surpassed and displaced. (1983: 147)

This thematic, with its further analyses of 'potlatch', the 'techniques of the body', Mauss kept strictly in the sphere of those societies which the

Durkheimians called 'polysegmental' but which Mauss developed (Allen, 2000: 61–74). Sociology may indeed, for Mauss, have been a 'lost cause' (Fournier, 1994: 527ff.). His lectures at the Collège de France in the 1930s which developed these ideas drew in new audiences and were to have effects in sociology which Mauss had not intended. But before examining these, it is important to focus on Mauss's writings on politics in this period, since they also point to his marked divergence with Durkheim, while indicating his critical distance from Marxism. Again, these writings he kept quite separate in what he called his 'written interventions in the normative sphere' (Mauss, 1983: 151).

Mauss: radical politics

The recently published collection of Mauss's political writings (Mauss, 1997) indicates two important aspects of Durkheimian social theory after Durkheim's death in 1917.[1] The first is that Mauss did not adopt directly Durkheim's theoretical sociology but uses *marxisant* terms for social classes. The second is that there is a very clear sense that Mauss's ideal and model for his notion of socialism is not at all a Marxist one but the development of socialist practical forms in Britain. Thus Mauss has a clearly individual voice both in sociology and in political philosophy, and it is not very obvious just what the scope of his divergence from Durkheim is. Is it a difference of emphasis, for example, more concern for practice over theory? Or is it more than this: a reconfiguration of Durkheimian sociology as a whole? On the one hand, Mauss is much more impressed with the theory of capital and capitalism than Durkheim was, and this gives certain parts of his writing a radical character. On the other hand, Mauss tends to look more for the practical processes of the development of socialism for example than to critique socialist theory (though he does this too of course), and this leads him to assess socialist progress on the ground which he claims is different from, and in advance of theory (Mauss, 1997: 254ff.).

Whereas Durkheim outlined a theory of social structures, developing notably the distinction between segmental and organic forms of solidarity, Mauss retains something of the principle but introduces the concept of the nation as the key mediating term. Thus, very simply, it seems that socialism is a modern idea and practice (after 1830) and is possible only as part of the development of the modern national form of organic solidarity. The project for a socialism where this form is absent, for example in Russia, leads to quite different results (for the social elements are more like heterogeneous segments in an 'imperial sack' [Mauss, 1997: 258ff.]). Mauss does not appear to give any great weight to the notion of social pathology, and so does not locate himself in Durkheim's scheme where the principal objective of theorists is to repair a social abnormality of structure through appeals to statesmen ('The work of the sociologist is not that of the statesman. We do not have to present in detail what this reform should be. It will be sufficient to indicate the general principles' [Durkheim, 1964: 23]). Whereas Durkheim stood at a distance from politics, even

> the social and moral crisis of the Dreyfus Affair in which he [Durkheim] played a large part, did not change his opinion. Even during the war, he was among those who put no hope in the so-called internationally organised working class. He therefore remained uncommitted – he 'sympathized' ... with the socialists, with Jaurès, with socialism. But he never gave himself to it. (Mauss citied in Durkheim, 1962: 34–5)[3]

Mauss did give himself to socialism: he was a founder member of the official voice of the Socialist Party, the journal *l'Humanité*, in 1904. He left it in 1920 when it became the organ of the Communist Party, just as he had left the radical journal *Mouvement Socialiste* when Sorel developed a violent campaign of the 'active minority' (Mauss, 1992: 213). Mauss kept the academic anthropology and the political idioms separate.

The phase of socialism which developed in Western Europe (particularly 1876–90) after the Commune revealed, says Mauss, a variety of practical developments of a new kind which left the heroic and utopian age of theory (Marx and Proudhon) behind. Mauss is therefore led to look very positively at small-scale local developments where democratic progress is the result of engagement and struggle, where liberties are won and defended in constructive encounters, and where organisations, economic and political, are built up through experience. He is not enthusiastic about a revolutionary strategy of taking society to a zero point, *tabula rasa*, on which a new society is suddenly implanted. Only from an existing nation can socialism be conceived as an internal progression of an organic type, but nonetheless this is revolutionary and requires a sharp transition, '*une modification organique*' (Mauss, 1997: 82) of bourgeois society. Thus the task for the proletariat within a nation is not primarily a political and revolutionary one, but a social engagement in building new organisations within and against the existing frame. This frame is not in itself an insuperable obstacle to this engagement as Marxists claim, but quite the contrary, it alone makes it possible. Mauss enthusiastically cites the formula of the Webbs – to build a 'state within a state' (Mauss, 1997: 173). It is the emergent socialist idea and spirit (*l'esprit socialiste*) which is the direct cause of the new movement in society and which is realised in trade union and cooperative organisations. Mauss is sent by *l'Humanité* as *envoyé spécial* to conferences of the cooperative movement in Hamburg, Budapest, Paisley and was sent on a research mission to Russia in 1906.

Mauss therefore took up a position which embraced the empirical and practical elements of the socialist movement and this led to an admiration for social developments in Britain in particular. This was unusual for a leading French intellectual in this period, as Fournier points out in his introduction to the political writings.[2] Mauss in this respect develops a sociological frame which is distinct from that of Durkheim. More empirical and concrete in its emphasis, this can even be traced in theoretical reflection. For example, when

Mauss presents socialism as a social fact in Durkheimian style, he very specifically departs from the classic definition. Social facts are essentially psychological, and not to be found outside individuals in their social context, he says (Mauss, 1997: 76). Durkheim's famous methodological definition of social facts as external to individuals appears abstract and theoretical against Mauss's formulation. Durkheim's distance from political engagement contrasts to the position of Mauss, especially compared to the latter's political tirades – first against revolutionary anarcho-syndicalism and direct action (1997: 184–9), and second, the ones launched against the French bourgeoisie from the point of view of proletarian socialism and in comparison with the more advanced forms of bourgeois politics found elsewhere, especially in Britain, which were so clearly admired by Mauss (1997: 230–9).

Mauss's position is, however, put to the test in the period running up to the First World War. It seems clear that Mauss, almost in Comtean terms, thought it impossible that there could really be deep-seated causes of war between advanced nations – by which he meant France, Britain and Germany. These were the great civilisations, the great nations. The diplomats and diplomacies of these nations he saw as democratic, not divorced from popular control (1997: 225). In the run-up to the war therefore, Mauss contrasts the political maturity of these nations against the autocratic and feudal regimes of Eastern Europe, particularly Russia, but also the primitive relations of Croats, Czechs, Austro-Hungarians to the 'Jesuit Order' in Vienna. His view is that Germany's ambitions are eastward and France will be drawn into war only because of a misconceived loyalty to Moscow (1997: 208) and naïve entrapments in 'infernal Russian intrigues' (1997: 225). Again Mauss does not look for abnormalities of structure (as Durkheim did in his war essays), but to different levels and complications in social development which are open possibly to political repair.

After the war Mauss took up a detailed analysis of the Bolshevik strategy in the Russian Revolution and its aftermath. His position was certainly a qualified support of the project, with clear distantiation from those who wished to condemn the experiment completely. His position remained very much a continuation of his previous reflections on Marxism and the nature of socialism. First of all, Russian Marxism did not add anything to theory or practice (1997: 258); it reproduced a utopianism which belonged to the first half of the nineteenth century and was already unable to deal with later developments. The classic errors were reproduced: fetishism of politics, attempts to construct complex social structures by fiat and violence, elimination of the market, etc. Mauss's analysis of the Soviet experience is therefore that Bolshevism took an early utopian form of socialism into a social context which was itself unpropitious for socialist development. His position was to advocate, along the lines of other socialist critics of Bolshevism, a more modest and evolutionary approach which centred on the idea that the Bolsheviks should have first attempted to create a modern nation and only then attempted to defined more advanced projects.

Marcel Mauss's essay on Bolshevism is written, he says, as an 'assessment' in a style of Comte, and it will 'criticise' in the style of Renouvier (Mauss, 1992: 170). He also notes that 'It would not be difficult here to pastiche Marx, to rewrite vis-à-vis this gigantic Commune his two famous pamphlets on the class struggles in France and on the Paris Commune. If I steer clear of such a parody, I hope I shall be allowed to follow fundamentally his example' (1992: 171). In fact Mauss's essay is close as an idiom to the one inaugurated by Littré in his attempt to learn the lessons of the first efforts at sociological prediction. He notes the curious lineage of Marxism to French socialism, eliminating all utopianism except 'the general apocalyptic thesis of the 'taking over of the administration of things' but taking up the main idea indicated in Durkheim's critique of Saint-Simon in two ways. First the idea of the Soviet corresponds to Durkheim's avocation of professional corporations as the basis of property statute. Second, 'the establishment of a moral and political law of the group formed out of the economic association of those united in the same production', that is the occupation as the basis for political representation and social status on the model of the guild or the university (1992: 172). Thus Mauss's interest, he says, combined both scientific and personal concerns: 'it was a socialism which among the options open to it had chosen my own, the professional organisation'; indeed 'Moscow seemed to many amongst us what it remains for many enlightened people … a kind of sanctuary incubating the very destiny of our ideas' (1992: 173).

His judgement against the Bolsheviks draws some harsh lessons. But first he asks the question: to what extent was Bolshevism a true social experiment? For Mauss, though he does not examine Bolshevik social theory, the Bolshevik revolution was more a creature of the crisis in Russia than the outcome of the will of a people. It was not 'methodically pursued … it is just a great adventure'; in fact, 'an accident, it has been grafted, overlaid onto the life of a people … it does not correspond to the movement of the mentality of the Russian people, any more than it is the pure realisation of the ideas of its leaders' (1992: 175). Mauss compares France of 1789 (with its bourgeoisie in place, 'already dominant') with the 'impotent bourgeoisie' in Russia. Even the February revolution of 1917, when Kerensky took power, was not the work of 'a living society creating for itself by force a constitution', and even the socialist revolutionaries destroyed what political and civic organisation there was. As for the Bolsheviks, 'at least they had willpower … savage will … not encumbered by any love for this immense people'. Like parasites, the Bolsheviks 'exploit' the revolution, they 'seized Russia' but the opposition is even worse and even less popular (1992: 178–9). Thus Bolshevism in Russia is explicable only by the conjuncture of the war crisis and the inability of other forces to resist it.

Mauss is very clear about the further lessons to be learned from Bolshevism. It proves that all social revolution 'must take a national character … it must be the work of the "general will" of the citizens'. Indeed, he concludes, the communist and terrorist period of the Russian Revolution was 'not strictly speaking socialist'. Socialism should organise the market and not attempt to produce a communism of consumption. Socialism cannot 'dispense with money' nor suppress the essential 'industrial and commercial freedom' or the modern economy. Essential to socialism is to maintain and to 'respect … intermediary collectivities'. Indeed, 'Durkheim's hypotheses about the moral and economic value of the professional group emerge further confirmed … The Soviets failed precisely because they undermined and destroyed this primordial organisational element' (1992: 187–91). Essential political conclusions follow. First that 'violence is only legitimate via the law, via the legal order whose reign it supports: it is not itself order, still less faith'. Second, 'naïve sociologists, the Communists believed that the order of sovereignty, the law, can create … from nothing … the law does not create, it sanctions' (1992: 198–9). Thus, Mauss concludes, the failure of Bolshevism in Russia teaches lessons, but it does not teach the lesson that socialism as a project is doomed to fail, only that it will fail under the conditions in Russia pursued as a project in the way the Bolsheviks pursued communism, for 'despite their violence, despite their strength, despite their energy and their daring, despite their power, political power, they failed' (1992: 199).

Towards the 1930s Mauss's political texts are more rare, although it is clear that he tried to come to terms with another series of political crises and another world war. In 1936 he wrote to S. Ranulf that the fact that 'great modern societies … could be subject to suggestion as Australian ones are by their dances, and made to turn around like children in a ring, is something we had not really foreseen. We did not put our minds to this return to primitivism' (1992: 214). In 1942 he wrote a short piece in which he wonders how to conceptualise the war as a crisis, how to 'find the means to express the sensations I have had during these long months' (Mauss, 1997: 771). He believed he had found the means as follows: the bonds which hold the social parts together come apart, so that 'irregularities are the rule' (1997: 772). This comment pushes Durkheimian notions of pathology to the limit, a genial reflection is followed by one also of 1942 on 'Origines de la Bourgeoisie' in which Mauss again seems to be developing a line of thought against Durkheim. In this short piece, again based on war-time reflections, he says that it is quite wrong to think of the bourgeoisie through the slogans 'Liberty, Equality, Fraternity' or through the notions of the fraternity of guilds, communes or corporations. Essentially, he argues, the bourgeoisie is the owner of funds, of stocks, which need to be protected; hence the development of the 'bourg', and the fortress. It is from this basis that the bourgeoisie forms an independent intermediary class able to sustain itself against other interests. It would be a mistake, he says, reflecting on the socialist project, to resurrect this class in the guise of a '*socialisme du ravitailleur*' (1997: 774).

Mauss therefore furnishes a remarkably coherent and consistent political engagement over many decades. It is a rationalist socialism adopting the theme of the class struggle between the proletariat and the bourgeoisie, though this is given a quite different frame from that of Marx and Lenin (whose theory he does not assess). Mauss retains from Durkheim the idea of organic solidarity, and this is related directly to the concept of the nation and emergent socialist forms. Whereas Durkheim considered the bourgeoisie as identical with the class formed in the corporation, Mauss's view is more in line with Marx. Whereas Marx thought the proletariat could overthrow bourgeois society in a political revolution, Mauss thought that it could only triumph through a long revolution of social construction – economic, cultural, political and moral. Mauss attempted to maintain a broad anthropology and sociology with political engagement. With the publication of this collection we are in a position for the first time to read the relation between these elements.

Bataille: heterology and theatricalisation

Born in 1897 in a village near Clermont-Ferrand, Bataille was brought up in Rheims, at the same school as Roger Caillois. He won his first baccalaureat in 1914, the second in 1915. He was called up, but when he was found to have TB was discharged. He was a fervent Catholic and wrote a piece on the bombing of the Nôtre-Dame of Rheims (in Hollier, 1992: 15–19). In 1917 he entered a seminary and intended to become a priest or monk, but by 1920 he had changed his mind after a stay at a monastery in the Isle of Wight. He wrote a thesis on Chivalry at the Ecole in Chartres in 1922. He was given a fellowship in Madrid in 1922, and at the end of 1922 procured a position at the Bibliothèque Nationale in Paris, when he also became a pupil of Léon Chestov, reading Nietzsche and others. He met Leiris, André Masson and others and entered into the circles of the surrealists. His publications began to appear from about 1927 and his ideas developed very quickly up to the outbreak of war in 1939. He wrote a number of pornographic pieces under pseudonyms, and was at the heart of the internal divisions of the surrealists, taking a position against André Breton. Bataille encountered the philosophers via the lectures on Hegel by Kojeve, the sociologists and Durkheimians via the lectures of Marcel Mauss, and he was politically aligned with the Democratic Communists lead by Boris Souvarine. Reconciled with André Breton, he formed with Caillois an anti-Popular Front group called Contre-Attaque in 1935. From 1937–9 he was actively involved in the Collège de Sociologie, and in the background the secret society Acéphale. In the war period he turned away from these enterprises, to more reflective and somewhat mystical works. He left the Bibliothèque Nationale in 1942 because of his TB. After the war he founded the journal *Critique*, and worked on the large-scale project called *The Accursed Share*, but he remained unemployed until 1949 when he became a librarian in Carpentras, then in Orleans. He became ill again in 1955, but recovered to write on eroticism, etc. He bought an apartment in Paris in 1961 from the proceeds of a sale of works by Picasso, Miró, Masson, Ernst, and others, and hoped to regain a position in the Bibliothèque Nationale, but he died on 8 July 1962 before this aim was realised.

Bataille was therefore an outsider to the mainstream of Third and Fourth Republic academic philosophy, sociology and anthropology. He later reflected (1946) that

> Until around 1930 the influence of Durkheim's sociological doctrine had scarcely gone beyond the sphere of the universities ... Durkheim had been dead for a long time when some young writers, coming from surrealism – Caillois, Leiris, Monnerot – began to attend a course given by Marcel Mauss ... It is hard to say exactly what they were seeking there ... There was a serious attraction for realities that ... are held to be sacred. (Bataille cited in Hollier, 1988: 383–4)

Caillois actually argued directly in 1938 that 'these last twenty years have seen as an extensive intellectual *turmoil* as one could imagine. Nothing durable, nothing solid, no basis: Everything crumbles already and loses its edges ... an extraordinary, almost inconceivable, *fermentation*: yesterday's problems posed again each day with many others that are new, extreme' (cited in Hollier, 1988: 9, italics in original).

Later Bataille was more specific: 'The theory of transgression is primarily due to Marcel Mauss whose essays dominate modern sociology. Marcel Mauss, unwilling to formulate his ideas too definitely, has merely expressed them periodically in his lecture courses' (Bataille, 1990: 208). But Caillois in 1938 had emphasised the fact that in founding the college,

> the precise object ... can be called Sacred Sociology ... There are certain rare fleeting, and violent moments of this intimate experience on which man places extreme value. From this given the College of Sociology takes its departure ... The ambitions that the community thus created exceed its initial plan, swing from a will for knowledge to a will for power, become the nucleus of a wider conspiracy – the deliberate calculation that this body find a soul. (Caillois citied in Hollier, 1988: 11)

Marcel Mauss was suspicious of such an adventure and remained at a distance. He wrote to Caillois in 1938 that this line of theory was a 'species of absolute irrationalism' (cited in Fournier, 1994: 709). *Sacred sociology* was therefore a project that does not evolve simply from the Ecole Normale or the Ecole Pratique des Hautes-Etudes. It goes beyond Mauss, in embracing de Sade, Marx, Nietzsche, Freud and surrealism; even the altruistic theory of the gift is developed from Mauss (by Bataille himself) into a proposed 'gift of self' in sacrificial suicide. The sacred sociologies prefigured in Saint-Simonianism were always 'positive', that is they concentrated on ideals, utopias produced from theologies where God or Humanity is an idealised presence. The negative theology of Bataille relates to the sacred atheologically, through radical otherness in both a science and the religion of heterology. The idea of the homogeneous totality here is placed in a cyclical relation with radical heterological otherness, just as in earlier positive theory organic epochs alternate with critical ones. The abstract genealogy established in orthodox positive and rationalist sociology did not deal with the realities of violent social transition as transgression, but only rational or religious conversion. The idea of transgression was initiated in the anthropological theories of Mauss and then introduced into a social theory which shifted decisively towards Marx.

Thus at the end of the 1930s Bataille represents the mediating link between Durkheimian theory, which was still dominant among social theorists and most creative in anthropology, and Marxist theory which was beginning to assert its hegemony over Durkheimianism in the late 1930s and 1940s. This is the moment of metathesis, the moment at which the Comte–Durkheim–Mauss variations of Saint-Simonian thought transposed by displacement into the Marxist idiom. It is the moment also when the Kantian influence is displaced by that of Hegel. For many years after the war, Bataille was truly the 'vanishing' mediator between the earlier French tradition and French Marxism (for example, there is no mention of Bataille in Poster's influential study of 1975). When the Marxist variant becomes clearly prominent, there are other elements which begin to assert themselves in the theoretical frame, most notably the theme of materialist philosophy, the Barzardian theme of exploitation of man by man, the theory of the mode of production, capitalist industrialisation, class struggle and proletarian revolution as the path to the realisation of the ideal 'from each according to his work to each according to his needs'. This, it was forgotten, was merely a formal and uncritical development of Comte's 1820 formulation 'each person obtains a degree of importance and advantages proportionate to his capacity and contribution' (Comte, 1974a: 104; 1998: 39). In Bataille, Marxist ideas are fused with the anthropological ideas of Mauss and crucially the notion of the spiritual authority from Comte remains central.

There are some idiosyncratic aspects to Bataille's fusion of these ideas since here it is the anthropological schema that predominates. He achieves this by conceiving of society as being divided initially into two realms, viz. the sacred and the profane, and the sacred into good and evil, along classical Durkheimian lines. Bataille needs, however, a further division, that between the homogeneous and the heterogeneous, which he also takes from Durkheim (Durkheim, 1995: 36; see Gasché, in Bolt-Irons, 1995: 157–208; Hegarty, 2000: 28–9). Bataille's ingenious solution to this metathesis is to argue that the tendency to homogeneity is always necessarily checked by the fact that within the homogeneous profane social body there are equivocal 'foreign bodies' or heterogeneous elements which have to be expelled if the body is to remain intact. Adopting a Sadean model, these are excremental elements, extreme, horrific, repellent, and so on, and they are violently expelled into the sacred either as dangerously pure or impure (evil) elements. Durkheim's sociology developed a theory of normal limits, and of the function of normal sanctions. It is as if Bataille and Caillois take as their key thematic (Comte's and) Durkheim's rules defining the pathological fact and treat the transgression of (normal) limits in each domain, but domain established within an anthropological problematic (abundance and consumption have priority over production and poverty). A kind of anthropological universal cycle, derived from Durkheim's theory of effervescent totemism (without the totems), is invoked: all societies must expel the heterogeneous elements within them if they are to survive. These elements must be then transformed by ritual sacrifice, which becomes the new productive principle *par excellence* into the sacred. Now the internal logic of the sacred tends to homogenisation if it is not renewed by the challenge of evil. Evil is always the active element in the sacred realm. Bataille comes to view revolution as a form of ritual sacrifice, of ritual expulsion of a foreign element. After the revolution there will be a new 'economic and political organisation of society … and an antireligious and asocial organisation having as its goal orgiastic participation in different forms of destruction, in other words, the collective satisfaction of need that correspond to the necessity of provoking the violent excitation that results from the expulsion of heterogeneous elements' (Bataille, 1985: 101).

This reading of Marx thus adopts the notion of the mode of production, but it is subordinate, secondary to the idea of destruction, or what he also calls 'expenditure' (1985: 116–29). Modes of 'consumption' are predominant. This is a theory in which the driving force of all cycles of renewal is the 'devil's' or the 'accursed share'. The exemplars are the practices studied by Mauss: potlatch, human sacrifice, but turned into a theory of radical evil, in a conception of divine regeneration derived from the movement of excremental heterogeneity – excremental laughter as much as pure shit (antisocial, he suggests 'like, for example, the great ritual destructions of goods in British Columbia, or … the pleasure of crowds watching great fires at night' (1985: 100). The revolution, Bataille says, must be understood as a moment of excretion in two phases, separation and then explusion (1985: 100). The moment of extreme suffering or revulsion is essential in this process, for 'without a profound complicity with natural forces such as violent death, gushing blood, sudden catastrophes … the fall into stinking filth of what had been elevated – without a sadistic understanding of an incontestably thundering and torrential nature, there could be no revolutionaries, there could only be a revolting utopian sentimentality' (1985: 101). The ideas clearly also draw from Nietzsche's the will to power (sovereignty), and paganism, Marx's critique of the violence of capitalism, and the surrealist critique of banality of capitalist culture.

Thus Bataille's idioms are themselves heterological to the social theory considered so far. The range of his writing includes: pornography, eroticism, politics, aesthetics (surrealism), a heterological sociology of religion and art, evolutional scheme of societies by modes of destruction, poetry, negative theology, etc. The idiomatic styles are also varied: essay, intervention, thesis, fragments. There are various tones: serious, playful, mediative, the moralistic, etc. The master idea however is the inverse of that of Saint-Simon: here the foundational thesis is that it is not utility and social justice and work which lie at the heart of the social; rather it is consumption. And, against Comte, it is not the ideal objects of a Religion of Humanity, order and worship which are crucial in religion. Nor is it Littré's and Durkheim's sacred. It is above all *sacrificial destruction* (all the fundamental modes of transgressive consumption) which is the key, since this is the transformative ritual which will produce the long-awaited spiritual authority identified by Saint-Simon. Bataille thus rejects Comte's notion of fetishism, and rejects Durkheim's concept of totemism as well. The programme to form a spiritual authority is linked, for Bataille, to the need for the direct experience of sacred *horror*. In a strange continuation of Durkheim's conception of social pathology, Bataille finds, that it is here at this transgression point that a society lives and renews itself.

Bataille's project is to liberate sovereignty, an original spontaneity. This is reminiscent of Durkheim, who at the end of *Elementary Forms* notes the possible return of the gods through social effervescence and energy. Bataille, however, predicts the rebirth of the gods through violent sacrificial acts. Roger Caillois, reflecting on this period (in 1967), wrote:

> I ... founded with Georges Bataille – specifically to break bridges with literature – the College of Sociology ... With Georges Bataille [a] conflict – which never broke out – bore on the possibility of conjugating and unleashing energies starting from the ritual execution of a consenting human victim. (Caillois citied in Hollier, 1988: 288)

Alongside the Collège was a secret society organised around a journal, which appeared only four times between 1936–9, called *Acéphale*. Its members debated human sacrifice. There were a number of members in the group who offered themselves up as victims. No executioner could be found. Much of the published discussions of the Collège concerns 'sacrifice', the 'executioner' etc. The secret society was the theatre in which the creation of the new spiritual organisation was to be accomplished. This was to be a ritual process along the lines Durkheim had defined, not a religion formed by Comtean fiat. Bringing the new religion into existence was to be achieved by means of vital sacralisation (for details of the group's practices see Surya, 1987: 253–8). For Bataille these practices bring experience face to face with radical otherness in the milieu of secret society, meeting at a sacred place, on the model of a primitive group.

The serious dispute between Bataille and Caillois at the end of the life of the Collège concerned the nature of spiritual power. What was at issue? At the very opening of the Collège a questionnaire was sent to a selected number of intellectuals. It asked two questions, the first was 'Do you think that spiritual direction is an organic function in human societies? Or, on the contrary, that the society of which we are members in which we are living has attained a sort of adulthood that permits it to do without spiritual directors?' The second question was 'Do you believe that the irruption into Western history of a new universalism is necessary?' (Hollier, 1988: 51–2 which includes replies from Klossowski, Duthuit, Gualstalla, Libra, Pauhlan, Wahl). The results were published in February 1939. By July the Collège leaders were already in dispute about the nature of the Collège [CS] itself. Bataille wrote to Leiris on July 3 about Caillois' ideas on the rules for the organisation: 'it is perhaps possible to speak of the project of achieving a structured organization in October, with bylaws defining the CS as an organization posing the question of spiritual power.' Leiris wrote to Bataille

> An order is not founded to produce a religion; it is, on the contrary, in the heart of religions that orders are founded ... if we take a sociological science as it has been established by men like Durkheim, Mauss and Robert Hertz as our reference, it is essential to stick with their methods.

Bataille wrote to Caillois, on July 20: 'I developed [the] theory of beings in the direction of a problematic of the gift of self. I attempted to show that starting from this point inevitably introduced the need for drama. My insistence on taking Nietzsche as my reference, alone, indicates the direction I am taking.' He then tackled the question of the purpose of the project:

> This organization can claim only to *pose* the question of spiritual power. It obviously has no answer beyond an assertion that a spiritual power is necessary ... a society is a being no less true and no less rich than the person; that this being that requires the gift of self must be *Sacred* that is to say, possessing the powers, the virtues, the seductions that sacrifice demands and entails. Now the consequence of this is that spiritual power cannot refuse to define itself as a being similar to those it describes as no less true and no less rich than the person. Insofar as it is such a being, it must therefore possess the power [*la vertu*] of provoking sacrifice; it must therefore aspire to the sacred. (Bataille citied in Hollier, 1988: 158)

Thus there are vast differences between Bataille, Comte and Durkheim. Bataille's thinking seems to centre on the importance of the limit of experience in diverse fields, excess, the ambivalence of good and evil. Here there is no worship to excess of a *Sainte Clotilde*, or an attempt to set himself up as Pope or to establish an order with a number of Popes. And no attempt to enter the university to establish a school. There is here no decision to remain within the confines of an established methodology – as Leiris suggested, noting that from a methodological point of view they may have worked against a rational method, that is from 'badly defined ideas, comparisons made between data taken from societies of profoundly different natures' (in Hollier, 1988: 354). Rather, this logic suggests that Bataille will offer himself up for sacrifice, and this will happen on condition that he produce the theatre in which the ritual event can occur, the executioner to perform it, and the individuals who will be initiated through it. His theorising is designed surrealistically, as an intellectual excretion to provoke an expulsion. Not 're-enchantment' but radical sacralisation. In the last meeting of the Collège on 4 July 1939, Bataille outlined his basic idea: 'it is necessary to find again the equivalent of the community in the form of a universal god, in order to extend endlessly the sacrificial orgy.' He finished his lecture with a series of questions: 'Is it possible to find any reason for fighting and dying other than country or class, any reason for fighting that would not be based on material interests? ... Could there be a society without a spiritual power, radically separate from temporal power?' (in Hollier, 1988: 340–1).

Conclusions

The political crisis in the late 1930s, for Marcel Mauss, is one in which things come apart, irregularities become the norm, a crisis characterised by *'le "dégel", c'est le départ des molécules de la gelée de viande sur le macaroni ... c'est l'état moléculaire'* (Mauss, 1997: 772). By that time in his life, the successor to Durkheim had become widely known as *'un homme bizarre'* (Bouglé). Paul Honigsheim reflected that he was invited to call on Mauss one Sunday morning at eight o'clock.

> [Mauss] was in his nightshirt when I arrived, he ordered me to take a seat and excused himself to look after some beans that were boiling on the stove. Presently he welcomed me with these words You have been a contributor to the reviews of von Weise and Max Horkheimer and now you will work with Bouglé. That is very appropriate because all of you are equally stupid. (Honigsheim in Durkheim et al., 1960: 310)

Bataille was in the village of Tossa in April 1936 writing a text called 'The Sacred Conspiracy' (in Hollier, 1988: 181). In it he says, 'I discover myself ... as a monster.' By June 1939 Bataille is practising – though it might be just an 'ecstatic contemplation' – 'an initiation into the exercise of a mysticism of "joy before death"' (in Hollier, 1988: 235ff.). It was but a short step to link this idea to the performance and to the logic of the spectacle as a means of conjuring the sacred corporation once again into existence (see Bataille 1990: 20). As Allan Stoekl reflects, 'the war broke out in September [1939] putting an end to [Bataille's] Collège de Sociologie and with it an epoch' (in Bataille, 1985: xxi).

Notes

1 Fournier's collection of political writings by Marcel Mauss (Mauss, 1997) might well be considered to be the long-awaited completion of the *Oeuvres* of Mauss which appeared in the 1960s (ed. V. Karady, 3 vols, Paris, Editions de Minuit, 1968–9). The collection is clearly dominated by the writings of the period 1920–5. This collection does not, as Fournier points out, include all of Mauss's political writings (it does not include Mauss on 'The Nation', for example, a previously unpublished but fascinating outline essay). Moreover, many of the minor pieces, even half a page sometimes, are genuinely minor observations on passing items of co-op news. Yet among these items there are occasional theoretical reflections of considerable interest. Take, for example, the penultimate piece, a short note of 1942 on crises. This note tries to conceptualise the idea of crisis and in so doing he remarks that 'to the great irritation' of his uncle he found the term 'anomic' too philosophical, too juridical, too moralistic and insufficiently concrete. This section of the chapter is drawn from my discussion of Mauss's *Ecrits politiques* (ed. M. Fournier) in *Durkheimian Studies*, 1998, vol. 4, ns., pp. 125–30.

2 The only parallel in French intellectual life is Elie Halévy (in Mauss, 1997: 37).

3 The translation in Durkheim (1962) at this point misses a clause from the passage from Mauss quoted. The full passage is given in Lukes (1973: 322).

The Third Cycle, 1940–2000

The Second Rebirth of Social Theory: Hypertelia

We are living in a state of having anticipated in some way our own ends, of having anticipated the ends of man, of having already realized them, or even of having passed beyond them, through a sort of hypertelic [*hypertélique*] process in which we will have gone faster than our shadow … in which we will have passed as living beings into a sort of transpolitical, transsexual, transaesthetic state (which is not at all the eclectic and derisory state of postmodern indetermination, but a tragic state of passing beyond our own finalities) and where in consequence it would no longer be possible to live or confront our own end. (Baudrillard, [1989] 1993b: 163)

9

Existential Theory

> French philosophy, which has formed us, scarcely knows more than epistemology. But for Husserl and the phenomenologists, the awareness that we have of things is not limited to a knowledge of them. (Sartre, [1939] 1947: 31)

There had been a growing interest in Marxism in the France of the Third Republic and French communism split away from the other socialists (taking the journal *l'Humanité* with it) in alignment with Bolshevism after the Russian Revolution of 1917. Mauss held that Lenin had been influenced by Durkheim (via Sorel), and, as we have seen, wrote a sociological 'assessment' of Bolshevism. Mauss's texts can be seen retrospectively to have recognised that there could have been a *rapprochement* between Durkheimian and Marxist theory, but the way that Leninism and Bolshevism developed towards autarchy made this impossible. During the inter-war period wide groups of intellectuals in France began to take up positions relative to Marxist social theory and the political divisions, particularly the division between Stalin and Trotsky after the death of Lenin, within the communist movement. As we have seen in the last chapter, Georges Bataille had attempted to fuse Marx, Durkheim and Nietzsche together into a 'sacred sociology'. Sartre and de Beauvoir, however, stood off from politics in the 1930s. Gradually the two moved to take up radical positions in social theory based on their reading of German philosophical attempts to remedy the ungrounded nature of positive social analysis.[1] It is not significant here to ask whether or not their philosophy would lead inevitably, as Aron has suggested, to radical egalitarian conclusions as a logical outcome of their presuppositions; it is only important to note that in different ways Sartre and de Beauvoir brought their own version of existentialism into contact with the Marxist variant of Saint-Simonianism to develop a new body of theory. In this chapter I examine Sartre's route to Marxism, and de Beauvoir's attempt to develop an existential ethics, before looking at examples of how de Beauvoir applied the method in two famous analyses (Poster's account of 1975 discusses in detail the various existential groups but ignores de Beauvoir, whose importance is still underrated in Gutting 2001: 158–80).

Sartre and de Beauvoir

Sartre was called into the army where his spent two years, and then he was imprisoned in a camp, Stalag, XII D, for nine months. This experienced changed him fundamentally. During his imprisonment he began lengthy discussions on political issues with the camp priest Father Perrin, who concluded that Sartre 'had decided to leave his ivory tower' (Cohen-Solal, 1988: 157). The new political programme Sartre had worked out 'owed a great deal to both Fourier and Saint-Simon' (1988: 158). When he rejoined de Beauvoir in Paris – he was released on the basis of a false medical certificate (September 1940–March 1941) – he appeared to de Beauvoir to be a changed man, with a marked 'accusatory' attitude towards her (Bair, 1991: 248). In place of the contemplative thinker, Sartre had become anxious for political engagement, and involved in resistance to German occupation.

Back in Paris, Sartre took up teaching at the Lycée Pasteur, but also began with Merleau-Ponty to set up a group called 'Socialism and Liberty' which by June 1941 had fifty adherents. In the summer of 1941 Sartre wrote a political document of about a hundred pages, now lost, which outlined his vision of a new social constitution for France. It was anti-communist, yet inspired by the utopian socialists. He proposed a currency based on labour value, a form of political representation through occupational groups, and a separation of executive from judiciary (Cohen-Solal, 1988: 169). The 'Socialism and Liberty' group dissolved soon after as the wider resistance movement became organised.

During the rest of the war, Sartre spent much of his time writing the huge manuscript which was to appear in 1943 as *Being and Nothingness*, at the same time his play *The Flies* was produced in Paris. The immediate postwar success of novels, plays and his philosophical publications, combined with those of de Beauvoir, was also matched with the success of their new journal *Les Temps Modernes*, which Gallimard agreed to finance in 1944. Gradually Sartre's theoretical position moved towards Marxism, but with carefully guarded independence from the French Communist Party (PCF), to what Merleau-Ponty called Sartre's 'ultra-bolshevism' (1974: 95–202), through the Cold War and the subsequent period.

Marxism and ethics

Sartre's Marxism was conceived from the beginning as a form of *verstehende Marxismus*. Marxism, Sartre held, had become immobilised in *cliché* formulas. The entire general theory developed by Marx needed to be reconstructed on the basis of an existential humanism, in which individual freedom was the guiding principle (Sartre, [1945] 1973: 23–56). Drawing inspiration from the recently published writings of the young Marx, Sartre developed his new interpretation around the concepts of *praxis* (man makes himself through his projects), and alienation (in the modern capitalist world the products of man's projects were reified and turned against him). Thus the Saint-Simonian call for a new morality and society, and the Marxist theory of the capitalist mode of production, were in the Sartrean vision combined with a theory which tried to reintegrate social science back into a humanist theory of action and to recast this as a general theory of history. The radical nature of this project meant, according to Sartre, that

> The dialectical knowing of man, according to Hegel and Marx, demands a new rationality. Because nobody has been willing to establish this rationality within experience, I state as a fact – absolutely no one, either in the East or in the West, writes or speaks a sentence or a word about us and our contemporaries that is not a gross error. (Sartre, [1957] 1963: 111)

The Ethics of Ambiguity ([1947] 1948) was de Beauvoir's major contribution to existential moral philosophy. Written by someone who was, scandalously, in revolt against bourgeois marriage, she became doubly infamous. First for living openly a life of an independent woman, gaining her own independent income from her intellectual work. But secondly, for establishing a relationship with Sartre that formed a privileged site for undisclosed discussions of the private relations with their other close sexual partners (as revealed in detail on the publication of de Beauvoir's letters to Sartre). In these letters de Beauvoir admits to Sartre in 1945 that at least one other person was deeply damaged on learning of the way she had been manipulated in these interpersonal experiments (see de Beauvoir, 1991: 389).

A literal translation of de Beauvoir's book on ethics would be 'For an Ethics of Ambiguity' (*Pour une morale de l'ambiguité*), and it examines from a number of points of view the consequences of recognising fundamental human free agency and responsibility for it. She considers the problem of whether this freedom is itself willed, or is the ultimate ground. Her conclusion is that 'my project is never founded; it founds itself' (de Beauvoir, 1948: 26). In this sense de Beauvoir can be read as one of the most radical of the existentialists, one who does not seek a ground for theory. At base, as it were, is not the will to freedom but *nothing*, and in order 'for meaning ... to justify the transcendence which discloses it, it must itself be founded, which it will never be if I do not choose to found it myself' (1948: 25). Freedom is not a 'thing or quality naturally attached to a thing', it is of the nature of 'the original upsurge of our existence' (1948: 25). In de Beauvoir's idea of existential morality then, the ground is a 'perpetual tension' not a kind of permanent substratum of the life-world. Thus the ethics of ambiguity in effect become de Beauvoir's ground. She is keen to take on the argument that the general idea of existential freedom is 'only a hollow formula and offers no concrete content for action' (1948: 78).

But de Beauvoir does not deliver a kind of existentialist ten commandments from her chosen ground. The argument is a complex one which arrives more at method than a positive content: 'Ethics does not furnish recipes ... one can merely propose methods' (1948: 134). It seems clear that the reason de Beauvoir's argument is complex is because she wishes to pursue a case that is based on a subtle dialectic of freedom, being and existence. Once one recognises the tensions inherent in human existence, then any ethical relation must recognise the situated necessity of the freedom of the other. Both the mystification of the oppressor and the oppressed lead to impossible denials, but so too do the misplaced modes of triumphalism associated with successful liberation movements which find their victories turn to new forms of repression. Thus the very definition of a specific and concrete ethical content would freeze agency into being. The method 'consists in each case of confronting the values realised with the values aimed at, and the meaning of the act with its content' (1948: 152).

Existentialist ethics turn on the assertion of freedom but in the framework of a recognition of the 'concrete thickness of the here and now' and of the fact that 'human adventures stand out against the background of time, each finite to each, though they are all open to the infinity of the future and their individual forms thereby imply each other without destroying each other' (1948: 122). The examples and illustrations she provides are not trivial ones: concrete issues of Stalinism, fascism, the dilemmas of the activists of the liberation in France, are considered from the point of view of the moving configurations of antinomies of action. For example, the Resistance is considered as 'a negation, a revolt', but after the removal of the force which brought a unifying target to the movement there is a revival of 'old divisions and hatreds' (1948: 96ff., esp. 132). De Beauvoir at one point appeals to the idea of 'permanent revolution' as the most adequate concept of the process of liberation: 'the truth is that if division and violence define war, the world has always been at war and always will be; if man is waiting for universal peace in order to establish his existence validly, he will wait indefinitely: there will never be any *other* future' (1948: 119).

By the 1950s, the existential programme had become the centre of the most theoretical debates in France, and its influence was felt world-wide. Several internal differences had become important and the way that existentialism as a philosophy was united with political tendencies, organisations and parties was widely reflected on. One such characteristic reflection was written by the young Lyotard in 1954. In 1954 Lyotard joined the *Socialism or Barbarism* Marxist group: it was the year of the French defeat in Vietnam (Dien Bien Phu), the year the Algerian war of independence began. But it was rare indeed for any of these debates within the Marxist groups in the 1950s to refer to de Beauvoir, even though her work, *The Second Sex*, had posed and successfully overcome many of the problems raised in these methodological controversies.

Simone de Beauvoir's analyses

Simone de Beauvoir wrote two important studies applying existential methods. *The Second Sex*, of 1949, is by far the best known; *Old Age* (1972) is another application, and deserves to be better known (Deutscher, 1999).

In de Beauvoir's eyes, philosophy was principally Sartre's invention; she 'took [her] cue from him' (in Schwarzer, 1984: 109). She emphasised in these interviews that '*The Second Sex* with its philosophical background of Sartrean existentialism was still exclusively the creation of *my* vision of women' (1984: 109). There has been considerable debate about just how far de Beauvoir influenced Sartre's own philosophical development. Some recent commentators have suggested that de Beauvoir might well be responsible for having created some of the key ideas hitherto thought to be Sartre's (Fullbrook and Fullbrook, 1993). But Sartre's dependence had already been suspected. Asked on these points in an interview, de Beauvoir replied that they had worked on many issues together and on specific points Sartre accepted her point of view. For example, 'in the first version of *Being and Nothingness*, he talked of freedom as though it were quasi-total for everybody ... But I insisted on the fact that there are situations where freedom cannot be exercised, or where it is simply a mystification' (in Schwarzer, 1984: 109). It seems clear that this Beauvoirean idea is worked out at length in *The Second Sex*.

Woman: être-pour-les-hommes

The Second Sex is probably best known for the proposition 'one is not born, but rather becomes, a woman' (de Beauvoir, 1972: 295). In this work this proposition is put to the test in the most thorough examination. The idea that all human beings possess the same fundamental freedom – the freedom to act, think, choose between a range of possible alternatives – is examined against the fact that half the human species are subordinate to the other half. How does this come about as an outcome of choice? For de Beauvoir is rigorous in her method; this inequality is not an effect of some 'biological, psychological or economic fate' (1972: 295). Her first chapters subject biological, psychological and economic theories to a severe critique; it becomes clear that both Freud and Marx are not found helpful in the analysis of gender since they fall into parallel forms of explanatory reductionism and determinism. Even the biological evidence, which de Beauvoir examines in detail and considers 'of first rank' does not establish for women 'a fixed and inevitable destiny' and these facts 'are insufficient for setting up a hierarchy of the sexes; they fail to explain why woman is the Other; they do not condemn her to remain in this subordinate role for ever' (1972: 65).

It is significant that in her discussion of the history of women in the nineteenth century there is only a brief mention of Saint-Simon and socialism: 'with the utopian socialisms of Saint-Simon, Fourier, and Cabet was born the utopia of the "free woman"; the slavery of worker and of woman was to be abolished, for women like men were human beings. Unfortunately this reasonable idea did not prevail in the school of Saint-Simon' (1972: 143). That is all there is on Saint-Simonianism, and no mention of the feminism which grew out of it. But there is more on Marx, and here her view was equally severe: 'between the cause of the proletariat and that of women there was no ... immediate solidarity' (1972: 147). Curiously, de Beauvoir gives Léon Richier the credit for being the 'true founder of feminism' (1972: 153). And her conclusion, after surveying the feminist movements, was that

> Feminism itself was never an autonomous movement ... Never have women constituted a separate caste, nor in truth have they ever as a sex sought to play a historic role. The doctrines that object to the advent of women considered as flesh, life, immanence, the Other, are masculine ideologies in no way expressing feminine aspirations. (1972: 160)

Yet in economic terms, 'men and women ... constitute two castes' (1972: 167). 'Women are still, for the most part, in a state of subjection [*vassalité*]'. They do not, according to de Beauvoir, make autonomous choices, but in relation to the definition man dictates, and that reflects directly women's being-for-men (*être-pour-les-hommes*) (1972: 169).

De Beauvoir provides a long account of men's myth of the feminine (1972: 171–292). But this only provides the essential background for the detailed analysis of the woman's life cycle which is the heart of the book. It is very extensive (1972: 295–741) and certainly rests on the problem: given the nature of human freedom at each moment, how is it that women are the second sex? It has appeared to many readers that the exposition is really simply a sham, since at the end of the book it is very difficult to see how such consistent patterns of inequality could be the outcome of individual choices. But this is a serious misreading of de Beauvoir's thesis, which is a sustained attempt to relate the concept of the human as always in a condition of existential freedom and the situations in which the complexity of the action of others is a necessary part of the way in which outcomes are made. Thus her thesis is that a 'new civilisation' is coming into existence and with it new possibilities and opportunities. Yet the old traditions and obstacles still exist: 'the truth is that her situation is out of equilibrium' (1972: 167). In her view the changing world cannot be grasped on the basis of a theory which reduces too quickly sex to biology or essence. But it was only later that she made explicit any connection of this 'lack of equilibrium' and new possibilities with socialism:

> At the end of *The Second Sex* I said I was not a feminist because I believed that the problems would resolve themselves automatically in the context of socialist development ... I am a feminist today, because I realise that we must fight for the situation of women, here and now. (de Beauvoir 1972 in Schwarzer, 1984: 32)

The general thesis of the book is that woman, having been object or Other for man, is in the process of becoming subject for man. In other words, women, having been that 'non-existent' that all patriarchal thought mythologises, is only now coming into being. De Beauvoir's political interpretation of this transition made her notorious. Women will not bring an (old) essence into existence, by reconstructing it, as a new 'partner' to man. This process is open, to be disclosed by projects to come. But the new conditions that make this possible are the same as those that make socialism possible: industrial capitalism, the formation of modern classes and citizens, and the radical reformation of masculinities which accompany these processes. The analysis seems often to read as an absolute, literal account of the facts of life, and hence have been misinterpreted as an attempt to describe the universality of gendered relationships. Thus in her famous analysis of sexual initiation it has often been read as if the woman is essentially alienated by the encounter. It is rare for her to declare 'in a sexually equalitarian society, woman would regard menstruation simply as her special way of reaching adult life'. Today, however, it throws her 'into an inferior and defective category' (1972: 340). But there is no analysis of individual experience, the discussion is in terms of men and women, of different ages, classes, etc. Yet this is not a positive sociology, since there is a philosophical and theoretical tension established in the analysis which forms the thematic throughout: these conditions are changing and this analysis, she argues, is a project in this very history.

Some of her theses seem to derive from her presuppositions directly, and some of these are the most shocking: 'the foetus is part of her body, and it is a parasite that feeds on it' (1972: 512); 'it is much more difficult for the woman than for the man to recognize an individual of the opposite sex as an equal' (1972: 701); her conclusion that real independence and liberty require a woman to abstain from marriage and motherhood. Part four of the book is called 'Towards Liberation'; its first chapter is a discussion of 'The Independent Woman' and it is soon clear that for de Beauvoir even that situation and condition of independence for women is different from that for men: 'she refuses to confine herself to her role as female, because she will not accept mutilation; but it would also be a mutilation to repudiate her sex' (1972: 691). At this point de Beauvoir's language becomes Durkheimian: 'because the concept of femininity is artificially shaped by custom and fashion, it is imposed upon each woman from without' (1972: 692).

This formulation, with its resonance of Durkheim's notion of the social as 'external constraint', seems to lead back into the very structures of sociology that de Beauvoir's method sought to criticise. But in what sense is de Beauvoir's analysis a resolution of these methodological questions, and the 'in' terms which, for example, Lyotard had sought to use? It seems evident that the study is aware of most of the main currents of nineteenth-century sociology, certainly the French tradition, and Mill, and of course the Marxist tradition, and is certainly not naïve. The study makes a unique contribution to sociology, not just because of its philosophical adherence to certain principles, but because it finds new resolutions to key problems. The analysis of the life-cycle of the modern woman could certainly not have been written by Durkheim and there is no direct application of the sociological method of that school. But it does come close to meeting many of the requirements identified by Lyotard's critique of phenomenology without violating Durkheim's rules. Although feminists have often criticised the text as giving the appearance that its author is above the struggle, not written by 'one of us', it is very clear that this is a monumental critique of the assumptions and outcomes of patriarchy and patriarchal power, even its continuing effects for those women who have struggled to achieve a degree of independence. It does not use the concept of social pathology for the condition of women. It does, however, present a sense of evolutionary development to a new situation. It does not present the coming of the woman's movement, and there is no sense in which de Beauvoir herself seemed to present herself as a new type of intellectual at the head of a new liberation movement. But this is not far from the surface of the text.

There is a clear methodological invention. It is to be found in her adoption of life-cycle analysis. Childhood, the young girl, sexual initiation, the lesbian, these chapters make up the first section on 'The Formative Years'. Then the second section focuses on the married woman, the mother, social life, prostitution and hetairas, maturity and old age and woman's situation and character. The next section is called 'Justifications' – the narcissist, the woman in love, and the mystic. The last section is called 'Towards Liberation', and has one chapter, 'The Independent Woman'. Thus: formation, situation, justifications, towards liberation. But these are transitions without ritual. The underlying presuppositions in the analysis are clear from the start: men and women are first human beings, not two different species (1972: 321). The account is thus posed in terms of a universal experience in which the body is encountered, as is the milieu, the social, culture, but always in terms of possibilities and choices – against the existence of 'external constraints'. It could be said, perhaps, that this massive study is one individual's own unique attempt to live and to make an individual 'ethics of ambiguity'. But there is no substantial ethics as a conclusion, only a recommendation that if a woman wants independence, then such and such are the costs: no family, no children. The conclusion is that men and women *should live out* 'the ambiguities of their situation … both should assume the ambiguity with a clear-sighted modesty'. She insists at the end that 'the fact that we are human beings is infinitely more important than all the peculiarities that distinguish human beings from one another; it is never the given that confers superiorities' (1972: 737). It is almost certain that

> sooner or later [women] will arrive at complete economic and social equality, which will bring about an inner metamorphosis. However … there will be some to object that if such a world is possible it is not desirable. When woman is 'the same' as her male, life will lose its salt and spice. (1972: 738)

De Beauvoir is quite conscious that she is dealing with a pivotal cultural transition. The transition from world of (symbolic) otherness, to that of identity and 'fraternity' (1972: 741). It is clear where de Beauvoir stands: she defines the culture of symbolic otherness as that world which has become oppressive, and 'nothing seems more debatable than the opinion that dooms the new world to uniformity and hence to boredom' (1972: 740).

Thus there is something in de Beauvoir's analysis which tries to capture the openness of the situation, a situation in which modifications in the man's world are making new demands on the sexual division of labour. In this context her analysis is retrospective, from the perspective of a universal in humanity, not from an analysis based on givens in a comparative sociology. This undoubtedly inserts values into the analysis as commentators (e.g. Aron) have suggested. And this idea provides something of an observation on modern social theory generally: it is universalising in its very presuppositions. The Sartre–Beauvoirean notion of the 'transcendental field' (nothing) of 'absolute consciousness' (Sartre, [1957] 1957: 106) forms the basis of ideas of liberation that are generalised out from specific historical situations (e.g. France after 1940), to human issues of liberation in a global context. Thus de Beauvoir maintains that it is not only in modern France that women may feel humiliation in certain relationships because of a certain structure of patriarchy or masculine privilege, but that in all patriarchal cultures a basic and fundamental conflict and tension exist, since in all the artificial structures of self–Other are, against resistance, imposed by patriarchy and thus individual men and women on women and men. In her conclusions, however, de Beauvoir is very careful to restrict her ethics to the situation in which her book was produced, and her remarks are phrased in utilitarian terms: 'there is no denying that feminine dependence, inferiority, woe, give women their special character; assuredly woman's autonomy, if it spares men many troubles, will also deny them many conveniences' (1972: 739).

Old age is 'unrealisable'

Some twenty years later, de Beauvoir went on to write an analysis of ageing and ageism. Her analysis does not adopt the developments in social theory that Sartre had been working on and which were published in 1960 as *Critique of Dialectical Reason* ([1960] 1976, volume 2 was published unfinished in 1985). Her analysis remains focused on the paradoxes raised by the refusal of all biological determinism, and in this case that ageing is not a simple process of physical decline. Her argument is divided in two parts that deal with the Durkheimian mode of objectivity and then goes beyond this into 'lived experience'. The first she describes as examining ageing 'from the outside' in its scientific and social determinations. But in the second, she examines ageing from the point of view of the 'intimate, inward knowledge' the individual has of this state and how the individual 'reacts to it'. Her aim, she says, is to 'examine what happens to the individual's relationship with his body and his image during his last years, to his relationship with time, history and his own praxis, and to his relationship with others and the outside world' (1977: 313). In order to do this she sets up a contradiction: her principal presupposition is that there is no universal transcendental consciousness outside of time – it is the body, and its image, which ages (1977: 15) and 'individuals understand one another, not inasmuch as they are all men in the abstract, but by means of the variety of their praxis' (1977: 243). Unlike aspects of an identity such as nationality, however, 'old age is something beyond my life, outside it – something of which I cannot have any full experience … my ego is a transcendent object that does not dwell in my consciousness and that can only be viewed from a distance' (1977: 324). Thus, in the case of old age it is never possible for me 'to coincide with the reality that I assume' (1977: 324).

As with the analysis of gender, the analysis of old age predates movements for radical changes by the elderly in society. Her analysis runs into many of the same issues: what is the connection between this kind of inequality and class relations? Again her analysis does not suggest that radical changes in the condition of old people can be made without radical socialist changes, but even here her conclusion is that the socialist countries 'still have a very long way to go' (1977: 603). In this sense, as with gender, the matrix role of the socialist struggle forms again for de Beauvoir the condition for radical restructuring of social relations. This problem seems to be completely new. In the early history of the socialist idea, utopian feminism was an immediate outcome. In the 1960s second wave feminism was in part inspired by de Beauvoir's analysis of women's inequality, but it was accompanied by the recognition of new problem of ageism as a form of oppression.

Looking at de Beauvoir's development from *The Second Sex* to *Old Age*, it seems that she came to embrace fully the idea of the social as external to individual experience and constraining. Clearly, however, in opposition to Durkheim, this approach did not rule out examination of individual experience – 'being-in-the-world' – as well. In fact her discussion of this side of her problem is quite different from anything Durkheim could have written. This is because she has recourse to the idea of the transcendental ego as produced by others and to which the inner experience is either in conflict or in concordance: becoming old is still 'particularly difficult to assume because we have always regarded it as something alien, a foreign species' (1977: 315). So it is that 'our private, inward experience does not tell us the number of our years … Old age is more apparent to others than to the subject.' So this awareness which comes from outside it is the 'Other that is myself' (1977: 316). The individual can 'adapt' to the changes in the body, and in this sense the individual 'does not notice the change' (1977: 316). Her analysis follows what she calls this 'assumption' of old age, the fact that the recognition by others of someone having become old is communicated to others or the person in question and comes as a discovery, a surprise, but 'whether we like it or not, in the end we submit to the outsider's point of view' but not without wavering. Indeed there is an insoluble contradiction between the obvious clarity of the inward feeling that guarantees our unchanging quality and the objective certainty of our transformation'. And this is why old age is an 'unrealisable' (1977: 323), a concept she did not use in her analysis of woman as other. One might say here that her formula would be 'one does not *become* old, it is impossible to realise it'.

The apparent logic of the development, then, of de Beauvoir's approach is that it seems to combine existential with the methods of positive sociology in an exemplary way. At the end of the book *Old Age*, the questions are not so much those that concern an ethics of ambiguity, though these are never far away for obvious reasons, but rather: 'What should a society be, so that in his last years a man might still be a man?' Her discussion here flirts with a certain utopianism:

> We may dream that in the ideal society … old age would be virtually non-existent … The last age would [be] a period quite different from youth and maturity, but possessing its own balance and leaving a wide range of possibilities

> open to the individual. We are far from this state of affairs ... It is our whole system that is at issue.' (1977: 603–4)

This casts retrospective light on the nature of the contradiction. For this 'unrealisable' between the inner experience of old age and the external 'transcendental ego' within modern society is not a universal condition. In fact de Beauvoir appeals (referring via Grotjhan) to Freud's notion of the unconscious to resolve this point, for the unconscious 'knows nothing of old age' (1977: 325). The rest of her examination of the assumption of old age discusses a host of instances where this ambiguity has been lived through (1977: 325–402).

Conclusions

Thus de Beauvoir reveals aspects of the Saint-Simonian idea as it is developed in its Marxist variant. Since the class struggle is seen as the central locus and pivot of what happens to the society more widely, first the other sites of inequality such as gender and age are seen as *dependent* sites, and second, they form there structures of inequality assumed an alienated mode (a contradiction between the imposed structure of the ego and inner experience). Some aspects of the nineteenth-century historical method are evidently transferred to these analytic sites. These include the static/dynamic analyses of a defined portion of humanity (the female sex which is the subject of the life-cycle analysis for example); how to theorise within existential analysis a transition from one state to another (one civilisation passing another is being born, de Beauvoir says). The analysis suggests that the key to this transition is the class struggle at the heart of industrial capitalism rather than a cultural logic. In theory this struggle comes first historically and causally. Gender and age relations, themselves fundamentally affected by capitalism, change as a consequence of more fundamental changes. By implication of course in the strategic calculations of political engagement, involvement in anti-sexist and anti-ageist movements is doomed to a limited horizon of reforms since they do not act on the causes of the problems of inequality in these domains. Gradually de Beauvoir broke with these latter assumptions.

Becoming clear now is a double articulation which rewrites the two principal aspects of Saint-Simonian theory and is much closer to its Comtean than its Durkheim variation. First a cultural transition between hierarchical symbolic cultures (relation to the Other), and modern cultures (relation to Other as same). Secondly, a social transition between societies whose structure rests on economic systems or 'modes of production', e.g. feudalism, capitalism, communism. Basic to existential theory is the attempt to understand the articulation between the sociological dimensions of social phenomena (constraining the individual), and the dynamics of inner experience with respect to the Other, or to others. De Beauvoir is crucial then in revealing how existentialism can be used as a method for radical social research in a way hoped for but never acknowledged by writers like Lyotard. Through her substantial studies of the forms of alienation of 'woman' and 'old age', she demonstrates how the aim of a fusion between the objective and subjective could be achieved.

There were many competing currents of existential social theory at the beginning of the 1950s; one of the most significant, which I turn to in the next chapter, was Lyotard's early political writings which provided an exemplary analysis of the Algerian war of independence which brought the Fourth Republic to an acute crisis.

Note

1 This was quite a different outcome from that of Aron's visit to Germany in the same period (Aron, 1964) and other thinkers such as Henri Lefebvre came to existentialism before Sartre (Shields, 1999: 127).

10

The Algerian War

> … a remarkable sociological situation: if French imperialism has not to this day managed to provide this society with any other mode of organisation than that of terror, it is because no institution can currently respond satisfactorily to the needs of the Algerians … Algerian society is 'destructured' [*déstructurée*]. (Lyotard, 1993b: 223)

After the moment of the Resistance and Liberation of the 1940s, the 1950s were dominated by the Algerian movement and war for independence. This again radicalised many intellectuals on the left. Baudrillard later reflected 'the Algerian War … had a vital part to play, a kind of Marxist-type politicisation' and for him the main influence in this was Sartre (1993a: 20). Sartre's own involvement was significant, but his writings reveal that his main concern was the 'colonial system' and the role of de Gaulle in the war and its resolution (Sartre, 2001). Sartre also played a key symbolic role for intellectuals such as Fanon (1967, 1970), and by his support for the development of journals such as Diop's *Présence Africaine*, and organisations and conferences like the Congress of Black Writers and Artists at the Sorbonne in 1956 (see Young, in Sartre, 2001: xx).

Other intellectuals like Bourdieu, who had done anthropological fieldwork in Algeria, composed studies such as *Sociologie de l'Algérie*. Bourdieu presented a survey of the different cultures and communities in Algeria, focusing mainly on the ones he had closely studied, but sketched his own picture of the colonial system (Bourdieu, 1958: 106f.), the imposed 'deculturation' it effected, and then presented a profile of an emerging new class structure. This, he said, was a completely 'original social classes structure' composed of an immense 'sub-proletariat, uprooted, and unstable' at the base of a hierarchy of proletariat, petite-bourgeoisie, and bourgeoisie arising around a very feeble industrial development (1958: 124–5). But this very passive objective sociological account was complemented, as was the anguished reflections of a writer like Fanon, in these years by the incisive theoretical analysis of Lyotard writing for the dissident Marxist journal *Socialism or Barbarism* (with its important contributions from Lefort and Castoriadis).

Lyotard

Lyotard (b. 1924) had graduated from the Sorbonne, where he had been friends with Deleuze, and took up a two-year teaching post in Constantine in Algeria in 1950. It was a fateful location. He went through a rapid process of political radicalisation under the aegis of Pierre Souryi from 1951. His militant involvement in the politics of the revolutionary left was long and profound:

> For fifteen years I neglected all forms of activity other than those directly connected to this cause. I gave up all writing except notes and studies on political topics that were published either in our review or in a mimeographed paper we gave out to workers early in the morning at the gates of factories. (Lyotard, 1988: 17)

The review in question was *Socialism or Barbarism*. He was invited to join the board with Souryi in 1954 (1988: 66). And it was the year in which his book on existential phenomenology appeared in which his version of Marxism constructively appropriated (Lyotard, 1997). But the appropriation was highly critical, for at the end of his study Lyotard's final conclusions were drawn in a surprisingly harsh way against a non-Marxist existentialism and phenomenology. First politically, Husserl's historical constructions cannot be sustained, and the phenomenological position either falls to the right (even fascism) or to 'infantile disorder' because of a resulting ambivalence. The 'third way', he concludes, has proved an illusion. Second, logically, phenomenology is caught between an attempt to identify 'originary' structures as given infrastructures of thought and an attempt to 'account phenomenologically for them', thus Husserl moves from intentional analysis only to a system of speculative history. Third, philosophically, existential phenomenology is a step back from Marx on the question of material structures, for in trying to establish the 'source of meaning in the interstices between the subjective and the objective, it has not realized that the objective (and not the existential) already contains the subjective as negation and supercession' (1991: 135). Fourth, theoretically, phenomenology is caught between a spiritualist subjectivism and a project that aims to recover humanity beneath the schemata of the objective social sciences. If Merleau-Ponty takes up Marx's formula that 'we cannot eliminate philosophy without realising it', Lyotard insists, against any incipient idealism, this realisation can only occur in the revolutionary transition to a classless society (1991: 136). 1954, the year of these conclusions, was the year of the struggle for liberation from French colonial control in Algeria; this became, although the French authorities never came to admit the fact, a war of independence.

Lyotard's contribution to *Socialism or Barbarism* principally concerned this war ([1989b] in 1993b). Was his writing betraying 'the invisible, but tangible presence of a Marxist theorist who, like a priest who has lost his faith, still dispenses a rhetoric of salvation' (Kroker 1992: 145)? Or was Lyotard committed to writing an eidetic Marxism, and through this to discover the depoliticisation of the proletariat in the heartland of capitalism, mirrored by the paradox of a social 'revolution without a proletariat' in Algeria?

Algeria

In his brief introduction to the republication of these essays on Algeria, Lyotard recounts the political orientation of the *Socialism or Barbarism* group.[1] The particular Marxist genealogy of the journal is traced from Trotsky's Fourth International, and the 1947 break-away group which developed a far more radical critique of the possibilities for socialism in the Soviet Union and indeed Western societies. It was this group which wanted to go beyond the framework of Leninism maintained by traditional Trotskyism, through a close examination of the immediate and concrete forms of opposition developed on the ground by workers themselves (Lyotard, 1993b: 166). The project was, he says elsewhere, 'to critique the class structure of Russian society and all bureaucratic societies [and] to analyse the dynamics of the struggles in underdeveloped countries' (Lyotard, 1988: 66). It seems clear that just as Lyotard was attracted to the promise of reconstructed Husserlian existential phenomenology as a specific critique of reified and alienated knowledge in a capitalist society, he was also attracted to those particular forms of Marxism not subject to the same process of reification, which could 'rebuild from scratch the framework of leading conceptions of workers' emancipation' (1993b: 166, trans. modified). His aim, he emphasised, was not to reproduce a scientifically 'true idea' but to identify, in the very grounded creativity of struggle, that 'secret from which all resistance draws its energy' (1993b: 167). The aim of the *Socialism or Barbarism* group was not to develop an institutional organisation or political party as such (thus it was free from constraints and the responsibilities of any practice of leadership). It was by intervening in a new way, by developing new forms of political analysis, to keep open and complex the spaces of resistance to oppression and injustice (1993b: 168).

Lyotard took responsibility for covering the Algerian War for *Socialism or Barbarism* from 1955 and his articles appeared from 1956 to 1963. It is clear, even from his first article, entitled simply 'The situation in North Africa', that Lyotard believed that the social conflicts in Algeria could not easily be allocated to any of the preconceived and available Marxist schemata. Algeria, a French colony since 1830, had very specific social structures and cultural divisions which made it quite different in character from other societies engaged in independence struggles. Drawing on his own experience in Algeria, his position from the start was that this was a paradoxical struggle. It was from a Marxist, or rather as he says himself, 'from the perspective of the global proletariat', one where 'the only solutions [were] solutions that none in the struggle can provide' (1993b: 172, 178). His objective is consistently to find that 'line the revolutionary movement ought to take' (1993b: 172) even in a struggle where a proletarian consciousness had not developed and was not likely to develop. He expected the revolutionary struggle in Algeria to evolve some kind of embryonic military and political bureaucracy which 'the scattered elements of the Muslim commercial and intellectual stratum' would likely join (1993b: 178). In this first very remarkable article, Lyotard outlines the stark contrast between the life of the French in Algeria and that of the majority Muslim community in its objective economic reality. The 'radical exploitation' that his analysis reveals appears to those engaged in struggle not simply as an economic one but as a cultural, even a racial one, for 'since class frontiers are almost exactly homologous with "ethnic" frontiers, class consciousness is impossible: a person is crushed for being an Algerian ... as much as for being a worker or a peasant' (1993b: 174). Thus if political power passed to nationalist forces, economic exploitation would not have been addressed, since the struggle was taking place at the purely cultural level. Yet this specific character of Algerian society led to the key problem of identifying the nature of the 'nationalist' forces, for here there is a remarkable vacuum, as the French 'cannot depend on any local bourgeoisie in Algeria' (1993b: 176). This mirrored the problem of the forces of the left in France, who could not find their equivalents in local organised forms of resistance. Lyotard thus concluded that the only tenable revolutionary position was to abandon any pretence to continue French presence in Algeria on the one hand, and to see that the course of the struggle would be 'determined by underground resistance forces' (1993b: 178).

This first article thus identified a number of very stark contradictions, and was written incisively in a sombre tone, a tone which continued for the remaining course of the revolution. Theoretically, he delivered cruel evaluations of both the orthodox communist (PCF) and Trotskyist analyses of these events, particularly of the way in which the theory of 'permanent revolution' was being applied. The communist line, which wanted a renegotiated union with Algeria, Lyotard stigmatises as a consequence of its dependency on the power strategy of the Soviet Union, and an attempt to juggle with the forces in Algeria to produce the best outcome for itself (a view endorsed by subsequent analysts such as Joly, 1991: 44–8). Marxist analysts believed that in such a process in a 'relatively backward' society, an industrial proletariat – however small – would form the principal force in the cities, and that it was to this force that the analysis should deliver a revolutionary programme. Such Marxist analysts thereby fell into a schematic Bolshevik formalism and sought the Algerian Lenin. Analysing the programmes of the various political groups in Algeria, Lyotard concludes that 'there cannot be any Algerian Bolshevism in the present state of industrial development' (Lyotard, 1993b: 208). Marxism loses its way, since it cannot grasp, on the ground, the peculiar features of Algerian society where class borders 'are buried under national borders' (1993b: 210). It was only by a certain kind of abstraction that it was possible to talk of class structure, and yet the basis of national consciousness was almost entirely a peasant one. For the Algerians every French soldier was an enemy and thus, for Lyotard, one must hear 'in this intransigence, which perhaps shocks the delicate ears of the French "left" (which is often paternalistic and always treacherous toward the Algerian people) the direct expression of the split that runs through, and tears apart, all the classes of Algerian society' (1993b: 212–13).

Lyotard and 'Stalinism'

It was at this point Lyotard began to question the right of Stalinism to claim to be a Marxism, indeed to be a science which resolved the critical problems posed by philosophy. What happens with the transformation of the critical dialectic into a science of dialectical materialism is that 'Marxism' becomes a means by which a certain state of society becomes legitimated as no longer alienated, no longer class divided. Things had changed around, for here theory had become the complacent tool of a certain bureaucratic class, and to make a critique of bureaucratic Marxism has to go beyond questions of theory: it would require a critique of a bureaucracy enveloped in 'Marxism' (1957: 59). For Lyotard, one could not be Marxist and Stalinist, since Stalinist Marxism was an ideology of a 'dominant class' and this condition introduced the very alienated separations which Marx denounced as alienating (1957: 59). A critique had to be made at the level of the 'human reality' of this system, of the very contradictions between theory and practice it introduced. Marxism is the practical critique of a dominant class ideology, not the process by which intellectuals established the laws of a social science in order to produce the legitimation of totalitarian social and economic planning (1957: 60).

Stalinism, in producing a social science, only ended up by suppressing a knowledge of the real dialectic of its own history. Lyotard claimed that from Lenin's *What Is to Be Done?* the capacity of the proletariat in the advanced countries had developed to the point that it could act for all society, and at that point socialist practice was not to be conceived as the suppression of private property or capital, a purely negative act, but of the effective installation of workers' control (1957: 60). This meant that Marxism developed a theory of this new relation, that is to say it was 'a new theory of political action' – this, he added, was a fact that neither Leninism nor Trotskyism had ever properly understood. It was here, then, that Lyotard detailed his own vision of a new political practice, a practice specifically related to the way practice and theory were outlined by Marx (1957: 60–1). What Lyotard was really seeking was not simply a method that would discover the realities of the fundamental level of human experience as an 'originary' sociality, but one that would find a theory/practice relationship which might escape reification and alienation, in exactly the same way he had tried to pose the problem of the theoretical and empirical at the heart of the phenomenological project. At this period Lyotard was, as critics have noted, developing and deepening the productivist thesis that 'man is the product of his works' (1957: 57; see also Descombes, 1980: 181; Pefanis, 1991: 87) in the context of a conception of the world as involved in an intensifying struggle which would lead either to socialism or barbarism. It was entirely consistent of Lyotard therefore, some years later, to question Althusser's conception of the relation of theory to practice as only partially adequate, for in eliminating the concept of alienation from theory, it tended also to eliminate its value in experience, its value in pointing to a theory of the experience of abstract universals (1984: 19ff.).

The key moment in French post-war history: the missed revolution

Lyotard was generally pessimistic about the outcome of the revolution in Algeria (from a communist point of view). He seized on the fact that, in contrast to the political settlements in Tunisia and Morocco (where the French negotiated with established bourgeois political groups), the situation in Algeria was more fluid: the 'bourgeois leadership is not strong enough to stand the growing hostility of the labouring classes supported by the dynamism of the Frontists (FLN)' (1993b: 213, trans. modified). He believed that radicalisation in Algerian society could produce new forms of resistance. But this was in a situation where the insurrections, the 'battle for Algiers' had been won by the French, the revolutionary organisations driven underground, a condition leading in May 1958 (the coup in Algiers) to an 'authentic totalitarianism' (1993b: 215). In his contribution to *Socialism or Barbarism* in 1958, Lyotard developed a close analysis of the situation in the French army, which he located at the heart of the growing contradictions in the French position: on the one hand, that between the ultra-right generals and the new political demands initiative from de Gaulle in Paris, and on the other, where in Algiers 'power is divided between the armed forces and the extreme right' (1993b: 215). Essentially this produces, though Lyotard does not use the expression, a double dual power conjuncture, in Algiers: 'an unstable political situation whose resolution will certainly involve the subordination of one group to the other', for the army (not even itself homogeneous) was effectively out of control.

It is probably in his analysis, not of the revolutionary movement itself, but – very surprisingly – of the army that Lyotard was able to produce his most insightful writing. The crucial contradiction is identified here, where the army is caught in a dilemma. On the one hand it believes, certainly from its defeat in Vietnam, that it is dealing with a guerrilla movement operating a classic Maoist strategy. On the other hand, the Algerian people cannot be defeated as such and have to be won over to the French position in a political and administrative struggle in the villages. The army was thus pulled in two directions, either towards building and maintaining a local elite, or to maintaining its own hegemony, and 'this is where the army splits apart' (1993b: 217). The logic of maintaining French hegemony also threatened to turn the whole of France itself into a totalitarian society in order to mobilise the materials and the ideological conformity necessary to the task in Algeria. But the Gaullist political faction was not totalitarian and thus the project was frustrated, and even in Algeria de Gaulle had a certain level of support as offering an honourable resolution to an intractable situation. If this resolution to the crisis was feared by the Ultras, since it would mean that all the army's work would have ultimately been in vain, says Lyotard, then the key to resolving the situation now lay in Paris.

His articles dealing with this complex situation from 1958, that is during the formative period of the Fifth Republic, chart carefully the changing balance of forces.[2] It is precisely at this juncture that Lyotard began to notice a phenomenon that would have crucial ramifications for his own position. He judged that in the crisis of the Republic, a dramatic process of depoliticisation of the proletariat itself had occurred in metropolitan France. It now became widely accepted in popular opinion in France that the solution to the Algerian problem was in some way bound up with de Gaulle himself as purely his 'personal problem' with authority in the army (1989b: 122). This intervention led directly to replacements of personnel at the top echelons of the administration and army. Yet this only further exposed the insoluble problem facing the army, namely its complete inability to build up local elites (1993b: 222).

For Lyotard's analysis, the key and determining structures of these political problems were revealed to be the specific character not of the army, but of the army's impotence in the face of Algerian society. After six years of war it was clear that the emerging elements of an Algerian bourgeoisie had still been excluded from socio-economic advance in the ruling bloc: its continuing 'political weakness results from its economic and social weakness' (1993b: 235). And it was this fact which accounts for the exceptional duration of the war and its intensity. On the ground Lyotard charts the resistance, the ways in which 'duplicity, laziness, ill will, the tendency to steal ... express at different levels, the refusal [of the Algerians] to take part in their own exploitation' (1993b: 236). In the absence of civil society as such, these forms of resistance do not and cannot 'constitute a dialectical negation of the society' (1993b: 227). Attempts to deal with this 'colonial non-society' by military or administrative means could only lead to a downward spiral of brutalisation. As soon as the Algerians began the uprising, the truth of this situation was revealed, since what was being rejected was the possibility of resolving the crisis on behalf of the Algerians. The spell was broken (*'la lutte armée a brisé le charme'* (1989b: 135)), while as yet the crisis could not be resolved.

All the uprisings since 1954, Lyotard suggests, had taken place in this social and political void, where 'the armed groups crystallised among themselves a nationalism that the situation of the Algerian bourgeoisie had prevented from finding expression ... [and then] this role [was assumed] by an organisation based directly on the peasant masses' (1993b: 239). In this struggle it was driven first underground, and then there developed among the insurgents the resolve to drive out the colonial power. The formation of these revolutionaries was different from elsewhere. They had been uprooted from traditional society and had spent years in France where they were 'stripped of their way of life' (1993b: 241), yet never integrated in metropolitan society even in left-wing organizations. In Algeria itself all radicals were ruthlessly deported. So the only active resistance left in Algeria was the tradition of peasant banditry. The evolution from these primitive forms of resistance since 1954 had been a gradual politicisation and involvement of wider sections of Algerian society into a struggle for national, not socialist, emancipation. This had become Algeria's specific 'revolutionary meaning', for it involved the intervention of these colonial workers 'themselves, practically and directly in the transformation of their own society … they break off, effectively, without asking permission from anyone … and provide an example of socialist activity to all the exploited and exploiters: the recovery of social humanity by its own efforts' (1993b: 251, trans. mod.). By contrast in France, the proletariat was becoming more and more passive and the vision of social transformation was gradually losing force.

In Algeria, from May 1958 to January 1960, the successive insurrections of the colonists had also become manifestly weaker and less resolved. Lyotard's analysis concentrates on the position of the army and clearly anticipates the army's crisis and the army putsch of April 1961: it is in 'this army that the contradictions of modern capitalist society are lived, if not thought more intensely than in any other fraction of the bourgeoisie' (1993b: 265, trans. mod.). Once more, Lyotard insisted that it was a fundamental mistake to define the army's position through the grid of a preconceived objectivist theory. This would identify in an ungrounded analysis the army's ideology as simply 'fascist'. The work of the army pivoted on an irresolvable dilemma: it was sent to 'pacify' a village, but it could neither build links with it on the one hand, nor destroy it on the other. The same dilemma faced de Gaulle: the administration of Algeria had become impossible, yet he cannot get rid of Algeria. Thus the Algerian war was 'exemplary because it crystallised and strips bare the most fundamental contradiction of the capitalist world, the only one which is insoluble within the system itself' (1993b: 267).

For Lyotard the real, the grounded, contradiction is discovered – through this specific form of analysis – to be not that of labour and capital, which is posed at a more abstract and secondary level, but within the system which required the working people to participate in the working of the system, but where this participation could never lead to direct popular control. Lyotard expressed this in relation to the developing situation in Algeria in 1960–1, as presenting the complete absurdity of the call for 'participation' of the Algerians in a French Algeria: 'the problem is not that of knowing whether the absurdity will really disappear, it is that of knowing whether one can act as if it did not exist' (1993b: 267). If the left (the French communists) invoked the word 'fascism' here, its function was simply an attempt to reinvigorate a fading energy, restore a lost solidarity in a new orientation which had begun to support independence, not to engage in political analysis (Joly, 1991: 52).

It is at this point Lyotard begins in earnest to examine the changes within the revolutionary movement in France itself. Proletarian organisations, and the proletariat itself as a class, were unable to find a way of confronting Gaullism: they could not oppose and they could not support it. This dilemma effectively neutralised them politically, a fact which set in train a shift to new de-radicalised forms of social integration in France itself:

> the idea of a global and radical transformation of society seems absent from the present attitude of the workers, along with the idea that collective action can bring about this transformation. The spread of this depoliticisation greatly exceeds implicit criticism of the parties and the unions. (Lyotard, 1993b: 269)

What was involved was 'an immense transformation in the everyday life of the working class'. Lyotard sketched the profound reasons for these changes as they began to affect French society in the early 1960s: the disintegration of family life on the one hand, the new consumerism and leisure, on the other, in a general process combining cultural homogenisation (1993b: 272). Significantly all protest, having become institutionalised, was being incorporated into this new prevailing order: for 'the ruling class assimilates it ... turns it against those same ones who have acted ... That is its function as an exploiting and alienating class: to place humanity in the past tense, in the passive mood' (1993b: 274). Yet in the face of this assimilation, inevitably, new forms of paradoxical 'resistance' mirroring those forms being left behind in Algeria turn into a new idiom of 'incredulity, lassitude, and irony' (1993b: 275). Lyotard presents this as a fundamental crisis facing all those who want to keep alive the revolutionary project. He did not pick up at this point the way in which the radical opposition within the communist movement and organisations which became marked at this time began a process which culminated in May 1968 (see Joly, 1991: 145–8), nor did he foresee the later rise of 'revolutionary' Muslim fundamentalism of the 1990s.

As Lyotard's analysis returned to the situation in Algeria, it is clear that there are strange ways in which the two situations reflect each other. In 1961 (in an article omitted from the English collection), Lyotard described how a new wave of resistance had swept through Algeria, which had consciously turned the traditional values and ways of life of the Algerians into defensive communal forms. This form is a revolt, he argued, but one that remains non-aggressive (1989b: 213). The new social agent that emerged here was a youthful generation that had been brought up in years of war; and it had begun to formulate the elements of a programme of a coherent Algerian revolution. In his penultimate article (1962) he posed the question: how are the French to leave? The prospect of a French secessionist regime was impossible, it would not be viable. The French presence had become unviable, yet the army could not withdraw. But the initiative no longer rested with France but had switched dramatically to the organisations that had grown up in the struggle; they remained eclectic and characterised by rapidly built compromises. The key question was how would they negotiate with de Gaulle? In his last article (1963) for *Socialism or Barbarism*, Lyotard surveyed the aftermath of French withdrawal and the immediate social collapse in Algeria. As predicted, the social and political void had become apparent once more as the effective entity (France) which sustained the Algerian compromises simply vanished. It became a 'society absent from itself' (1993b: 318ff.).

Perhaps what is crucial in this account is not so much the internal life of the revolt in Algeria (which Lyotard is only intermittently able to describe directly); it is in effect the transformation that occurs in France itself. Lyotard believed that the crisis of the Fourth Republic presented a revolutionary opportunity for the revolutionary left. His essay 'The State and Politics in the France of 1960' is the high point of his political disenchantment: 'France is politically dead' (1993b: 252). The various political defeats of France as an imperial power crystallised into a political crisis, provoked not as Marxists had expected from the left, but from the extreme right. De Gaulle's success was premised on the fact that there was during this crisis no threat from the left; 'the proletariat left capitalism at leisure to resolve the crisis ... the workers did not attempt, during those few days when the decayed state ended up in the streets, to destroy it and impose their own solution' (1993b: 255). In that crisis it became evident to Lyotard that the project of revolutionary socialism in France no longer existed as a real project, for the viability of the Fifth Republic was in a very fundamental sense built on a process of disenchantment, disillusionment and the neutralisation of proletarian initiative, and the theoretical and political failure of Marxism. At the same time, paradoxically, the fact of independent Algeria had vindicated the reality of self-directed emancipation as an exemplary form – but in the absence of any revolutionary agency or theory.

Conclusion

It would not be facile to draw a simple structural comparison between Lyotard's critique of phenomenology, its emphasis on finding a way of counteracting the tendency to impose 'truth' on lived experience, and the revolutionary process which discovers at the level of lived experience the real forms of resistance to the 'truths' imposed, as universals, by ruling classes and bureaucracies. Yet in both these forms of critique (and this enables us to answer the question posed at the beginning of this chapter) Lyotard holds not only to the programme of recovering direct and lived experience as the basis of truth and justice (for there is no real separation between truth and practical criticism), but also during this period they are bound together in a conception of the experience of proletarian emancipation as the touchstone of political analysis. In the introduction to the re-publication of his Algerian articles, he notes that if one compliments the *Socialism or Barbarism* group for its 'not having been too much in error', this only 'perpetuates the very thing against which the group fought' (1993b: 166), and it 'perpetuates the forgetting of what is and what remains absolutely true and about what was at stake'. He adds:

> True even today, when the principles of a radical alternative (i.e. workers' power) must be abandoned (something that allows many people, innocent or guilty, to relinquish all resistance and surrender unconditionally to the state of things). This stake, which motivates the carrying on of resistance by other means, on other terrains, and perhaps without goals that can be clearly defined, has always been and remains the intractable. (1993b: 166–7)

Indeed one could read the lesson to be learnt in the encounter between existential Marxism, and the experience of the paradoxes of the Algerian struggle for emancipation: truths were discovered within the experience (and not detachable from it) of a critical confrontation: an 'originary' sociality against 'universals'. One might call this Lyotard's critical existential method, but in the late 1960s and early 1970s he tried to recast his own 'problematic of alienation' by ruthlessly eliminating all religious implications from its humanism and its complement: the theorist as saviour (1993a).

Lyotard often returned to the example of Algeria in later writings. A significant example took place at a meeting in London on Postmodernism in 1985. Accused by Terry Eagleton of abandoning any concern for the real condition of the oppressed and the poor, especially in the Third World, Lyotard's reply was characteristic:

> I protest against the idea that political progressivism consists in referring to the poor of the Third World the revolutionary task. I think that if the intellectuals of the developed countries [do] this ... they are behaving in an absolutely irresponsible manner. Their task is that of confronting this question head on, and of elaborating it ... This does not mean that we don't have to concern ourselves with Third World struggles. But we can only [do this] on an ethical basis, not a political one. As a long-standing militant, I helped ... the struggle of the Algerians, but knowing very well that nothing revolutionary would come out of that struggle ... So one can contribute on an ethical basis. But that basis must not be confused with a political line. I think that the intellectuals should carry out this work of distinction between discursive genres (here the ethical and the political): that's part of the complexification of our situation. (Lyotard, 1986: 11–12)

His analysis of depoliticisation at the origin of the Fifth Republic was, as he has recently noted, 'in fact the announcement of the erasure of this great figure of the alternative, and at the same time, that of the great founding legitimacies'. And he notes, 'this is more or less what I have tried to designate, clumsily, by the term "postmodernism"' (Lyotard, 1993b: 169).

Before turning to the way in which Lyotard's conclusions were to be later worked out in theory, it is important to note that the period of the 1960s was dominated by a significant shift in Marxism, from existential to structural problematic. The structural current had of course been a serious if secondary one in the 1940s, with the work in anthropology by Lévi-Strauss (1987) most prominent perhaps, but in something of an alliance with psychoanalysis (Lacan) and the French epistemological tradition represented by Bachelard and Canguilhem. The latter came to occupy an important institutional position overseeing philosophy, in the University system. Canguilhem was, initially, strongly influenced by Comte and Durkheim, but in the 1940s launched a critical Nietzschean attack on the category of pathology, which had been so important in the theory of the earlier cycles. In the next chapter I examine the way in which Canguilhem's project itself became ambivalent as structural Marxism displaced existential Marxism in French social theory.

Notes

1 In 1950 Lyotard was in Constantine in French Algeria as a teacher (as described later in the essay 'A Memorial of Marxism' [1988: 45–75]). It was, he says, at a union meeting around 1950–1 that he met Pierre Souryi, and he 'had the good fortune, while the great century of Marxism was already declining, to learn ... that the historical and materialist dialectic could not

be just the title of a university chair or responsibility in a political bureau, but rather the name or form of a resolve' (1988: 65). I have drawn in this chapter on 'Lyotard's Early Writings: 1954–1963' (in Rojek and Turner, 1998: 139–57).

2 The English version of Lyotard's account of the mobilisation of the extreme right in Algeria omits key passages at this point (see note 1, ch. 30, 1993b: 335).

11

From Pathology to Normativity

> Health is more than normality; in simple terms, it is normativity (Canguilhem, 1994: 351)

The French tradition of social theory, which begins with Comte and continues through Durkheim, attempted to make the connection of theory and practice through the identification of 'social pathology'. With one or two notable exceptions, writers in the third cycle, dominated in the initial phases by Marxist ideas, did not adopt this concept. In fact, one important strand of social theory which runs through this last period sought to draw the line between the sciences and the sphere of social philosophy or literature, not between the objective and subjective, nor between the exact or natural sciences and the cultural sciences, as was the pattern in German thought, but between that sphere of the life sciences which studied biological and genetic processes and that which might be called the sphere of the therapeutic. The main contributors to this strand of theory were Canguilhem and Foucault, and it challenged not only the idea of a 'scientific' field of pathology, and by implication the Comtean view of the hierarchical system of the sciences, but also the idea of a scientific (Marxist) politics.

Canguilhem

Canguilhem was born in 1904. While under the supervision of Celestin Bouglé, he wrote a thesis on Auguste Comte's notion of 'order and progress' when he was in his early twenties. Between that dissertation and the first doctoral thesis, *The Normal and Pathological*, completed when he was almost 40, he wrote prolifically on politics and culture, in close association with Alain (E. Chartier) whose nostalgic Comteanism is evident throughout his extensive writings (see Sernin, 1985: 453; Muglioni, 1995: 133–48). It is perhaps to Bouglé that some attention should be given, for his work is the link between Comte, the French sociological school, and Canguilhem's project.

Bouglé was not a marginal Durkheimian, but a central 'pleiad' member of the school (Nandan, 1977: 232–42). Bouglé was famous for works on caste and equality, and he wrote an important study of science and democracy (*La Démocratie devant la science*, 1904) which tackled the problems raised by treating society as an organism. The French sociological school was well aware of the dangers inherent in a simplistic organicist sociology, and Bouglé presents a withering critique of such sociologies from a Durkheimian standpoint.

Bouglé introduces new terms, and in discussing the thesis of the sociological importance of the process of the division of labour, he distinguishes between social differentiation (an automatic process) and social complication (a social process). His objective is to demonstrate the weaknesses of the sociology produced by organicists who opposed the democratisation of the French state on the grounds that it was a pure utopia which could find no basis in social science (his target is Charles Maurras amongst others). Paradoxically, while the organicists found support for their position in Comte's writing, Bouglé used Comte's own term 'complication' to break out of such organicism. (Comte (1975: 194) had distinguished between natural organic regulation in the domestic union, and the invention of new forms of government for larger-scale social complication arising from the division of labour.)

In 1924 Bouglé wrote a key introduction to a selection of texts by Durkheim (just at the time Canguilhem was preparing his thesis on Comte under his supervision) in which he emphasises just 'how far the philosophy of Durkheim takes us from the materialist and organicist philosophies' (Bouglé in Durkheim, 1953: xli). Although Canguilhem does not refer extensively to Bouglé or Durkheimian sociology, there are many grounds for thinking that Canguilhem's project was never restricted to producing a history of the biological sciences.

The normal and the pathological

Canguilhem was interested in the writings of Auguste Comte because Comte not only coined the term 'sociology' and provided it with its first systematic content, but he also played an important role in the definition of the science of biology. More specifically, he took from Broussais a conception of the relation between normal and pathological phenomena which was to have wide ramifications in medical and social thought in the nineteenth century.

Broussais' idea was that there are no special causes of pathological facts, no domain of bad causes with a comparable domain of good causes. Michel Foucault charted the complex sequence of developments which led to this idea in *The Birth of the Clinic* (ch. 10), noting specifically:

> Bichat's pre-occupation remained that of finding an organic base for general diseases: hence his search for organic universalities. Broussais dissociates doublets, a particular symptom – a local lesion, a general symptom – and an over-all alteration, intersects their elements, and shows the over-all alteration in the particular symptom, the geographical lesion in the general symptom. From now on, the organic space of localisation is really independent of the space of the nosological configuration ... This represents a new organisation of the medical gaze in relation to Bichat. (Foucault, 1991: 186–7)

Foucault calls this revolution the birth of 'the new science', which for the first time aimed to define the cause of diseases and for which 'there are no longer either essential diseases or essences of diseases' (1991: 188, 189). Foucault expressed this in a surprising way: 'The medicine of diseases has come to an end; there now begins a medicine of pathological reactions ... the historical and concrete a priori of the modern medical gaze was finally constituted' (1991: 192).

Foucault notes – one-sidedly as Canguilhem pointed out (in Gutting, 1994: 87) – the 'frenzied' viciousness of the attacks on Broussais (Foucault, 1991: 191), but not the glowing review of Broussais' *De l'irritation et de la folie* (Paris, 1828), written by Comte in 1828. Foucault characteristically ignored Comte. In his *Order of Things*, Foucault omits to mention the independent development of Comte's notion of 'man' and 'humanity' by focusing on Kant. Here Foucault failed to note that Comte acclaimed Broussais as developing the ideas of Brown, the true 'founder of positive pathology' which Comte defined as the 'science which connects the perturbations of vital phenomena with the lesions of organs or tissues', so 'almost all recognised diseases are only symptoms, and that functional derangements cannot subsist without the lesion of organs or rather of tissues' (Comte, 1974b: 649). Comte claims this as a profound attack on the lingering metaphysics of medical practice which seemed trapped in trying to 'determine the precise seat of each of the maladies considered to have no special seat' (1974b: 649). Even if Broussais was wrong in his precise locations, 'it was better for pathology, and even for therapeutics, to propose a seat at variance with the true one than none' (1974b: 650). Progress requires the control of imagination by observation, says Comte, and the idea that disease is the 'excess or deficiency of stimulation ... either rising above or below the degree which constitutes the normal condition' opens the way to the analysis of pathology as a study of 'intensity in the action of stimulants indispensable for maintaining health' (1974b: 650).

Canguilhem's famous discussion in *The Normal and Pathological* ([1943] 1989) clearly presents the problems considered in the very questions asked: 'Is the pathological state merely a quantitative modification of the normal state?' 'Do sciences of the normal and the pathological exist?' These are the two fundamental questions posed by Canguilhem, and the aim of the work is to provide an attack on the very possibility of a scientifically based study of pathology. These projects are held to import into the sciences an extra-scientific dimension of normalisation. Canguilhem adds that what is remarkable is that the very society from which these ideas come is also the society in which 'normalisation' processes became a common feature. And Foucault's later studies take these normalising processes as an object of investigation, inaugurating an interesting counterpoint to the work of Canguilhem.

Canguilhem suggests that Comte promotes Broussais' principle into something equivalent to Newton's law of gravity (Canguilhem, 1989: 48). He notes Comte as saying 'Broussais established that the phenomena of disease coincided essentially with those of health from which they differed only in terms of intensity' (1989: 49), a 'principle of nosology vested with a universal authority that embraces the political order' (1989: 50). Comte takes the principle as a basis for the claim that pathology could play the role of experimentation, albeit indirectly, in domains where experiment was inherently difficult. Pathology could aid the discovery of laws based on observation and empirical verification. Canguilhem remarks that Comte aimed to divide pathology into anatomical and functional forms but Canguilhem is immediately suspicious that Comte provides no examples, and provides little methodological help in determining what might be the norm, except to appeal to the principle of natural balance and 'harmony'. This position is taken by Canguilhem to be an evident moral judgement. Things are actually more complicated than Canguilhem suggests, since although there is an implicit qualitative judgement here, the distinction rests on a purely quantitative criterion (degree of deviation from a norm). Canguilhem reviews the antecedents of Comte's argument to show that the elements of this position had been available for some decades, and (somewhat against Foucault's analysis) could be found in Bichat (Canguilhem, 1989: 61–3). A vitalism found in Bichat balances the purely logical position of Broussais (1989: 64) and from this point Comte works towards a position which subordinates Broussais principle to system. Canguilhem sums up Comte's position as one that holds that the 'cure for political crises consists in bringing societies back to their essential and permanent structure, and tolerating progress only within limits of variation of the natural order as defined by social statics' (1989: 64). Sociology as a discipline was thus constituted by taking up the project of trying to define abnormal social phenomena by relating them to normal social states (Comte's law of the three states).

Canguilhem's discussion continues however via and against Claude Bernard to René Leriche. Leriche's view that 'health is life in the silence of the organs, that consequently the biologically normal is revealed through infractions or the norm and that concrete or scientific awareness of life exists only through disease' is accepted as the most adequate position at this point in Canguilhem's thought. He adds a number of additional ideas: disease isolates (Sigerist), pathology is an individual norm (Goldstein), life is a dynamic norm, a judgement of value (Ey), and this latter idea Canguilhem accepts as the 'correct definition' (1989: 119). The first part of his book ends with the symptom-centred observation that if doctors talk about diseases, it is because they have a 'relationship with the patient and his value judgements' (1989: 122).

The second part of his thesis of 1943 discusses norm and normativity directly, and leads to the idea that

> there is no fact which is normal or pathological in itself. An anomaly or mutation is not in itself pathological. These two express other possible norms of life. If these norms are inferior to specific norms in terms of stability, fecundity, variability of life, they will be called pathological. If these norms in the same environment should turn out to be equivalent, or in another environment superior, they will be called normal. Their normality will come from their normativity. The pathological is not the absence of a biological norm: it is another norm which is, comparatively speaking, pushed aside by life. (1989: 144)

Canguilhem remarks that the relation between the functional norm of the living being, and the norms concerning the conditions under which these norms are normal (1989: 145), forms a crucial issue for any experimental science. Canguilhem quickly moves through a consideration of the norm and the average, the work of the quantitative tradition from Quetelet to Halbwachs (1989: 156–62), to conclude, characteristically and somewhat dogmatically, that 'physiology has better things to do than to search for an objective definition of the normal, and that is to recognise the original character of life' (1989: 178).

We should note that Canguilhem's concern has shifted, for he begins to assert a very specific way of thinking about norms and physiology: 'the true role of physiology ... [is] to determine exactly the content of the norms to which life has succeeded in fixing itself without prejudging the possibility or impossibility of eventually correcting these norms' (1989: 178). Indeed, against the view that pathological facts are purely harmful, they may express a diversity, or a 'negative vital value' (1989: 181). Canguilhem implies a methodological rule: do not bring in norms too soon. A different and highly paradoxical view of illness is implicit here: the 'sick man is not abnormal because of the absence of a norm, but because of his incapacity to be normative' (1989: 186). And this view (perhaps best described as Nietzschean) is quite different from that of Comte, for here 'disease is a positive, innovative experience in the living being and not just a fact of increase or decrease' (1989: 186). For Canguilhem, in 1943 at any rate, health is conceived, through paradox and tautology, as the 'boundless capacity to institute new norms' (1989: 196) so that 'to be in good health means being able to fall sick and to recover, it is a biological luxury' (1989: 199). Canguilhem pushes this idea to the limit: 'hemophilia is really nothing as long as a traumatism does not occur' (1989: 199). And even more paradoxically, even the 'temptation to fall sick' is essential to health. Against positivism, Canguilhem suggests that the attempt to reach a specific state called normal health may be paid for by 'renouncing all eventual normativity' (1989: 200).

Canguilhem nevertheless wants to safeguard the study of biological and social values. Instead of this falling to the sciences of biology and sociology themselves, it is the genuine terrain of philosophy. At this point, rather strangely, Canguilhem introduces his own version of Comte's law of the three states, and the regulative role of philosophy:

> Before science it is technologies, arts, mythologies and religions which spontaneously valorise human life. After the appearance of science these same functions still exist but their inevitable conflict with science must be regulated by philosophy, which is thus expressly philosophy of values'. (1989: 221)

The critique of Comte has thus an unexpected outcome. Instead of raising metaphysical philosophy to the status of a science, Canguilhem proposes that 'in looking for what is the vital significance of these constants, in qualifying some as normal and others as pathological, the physiologist does more – not less – than the strict work of science' (1989: 222). This point is underlined more than once: 'to fail to admit that from a biological point of view, life differentiates between its states means condemning oneself to be even unable to distinguish food from excrement ... What distinguishes food from excrement is not a physicochemical reality but a biological value' (1989: 220).

Canguilhem's intervention then is surprising. It does not attempt to eliminate the distinction of the normal and pathological as might appear at first glance, but to redefine it, and to situate the problem in philosophy, not biology or sociology. And in so doing, Canguilhem constantly plays with paradoxes, with inversions of expectations, even with outright contradictions: to fall sick is normal, to be normal may be a sickness. Normativity is the key to the judgement of norms for it appears to be the highest value. Such a study imports norms and thus values into the assessment itself and so lies beyond science. Curiously these values are not human values, since they exist for all life, all living beings, and they do not lead Canguilhem towards theoretical humanism, existential or otherwise.

When this book was republished in 1966 it was accompanied by a further section called 'New Reflections on the Normal and the Pathological' (1989: 233–90). It seems that Canguilhem had the intention of writing on the social implications of his position and these were completed only twenty-three years later, when he announced 'I am allowing myself some forays into the social' (1989: 235). What is remarkable in this excursion is that all other efforts to examine the problem of social abnormality are consistently ignored. The discussion drifts towards Marx, a consideration of ideological norms and the process of 'standardisation' of commodities, and drifts towards Bergson's notion of evolution and *élan vital*. At a crucial point in the discussion Canguilhem chooses to confront Comte's insistence that society should be treated as an organism.

Social theory: modernity is normativity

It is possible to regard the 'New Reflections on the Normal and the Pathological' as the long delayed contribution to the critique of sociology that had been begun many years previously. But there are many differences between Canguilhem's 'history' of biology and his reflections on sociology. Canguilhem wrote many excellent commentaries on Comte's work, notably an excellent essay on the concept of fetishism ([1964] 1983: 81–98). This essay considers the sources of the idea of fetishism, but it cannot be thought in any way a preliminary to a sociology of religion. Indeed instead of considering Durkheim's famous *Elementary Forms of the Religious Life* (1912), Canguilhem takes into account only the writing of Müller and Dilthey (Canguilhem, 1983: 97). Whenever Canguilhem approaches Comte's sociology, it is to stress its purely evaluative idea of a normal social state as one characterised by harmonic consensus of its parts. He is highly respectful of Comte's thought, defending the rational opposition to cell theory (Canguilhem, 1975: 64–6), and his support of phrenology (Canguilhem, 1983: 268). But Canguilhem stops well short of adhering to Comte's programme for sociology, in fact there is no discussion at all of the main elements of Comte's sociological analyses, and the law of the three states as such. Canguilhem's thought seems caught up in some of the principal illusions generated about his own work by Comte himself, and in this he is followed directly by his interlocutors such as Renard (1996: 132–5). It is important to clarify Comte's matrix of social statics and dynamics.

The Comtean illusion, or perhaps paradox, is that although his sociology sought to establish a method of social statics by defining (via the theoretical control of the biological notion of the 'organism') the character of a normal state, a normal state is only perceived by Comte to have existed for two or three centuries (eleventh to thirteenth centuries AD) in European history since the Romans. Here a consensus of the parts was visible in a monotheistic social formation, and even this, he had to admit (against the examples of the Islamic and other forms), was exceptional in structure. Comte analyses the decomposition of this polity from the thirteenth century through his conception of the metaphysical state, conceived as 'transitional' in his social dynamics – leading up to the French crisis of 1789 and to the threshold of the positive polity, the third and final state. In no sense then does European history from the thirteenth century have the character of harmony and consensus, and Comte's theory of the metaphysical state (as one of transition) sits uneasily against his specifications of what counts as a state in his three-state law. Canguilhem does not examine this problem directly and explicitly, even in his late paper on progress. In instance after instance he casually adopts oppositions such as ancient/modern, traditional/modern, primitive/advanced, in order to draw out sociological conclusions of one sort or another in what is, in truth, a rather ad hoc discussion of the changing character of sociological interpretations.

Instead of locating his discussion of the externality of the organisation of social complication, the effects of the division of labour, with reference to Bouglé, Bergson is described as the only philosopher who managed to conceive 'mechanical invention as a biological function, an aspect of the organisation of matter by life' (Canguilhem's position is clearly presented in his 1946–7 discussion of the ideas of 'machine and organism' ([1952] 1975: 101–29). What Canguilhem attempts to do in his excursion into sociology is to reflect on the difference between social organism and social machine, and the appropriateness of these concepts. By the 1960s, these reflections had taken on a distinctly Marxian flavour. In his 'New Reflections' he writes:

> Between 1759 when the word 'normal' appeared, and 1834 when the word 'normalised' appeared, a normative class had won power to identify – a beautiful example of ideological illusion – the function of social norms, whose content it determined, with the use that that class made of them. (Canguilhem, 1989: 246)

Canguilhem notes the commercial codes as an example of economic and technological normalisation (1989: 246–7). And these 'norms are relative to each other in a system, at least potentially. Their co-relativity within a social system tends to make this system an organisation' (1989: 249).

Yet Canguilhem hesitates: is this idea a metaphor or general concept? It is highly significant, he notes, that the social is not an automatic system but one that occurs through representations. He turns, at a crucial moment in the discussion, to the point of departure – to Comte's own formulation which distinguishes between the social articulation of parts and the action of power in organising them (1989: 250). New organs are required, says Comte, to regulate newly evolved specialisation of functions, giving rise to phenomena which are artificial but not arbitrary in the harmony of the system. Canguilhem quotes Comte's formulation of 1852: 'the collective organism, because of its composite nature, possesses to a higher degree the important aptitude ... the ability to acquire new, even essential organs.' These remarks by Comte are a recapitulation of the discussion of social complication, from the *Course in Positive Philosophy* (taken up by Bouglé noted above) for Comte's revised version of the sociocracy. Canguilhem sums up this project of a new religion of humanity in terms of a search for such a new organ: the 'spiritual power', the 'general art of man's action on himself', the organ now is the 'priest whose temporal power is merely a subordinate means' (Canguilhem, 1989: 251).

Of course, Canguilhem immediately distances himself from this conception: 'we shall say otherwise ... namely that society is both machine and organism' (1989: 252). An organism functioning more or less effectively is homeostatic, its needs are expressed through 'the existence of a regulatory apparatus' (1989: 252), such as through a nervous or endocrine system. Here all is co-presence and internality. But social organisation occurs through the invention of organs, where even the processes of normalisation create planning mechanisms, information and co-ordination, a process more and more subject to computerisation (1989: 253). Altering a famous phrase by Durkheim (that the social is external to the individual), Canguilhem says that the idea of society – and here the target without doubt includes Bouglé – determined by processes emanating from an 'internal milieu' conceived on the model developed by Claude Bernard – is quite inappropriate. Social evolution occurs on a different plane: societies have 'spread their means of action in spatial externality ... adding machines to tools ... archives to traditions' (1989: 254). Societies, he says, now inverting a famous phrase by Marx, 'must always solve a problem without a solution' (1989: 255). So 'to propose a model of the organism for human societies in search of more organisation is essentially to dream of a return not even to archaic, but to animal societies' (1989: 255). Canguilhem forces his point: if societies were organisms, 'we should be able to speak of a society's needs and norms as one speaks of an organism's vital needs and norms, that is, unambiguously.' Society is 'far from setting itself up as a whole' as a total consensus. He supports his position here in a disconcerting shift of focus, with an appeal to the work of Lévi-Strauss, and notes that there is perhaps 'a specific inertia in social life resistant to all attempts at organisation' (1989: 256).

It is clear that Canguilhem's target is the conception that social organisation can in any sense be conceived as an unproblematic self-regulated process arising from the automatic functioning of the social body – which might, if necessary, be either self-correcting or capable of being corrected through some sort of intervention. The basis for this critical position is in some way linked to his considerations of the normal and pathological in biology and medicine: not only is health in the individual associated with normativity, but, as revealed by the extracts from his manuscripts (in Canguilhem, 1994):

> Modernity is not normal in the sense of having achieved a definitive superior state. It is normative, however, because it strives constantly to outdo itself … Modern man is experiencing a crisis in the sense that domination and mastery of the environment elude his grasp. But the resolution of that crisis does not lie in the past. It does not exist in ready-made form but remains to be invented. (1994: 368)

Canguilhem could be talking either of the individual or a society. What characterises his position is the consistent critique of the conception of well-being as a fixed norm, of health as a state of being, of development as progression through necessary sequence of such states.

Canguilhem's increasing ambivalence

As Canguilhem developed his reflections on biological and social pathology, the biological sciences entered into a period of rapid change. Canguilhem registers in a detailed empirical history these developments in physiology, bacteriology, endocrinology and neurophysiology (1983: 226–71), but also in genetics following the discovery of the structure of DNA. His response to these developments is a complex one, and as far as I know is nowhere adequately presented and examined. In the first instance, in the 'New Reflections' of 1966 (1989), he defended his position on the basic definition of normativity, claiming that however much it had appeared 'rash' in 1943, it had been confirmed by subsequent studies: 'human norms … are determined as an organism's possibilities for action in a social situation rather than as an organism's functions envisaged as a mechanism coupled with the physical environment' (1989: 269). Against the idea that the normal could be conceived statistically, his insistence on normativity had been correct: 'it does not seem to us that we must profoundly modify our analysis', he concluded.

But there was something new: genetically determined pathologies. In 1943 there were few such instances, but by 1966 it was recognised that there were many such instances. At first it was a metaphor, then it became an analogy (1989: 276). Canguilhem was concerned to reflect on the specific features and character of this kind of pathology. He suggested that they were pathologies produced through false copying of genetic information: error. He notes in a comment which indicates how considerable this shift had been: 'It is not too serious if it is only a matter of error in the metabolism of fructose … It is more serious if it is a question of hemophilia arising from the lack of synthesis of a globulin' (1989: 279). He also notes that such biochemical diseases can lie 'hidden as non-activated tendencies' (1989: 281). The change in conception is not registered in the text but it is clear that in 1943 Canguilhem could refer to the formula of health in 'the silence of the organs' while now there is an 'original abnormality' (1989: 281). The change in the function of the example of hemophilia from that earlier text goes without a remark from Canguilhem. Yet he is conscious that the very idea of the 'wisdom of the body' is thrown into question, and he muses philosophically on the possibility of a new species of 'gene police' in the absence of any existential possibility of 'progress towards rationality in negative values' (1989: 279).

In the 1960s Canguilhem seems to have moved towards an acceptance of the possibility and probability of considerable further development and progress in the biological sciences. If anything his position seemed to move closer to that of Bachelard and Althusser and away from Foucault. As he later noted, he began to introduce the concept of scientific ideology into his lectures from 1967. In his *Ideology and Rationality in the History of the Life Sciences* (Canguilhem, [1977] 1988), this concept was accorded an important role in understanding the emergence of the sciences. This argument seems remarkably similar to the notion of the metaphysical stage in Comte's analysis of scientific revolution. Canguilhem had no difficulty at all in accepting the general idea of scientific revolution and the installation of new sciences in physics and biology. Scientific ideologies are not, however, 'false' sciences, but are characterised by their refusal to acknowledge falsehood or falsifiability (1988: 33). They form the early stages of a science and mark out a territory, but 'when science eventually supplants ideology, it is not in the expected location ... What science finds is not what ideology suggested looking for' (1988: 34). Canguilhem's examples are interesting, particularly his choice of Herbert Spencer's evolutionary sociology. The analysis rests almost entirely on the presumed existence of scientific progression in sociology. His critique of Spencer follows almost exactly, and ironically, that of Emile Durkheim. Spencer claims to have generalised the principles of embryology together with the law of the conservation of energy to support an evolutionary sociology, but he produced merely a justification of English political individualism which could be used to support a colonialist and imperialist practice (actually Canguilhem is in error here, as Spencer refused to follow this course, emulating Comte's own rejection of French colonialism). His sociology is now only a curiosity, 'merely an inoperative residue in the history of the human sciences' (1988: 36–7). What progression has occurred in the human sciences, Canguilhem fails to define.

Canguilhem also uses the concept of scientific ideology to rethink the problem of pathology introduced by Broussais at the beginning of the nineteenth century and to produce a more rounded appraisal of the medical revolutions that followed it. In effect it is an attempt to complete the analysis by Foucault already referred to. It entails not only a critique of Comte by implication, but also of Canguilhem's own 'fundamental idea'. Canguilhem notes that within a couple of decades, Broussais' notion of pathology (in terms of intensities) was considered by experimental biologists such as Bernard as having accomplished merely progress in a 'way of looking' at pathology, that is the medical gaze not the science. Broussais' substantive conceptions of pathology were quickly refuted and replaced in a series of progressive developments (Canguilhem, 1988: 54–73). He sums this up by saying that

> new clinical schools in Austria, France and Germany exploded such ambiguous pathological concepts ... [By] combining pathological anatomy with clinical practice, doctors learned to make differential diagnoses and to identify individual syndromes ... a necessary but not sufficient condition for the development of the idea of a specific etiology – nothing less than a conceptual revolution. (1988: 72)

Thus Canguilhem's judgement indicated that 'the new medical model' (as pursued by Broussais and others) 'remained an ideology. If the goal of the programme was eventually achieved, it was by a detour, by routes quite different from those envisioned by the programme's authors' (1988: 55, trans. modified). Elsewhere he repeated this view that

> if medicine has attained the status of a science, it did so in the era of bacteriology. A practice is scientific if it provides a model for the solutions of problems and if that model gives rise to effective therapies ... A second criterion of scientificity is the ability of one theory to give rise to another capable of explaining why its predecessor possessed only limited validity. (Canguilhem, 1994: 146)

The elaboration of this position seems to bring Canguilhem back from Foucault (and Nietzsche) towards Bachelard (and Comte).[1]

Conclusion

If we turn finally to Canguilhem's late paper on 'The Decline of the Idea of Progress' (1998), we can see that what concerns him is the way the value of the term progress is bound up with dominant scientific theories and the ironies entailed in such progress. Such ironies can also be found at the heart of Canguilhem's work. Two paradigms are identified as decisive. The first is the 'conservative' model taken from Newtonian and Laplacian celestial mechanics, which deals with invariant structures and predictable orbits. The second is the model taken from the invention of engines, which was worked out in the theory of thermodynamics and which introduces the notion of inevitable dissipation of energy, of loss, not found in the first model. Comte, influenced by Condorcet, adopted the principle of the perfectability and harmony. A number of developments occurred which complicated this vision, notably the recovery of the significance of childhood for individual maturation (Freud), the problematic effects of mass media and consumer society (McLuhan) and the invention of weapons of mass destruction. However, it seems for Canguilhem that it was principally the emergence of the model of thermodynamics which led to a decisive shift. Canguilhem moves, finally, to a consideration of a western Marxism (he discusses Lévi-Strauss, Sartre, Habermas) which he believes could explain, in a way comparable to psychoanalysis, the apparently inevitable combination of progression with barbarism. And so what Canguilhem produces here is an impossible irony on Bachelard's conception of progress, observing that scientific and technical revolutions produce the grave-diggers of the notion of progress in the very content of their discoveries. He also produces an impossible irony on Comte's demand for progress with order, borrowing from the discipline of psychoanalysis (which retains the ideas of progression and pathology) the desire to theorise the inherent complexity of development. To say, with Dagognet, that the positions of Bachelard and Foucault form two poles between which Canguilhem's thought moves is perhaps an oversimplification of a strategy marked by complex ambivalences. Canguilhem tried to understand the way that ideological practices became sciences. He found that in the domain of biology they did so in ways that no one had the means of anticipating. As for the domain of sociology, his last writings suggest that in emphasising the need to analyse social development as the complex combination of *progress with barbarism*, his reflections were still concerned more with philosophical irony than with a social theory of normal and pathological phenomena.

And one is led to ask: what was it in Canguilhem's work which produced a sustained critique of Comte, an avoidance of Durkheimian sociology, yet a strange highly contradictory rapprochement with the 'scientific Marxism' of the Althusserians which I discuss in the next chapter?

Note

1 The idea that there are important shifts in Canguilhem's thought is often discussed in recent commentaries but almost always rejected in the same terms Canguilhem himself used (1994: ix–xi). Gilles Renard asked explicitly: 'Is there a rupture in Canguilhem's thought?' (1996: 152), while François Dagognet (1997) asked rhetorically whether Canguilhem did in fact 'renounce' his 'fundamental idea'? Both of these recent essays answer negatively, although Dagognet suggests the curious, but entirely likely, possibility that Canguilhem's thought 'circulates' between the positions of Bachelard and Foucault (1997: 16). Paradoxically then, Canguilhem – this writer on intellectual discontinuity, paradox and irony – seems relatively unproblematic to his recent French interpreters. And this was his own judgement on himself (Canguilhem, 1988: Preface). I draw in this chapter on M. Gane, 'Canguilhem and the Problem of Pathology', in *Economy and Society*, 1998, vol. 27 (2–3): 298–312.

12

Structural Theory

> By means of what concept or what set of concepts is it possible to think the determination of a subordinate structure by a dominant structure; in other words, how is it possible to define the concept of a structural causality? (Althusser, in Althusser and Balibar, 1970: 186)

The social theory which developed after the Second World War worked in a complex continuation of the framework of Saint-Simonianism with its Marxist additions: economics (transformed into a theory of modes of production) and dialectics (idealist philosophy transformed into the logic of historical materialism). The coin had been turned in postwar French theory: the sociological, socialist, Comtean, Durkheimian development was replaced with the German, Russian, then Chinese developments of Marxism. After the war, in other words, that side of the Saint-Simonian legacy which had been on a journey to other parts of the globe, came home to France. First theoretical Marxism in France was worked through in an encounter with German existentialism and phenomenology. From the 1960s it was worked through from the materials available from the French epistemological tradition shorn of its references to 'sociology' but not to 'anthropology': in a word, it became structuralist in one form or another (just as there had been rival forms of existentialism). Many Marxist existentialists made the transition to the new methods and problematics, but there were many, such as Edgar Morin, who held on and resisted the new fashion with increasing bitterness (Kofman, 1996: 11–16), just as there were some who remained loyal to structural Marxism (such as Bourdieu) after its general collapse in the 1970s. The irruptive force of structuralism was due to the fact that across a number of disciplines new and brilliant writers appeared together: Althusser, Barthes, Baudrillard, Bourdieu, Derrida, Deleuze, Foucault, Kristeva, Serres and many others. Serres, usually so tolerant and once described as 'perhaps the only philosopher in France whose work is consonant with the spirit of structural analysis' (Descombes, 1987), said of Sartre that he 'crushes everything and understands nothing … he delayed the arrival of all the real innovations' (Serres, 1995: 41).

The linguistic or structuralist turn and the moment of 'theory'

Although 'structuralism', as a method, developed from a number of sources – linguistic, anthropological, mathematical – it did not become effective as a movement in social theory until the 1960s, when it dramatically displaced 'existentialism' from its dominant position in French thought. The problem of the precise nature of structuralism has been discussed many times, and there is still an ongoing debate (see the self-critical remarks of Descombes in Yamamoto, 1998: 464). For those commentators wedded to existential philosophy, the upsurge of this new set of ideas came as an 'invasion' (Gutting) into the genuine centre of French thought which will always be existentialism. However, as can be seen from the previous analysis, it is existentialism which came from outside (Husserl, Heidegger, Lukacs, Marcuse, and many others). And if the works of Durkheim and Mauss were claimed by various existential writers (e.g. Lyotard) as representing a tradition to be drawn towards their own position, this was done in the face of anthropologists such as Lévi-Strauss and Dumezil who, from the death of Mauss in 1950, claimed that tradition was structural not existential (Lévi-Strauss, 1987). This challenge provoked the famous debate between Lévi-Strauss and Sartre; Sartre was never able to find the means to launch a counter position (Sartre, 1971).

The 'structuralists' emerged into prominence suddenly and triumphantly with key works on methodology by Lévi-Strauss, Roland Barthes, Serres, Foucault, Lacan, Althusser, followed by analyses by Bourdieu, Baudrillard, Kristeva, Sollers, etc. In fact this movement was very varied, and it placed *theory* centre stage. The transition was complex as Baudrillard later pointed out. His books, *The System of Objects*, and *Consumer Society*, published in France in 1968 and 1970 respectively, maintained a perspective which he suggested was a critical Marxism: semiology and sociology organised together within the existential problematic of alienation and the society of the spectacle (1988b: 77–8). Theory still gave importance to the centrality of the acting subject, the subject's imaginary, and the scene cast in theatrical terms. Resistance to capitalist society was conceived as the 'transgression of the categories of political economy: use-value, exchange-value, equivalence' (1988b: 77). But this problematic had already been challenged in 1960s by the new Althusserian structuralist discourse which by 1968, as Derrida later confirmed, had become 'the dominant discourse ... of the Marxist intelligentsia' (Kaplan et al., 1993: 200). It then widened its influence in politics (Poulantzas), economics (Bettleheim), and was highly influential for a short time in literary theory (Culler, 1975). In particular, the structuralist discourse was taken up by the avant-garde artists, musicians, writers and cultural theorists who contributed to the journal *Tel Quel* (the works of Sollers, Barthes, Todorov, Kristeva, Genette, Faye, etc.), which was drawn into debate with leading PCF intellectuals.

This chapter examines Kristeva, Althusser, Foucault, Deleuze and Guattari, as representing the key figures in the debates of this moment, when 'structuralism' attained its complete hegemony over social theory in France, and then began to accommodate itself to the failure of May 1968 and the revolutionary project that theory had set itself. (The 'structuralist controversy' is reported in Macksey and Donato, 1972, and is critiqued by Anderson, 1983, and Merquior, 1986.) What is striking in the perspective of this analysis is that structuralism not only brought with it the epistemological heritage of the French tradition, but it also brought a keen interest in ideological or 'spiritual' authority.

From de Beauvoir to Kristeva

Julia Kristeva (b. 1941) became the most prominent feminist theorist when existentialism gave way to structuralism in the 1960s. She is associated with structualist theory in the same way as de Beauvoir was with existentialism. For Kristeva, de Beauvoir is 'a chronicler who knew how to construct an entire cultural phenomenon' (existentialism). Prolific author of novels, at least one of which is autobiographical, Kristeva was associated with Philippe Sollers in a relationship many compared with that of de Beauvoir and Sartre. But instead of *Les Temps modernes*, Kristeva's journal was *Tel Quel* (which lasted from 1960 to 1982). Indeed Kristeva herself even made the comparison and to her own advantage, asking if it was not the 'austere and cutting pen of this feminist in search of rationalism that gave *Les Temps modernes* its true erotic consistency?' By contrast, Kristeva writes of 'complicity, friendship, love':

> The eruptions, encounters, loves, passions, as well as more or less liberated or controlled eroticism that have shaped each person's biography constitute ... the deepest influences on an individual path ... Only a diary, a novel, could perhaps one day restore the wild indecency of it' (cited in Stanton, 1987: 219–20, 234).

Even if Kristeva had a university career and was a leading member of a journal *Tel Quel* (which was far from the sole preserve of university academics), it was a different career from that of de Beauvoir. Kristeva was trained in linguistics and psychoanalysis, and became a mother. Kristeva appropriated a scientific mode of analysis, and became a leading pro-Chinese Maoist intellectual. She applied Althusser's notion of theoretical modes of production to the analysis of textual as a process of production in its own right (French, 1995: 160–78). But she chose to base herself not in Althusserian circles but in 'the revolutionary aestheticism of *Tel Quel*' (Stanton, 1987: 229; for the politics of this group, see Marx-Scouras, 1996).

In the end she came to regard her involvement and the action of this group as a *perversion*. She defines it thus: 'a coherent structure determined by an ideal (this ideal was *theoretical* for us ...) which nevertheless uses the abjections of a reality, one that is neglected or even foreclosed, on behalf of libidinal or sublimated gratifications.' Kristeva, moving more and more from Marx to Freud, saw, she said, a society turned into a 'killer mechanism of individual difference. '"Society is a crime committed in common" ... we have never ceased observing the truth of Freud's famous statement' (cited in Stanton, 1987: 232). Maoism in France at that moment, she held, was an antidote to this process of homogenisation.

Kristeva, in the last phase of her Marxist career, went to China with a group from *Tel Quel* in April–May 1974 and wrote a book entitled *About Chinese Women*, in which her social, rather than psychoanalytic or linguistic, theory was in evidence. She has not sought to express regrets about her Maoist period: 'I would do it again ... [we] were in search of a utopia' as 'a way of asking questions about the Western tradition' (Kristeva, 1992). Kristeva's journey to China described in her book is of considerable interest (even if it has been criticised by some as being condescending; see Spivak). The book is in two parts. The first is a statement of Kristeva's theoretical presuppositions guiding her analysis. The second part is her analysis of the situation of Chinese women and a report on her visit. As a Bulgarian, raised in a communist culture, she 'recognised' her own 'pioneer komsomol childhood in the little red guards' – yet the experience was one of an encounter with a 'unique logic that no exoticism can account for' (Kristeva, 1977: 12). She spends some time deciding how to locate herself as a writer on China: not as a militant writing propaganda, but as someone who tries to make the *otherness* visible from a position where 'our capitalist monotheistic fabric is shedding, crumbling'. She writes from the 'underground', alongside those who 'speak differently' (1977: 14); a woman but not a woman locked up inside a 'secret society of females'. She speaks as one who is 'fed up' with being, through European culture, a 'Jewish mother, Christian virgin, Beatrice beautiful' (1977: 15). 'To relieve her of this weight ... it is equivalent to a second Renaissance' that is not a ministry for women's affairs.

Her analysis of the Western experience is primarily an account of the place of woman in religion (1977: 17–33) and the symbolic temporal order (1977: 34–8). Her analysis suggests that

> one betrays, at best, one's naïveté if one considers our modern societies to be simply patrilinear, or 'class-structured' or capitalist-monopolist, and ignores the fact that they are at the same time (and never one without the other) governed by a monotheism whose essence is best expressed in the Bible: the paternal Word sustained by a fight to the finish between the two races (men/women). (1977: 22–3)

Her solution to the problem of monotheism: 'to go on waging the war of the sexes' which must revolutionise 'our entire logic of production (class) and reproduction (family)', that is 'without a perverse denial of the abyss that marks the sexual difference'. 'Once this total change is effected', China will be understandable, but without it 'susceptible ... to being cast as another perversion' (1977: 23).

Thus her critical analysis rests almost entirely on her analysis of monotheism:

> There is one unity ... This unity that the God of monotheism represents is sustained by a desire that pervades the community, making it run but also threatening it. Remove this threatening desire – this perilous support of the community – from man; place it beside him: you have woman, who is speechless, but who appears as the pure desire of speech, or who ensures, on the human side, the permanence of the divine paternal function. (1977 19)

The decisive addition here to the main accounts of the development of monotheism in sociological terms is the explicit analysis of its sexual dimension, here taken from Ernest Jones's psychoanalytic analysis of religion.

However, in Kristeva's case the analysis leads to the conclusion that 'militants in the cause of their fathers ... are dramatic figures where the social consensus corners any woman who wants to escape her condition: nuns, "revolutionaries", "feminists"' (1977: 32). The term which Kristeva introduces again at this point is that not of deviation but one drawn from the vocabulary of pathology: *perversion*.

Thus Kristeva takes a different theoretical route from that of de Beauvoir, one which might be called social-psychoanalytic and in fusion with the symbolic cultures of the Other (precisely critiqued by de Beauvoir as producing Woman as Other). Although this route does join up with Marxism, it does so with the considerable inflection which Bataille, and indeed eventually Althusser, gave it – towards a Catholic-anthropological thematic. And this became more and more influential as Kristeva's career developed as she broadened the anthropological influences to include Mary Douglas, most notably in her study *Powers of Horror: an Essay on Abjection* ([1980] 1982) which recasts her theory of gender as an psychoanalytic anthropology of religion which has as its object the 'solutions given for phobia and psychosis by religious codes' in a critical reading of Céline (1982: 48). At the end of the work she refuses that feminism which conserves the power of horror as the 'last of the power seeking ideologies' in order 'to go through the first great demystification of Power (religious, moral, political, and verbal) that mankind has ever witnessed' (1982: 208, 210).

Althusser: 'high priest of Marxism'

Althusser, looking back from the 1960s, suggested that no French intellectual had written a history of philosophy in France because it was so second rate:

> It takes some courage to admit that French philosophy, from Maine de Biran and Cousin to Bergson and Brunschvicg, by way of Ravaisson, Hamelin, Lachelier and Boutroux, can only be *salvaged* from its own history by the few great minds against whom it set its face, like Comte and Durkheim, or buried in oblivion like Cournot and Couturat ... [and those] few conscientious historians of philosophy, historians of science[1] who worked patiently and silently to educate those to whom in part French philosophy owes its renaissance in the last thirty years. (Althusser, [1968], 1971: 33–4)

Althusser himself, born in 1918, moved to Marxism after an early period of intense involvement in Catholic movements. His mentor for a time was Jean Guitton, who later wrote a book on the Virgin (*La Vierge Marie*, 1957). Althusser was taken, while a 'strong believer' at the end of the 1930s, to Paris as Jean Guitton's protégé, where he condemned 'materialism in philosophical terms [with the help of Revaisson] in front of an audience of nuns' (Althusser, 1993: 93). The church had reacted strongly against what it saw as a considerable challenge to its 'mission', and condemned Marxism in 1937 as 'intrinsically bad', and again in the 1940s which led to a policy in 1949 of excommunication for those espousing communism. In 1946 Althusser had taken up a radical proletarian position within the church, and was quoting Marx: 'for the Christian who does not usurp God's place, the human fatherland is not the proletariat of the human condition, it is the proletariat *tout court*, leading the whole of humanity towards its emancipation' (1997: 27). Within a Hegelian and Catholic framework, Althusser allied himself early on with the proletarian class as the vanguard agency (1997: 30). He joined the French Communist Part (PCF) in 1948 at the moment paradoxically of 'his closest collaboration' with a religious group called 'The Community', founded by a Dominican father, even though in 1947 he had ceased being a 'firm believer'.

With Althusserian Marxism – and it was a significant school – social theory was again reconstructed, this time on the basis of epistemological concepts such as structural causality, overdetermination, condensation and displacement. This was a project conceived within the tradition established by Comte and Durkheim, transmitted by Bachelard and Canguilhem but introducing from outside these key Freudian-Lacanian terms. The early nineteenth-century model developed by Comte identified the irruption and struggle of positivities (science and industry) against theology, thereby inducing by displacement new revolutionary (metaphysical) formations. In both Comte and Althusser an elaborate methodology was required to formulate an abstracted theoretic locus within which these processes of displacement occur. For Marx (Althusser) it was the 'social formation'; for Mauss it was in the advanced societies 'the nation'; and for Comte it was 'Humanity'.

For Althusser, as for Comte, theory in the domain of science was no passive reflective process; on the contrary, it was an active practice, a practice which put to work to produce knowledge. Just as there is an economic mode of production in Marx's social analysis, so there are theoretical modes of production (Generalities II) which work to transform conceptual raw materials (Generalities I) into the finished bodies of abstract and concrete conceptual knowledge (Generalities III). Theories are dynamic motors; they are the means of production in science, making a systemic conceptual machinery which is applied in a process guided and regulated by methodological rules, and unified by epistemological solidarities. Thus there are new conceptual elements which work together in a new way whenever a scientific revolution occurs. If Althusser was drawn into Marxism through an involvement in Catholic Action and coming to face with the 'social question' (1993: 205), his redefinition of the social was crucial to what became known as Althusserianism: Marx's new object of analysis was not the social as such but the 'social formation', within which the economic mode of production was determinant in the last instance. This was reframed in a new idea of how causality is effective within such a totality: the economic is an absent or 'metonymic cause'. When Jacques-Alain Miller proposed this term it was immediately adopted by the group.[2]

Althusser proposed different kinds of 'theory' which could be identified by using the term in different ways, as Ben Brewster once tried to define:

'a distinction is made between "theory" (in inverted commas), the determinate theoretical system of a given science, and Theory (with a capital T), the theory of practice in general'. Althusser replied to this definition to give more precision via a corrected conception of theory:

> I now regard my definition of philosophy (Theory as 'the Theory of Theoretical Practice') as a unilateral and, in consequence, false conception of dialectical materialism. ... the new definition of philosophy can be resumed under three points: (1) philosophy 'represents' the class struggle in the realm of *theory*, hence philosophy is neither a science, nor a pure theory (Theory), but a *political practice of intervention* in the realm of theory; (2) philosophy 'represents' scientificity in the realm of political practice, hence philosophy is not *the* political practice, but a theoretical practice of intervention in the realm of politics; (3) philosophy is an original 'instance' (differing from the instances of science and politics) that represents the one instance alongside [*auprès de*] the other, in the form of a specific *intervention* (political-theoretical). (Althusser, in Althusser and Balibar, 1970: 321)

Thus Althusser defines a complex intersection between social science (the realm of theory) and politics, as the junction (Theory) of a double intervention. Later still he reflected that the tendency to give primacy to theory was a 'theoreticism', a particular Marxist 'deviation' (see Althusser, 1976: 124). But the main deviation called 'theoreticism' was 'buried beneath a secondary deviation (and problematic), structuralism' (1976; 127). Derrida once again pointed out that there was a risk that 'the move to eliminate theory with a capital "T" or theory of ideology as well as ideology from history [was] problematic until such time that a concept of history were produced.' Althusser's critique of 'the metaphysical concept of history did not mean "there is no history"', said Derrida (in Kaplan, 1993: 193).

What Althusser did to resolve his 'theoreticism' was to argue that the process of the production of theory is not a pure action of thought, but that for Marx 'the conjunction of the three theoretical elements (German philosophy, English political economy, French socialism) could only produce its effect (Marx's scientific discovery) by means of a *displacement* which led the young Marx not only onto proletarian class positions but also proletarian theoretical positions' (Althusser, 1976: 160). Very soon, by 1978, even the thesis of the three sources of Marxism came to be criticised because it too rested on the idea that the process of intellectual production was purely one of inversion or conjuncture rather than a complex set of interventions, including a political one that was worked out 'on the terrain of working-class struggle' not imported into the movement by an intellectual from the outside (in Elliot, 1987: 316).

Althusser had also worked to a new position in considering the relation of theory to truth. In his paper 'On Theoretical Work' ([1967] in Althusser, 1990) he argued that theory exists 'in the practical state' in the political practice of political parties. These are principles, and even 'theoretical content' which may be 'in advance' of their theoretical reflection. This idea led Althusser to some extreme formulations, because he was immediately drawn to the conclusion that

> The political practice of a revolutionary party, the structure of its organisation, its objectives, the forms of its action, its leadership of the class struggle, its historical achievements, etc., constitute the *realization* of Marxist theory ... As these principles are theoretical, if this realization is *correct*, it inevitably produces results of *theoretical* value. (Althusser, 1990)

The materials of this theoretical productivity include

> resolutions fixing the party line, political discourses defining it and commenting on it, programmatic slogans recording political decisions or drawing out their conclusions. These can be actions undertaken, the way they are conducted as well as the results obtained. These can be forms of organization of class struggle ... These can be methods of leadership ... the way problems of the union of theory and practice in the union of theory and practice ... are resolved. (Althusser, 1990: 65)

Althusser noted that where the practice is *incorrect*, the analysis should take the form of 'historical pathology' of deviations (1990: 65). Thus one can be in the truth without being able to speak the truth, and one can be in error without being able to speak error. By 1978 Althusser had launched a massive critique of the French Communist Party, a party that was in crisis, as was Marxist theory in general. Althusser attacked the way the leadership of the Party regarded its precious possession of political truth which it could bring to the masses from the outside, indeed from above. The Party apparatus, and the relation of theory to practice, had become a mirror image of the bourgeois state itself (see Elliot, 1987: 301–2). Althusser also condemned the prevailing forms of theorising in the USSR, with a carefully aimed attack on how mistakes were dealt with, and how the political process failed to learn from the direct experience of proletarian struggle. He concluded that the Soviet style of practice was an example of a 'deviation without a norm' (in Lecourt, 1977: 10).

Theory and power

Althusser claimed in his last writings that it was his theory of the Ideological State Apparatuses (ISAs) which had been his central achievement. The seeds of the idea can however be found in other writers like Barthes, who had already noted the importance of 'interpellent speech' ('*parole interpellative*'; Barthes, 1973: 125), a term which Althusser was to make central to his theory of the state. Althusser provided the general theory in a sense for Barthes' analyses and this turned out to be his major theoretical innovation in the field of social analysis. In his autobiography Althusser refers to his own experience in the family – for him an experience of an ideological apparatus of the bourgeois state – during which his parents instilled into him 'the supreme values prevailing in the society in which I was growing up: absolute respect for absolute authority'. He elaborates on this theme:

> In addition to the three great narcissistic wounds inflicted on Humanity (that of Galileo, that of Darwin, and that of the unconscious [Freud]), there is a fourth

> and even graver one which no one wishes to have revealed (since from time immemorial the family has been the very site of the *sacred* and therefore of *power* and of *religion*). It is an irrefutable fact that the Family is the most powerful ideological State apparatus. (Althusser, 1993: 104–5)

This theory of the ISAs was essentially Althusser's way of confronting the problem that knowledge does not flow in a vacuum but is implicated in complex ways with the structure of power and authority in society. This problem 'refers us to a theory of the material (production), social (division of labour, class struggle), ideologies and philosophical conditions of the processes of production of knowledge' (Althusser, 1976: 156). Althusser's paper on the ISAs was published with the title 'Ideology and Ideological State Apparatuses (Notes towards an Investigation)' (1971). It was written in 1969 and was 'no more than an introduction to a discussion' (1971: 123). The essay was originally conceived as parts of five chapters of an eleven chapter book (the first of two volumes) on the concept of the superstructures in Marxist theory. This was drafted out in full but remained unpublished. The basic idea was to set out the nature of Marxist philosophy as both a theoretical and political intervention. The ISAs paper constituted 40 pages out of a 150-page manuscript, nevertheless its formulations were remarkable (Gane, 1983, includes Althusser's defence of the ISAs thesis).

The main theme of the paper is that the State, in Marxist theory, is divided into ideological and repressive aspects, and functions to reproduce the conditions and relations of production for the dominant social class. As there are ideological formations that function to maintain the position of the dominant class, they should, according to Althusser, be regarded as State apparatuses. No examples of the (R)SAs were given in the published version of the paper, though it is suggested they function by violent means primarily. Althusser provides a list of the formations which function primarily by ideology: the religious, familial educational, legal, trades-union, media and cultural apparatuses (the drafted book has chapters on the legal and trade union ISAs). The unity of this set of formations is to be found in their function, which is to reproduce the class hierarchies. The paper provides a new conception of ideology as a process that works by 'interpellation' or hailing of individuals into subjecthood, in both the sense of individuality, and as subject (subjected to a Subject (authority in some form)), of inter-individual and self-recognition, and a guarantee of the reality of the individual as individual in a world of things (1971: 169). There is an analysis of a key ISA, the Christian faith and its rituals (1971: 165–70), but the main thesis of the paper is that it is not the political ideologies of bourgeois society that are fundamental but rather the unsuspected 'educational ideological apparatuses'. Althusser in this analysis draws on the anthropological and theological concept of ritual and applies it indiscriminately across a range of activities, particularly to 'rituals of ideological recognition' (1971: 162). But it is a short step to begin to consider the higher educational institutions as a crucial site of struggle, as Althusser did in his analysis of the student revolt of May 1968 (Macciocchi, 1973: 301–20). Subsequently it is also a short step for

Althusserians after Althusser to consider that there may be a 'theoretical state apparatus' (Zizek, 2001: 225ff.).

To retrace steps: included in Althusser's original ISAs paper is a brief historical sketch of the evolution of the French social formation. In the pre-Revolution period the social criticism was located in an anti-clerical and anti-religious struggle, since it was the religious ideological apparatus which embraced a range of functions including education. The French Revolution effectively transferred power to the new 'merchant-capitalist bourgeoisie' and replaced the old repressive apparatus with a new one, the popular army. The struggle was a much more protracted one in the field of education itself, involving a 'long class struggle between the landed aristocracy and the industrial bourgeoisie throughout the nineteenth century for the establishment of bourgeois hegemony of the functions formerly fulfilled by the Church'. Althusser's analysis of this struggle was that although the bourgeoisie could accommodate itself to various types of political regimes in France, it principally 'relied on the new political, parliamentary-democratic, ideological State apparatus [the Third Republic] to conduct its struggle against the Church and wrest its ideological functions away from it (1971: 144). Normally the transition from feudalism to bourgeois society sees a displacement between the alignment of institutions: from the dominance of the Church-Family to that of the School-Family alliance (1971: 146).

If the transition from feudalism to capitalism involved this kind of social reorganisation of institutions, there would essentially be a further displacement in the transition from capitalism to communism, and this would involve the abolition of the 'bourgeois school' and the 'bourgeois family'. Althusser did not though outline what the new alignment would have to be. He was, he said, trying to rectify the thesis that the epistemological break occurs in pure thought, through the action of pure reason, and subject only to the principles of a logic of discovery, by placing theory within the framework of power and the State. The framework as elaborated by Althusser was defended and developed by Althusser's former students Baudelot and Establet, and by Bourdieu. It came under direct criticism from another of Althusser's former students, Foucault.

Foucault's alternative to state theory

The main impact of Foucault's intervention among sociologists and Marxists has been to question the role and value in analysis of all 'systemic' approaches, whether sanctions are seen as primary means of social integration, or whether the 'social formation' is conceived as a totality in which the State (RSAs and ISAs) is always linked to objective functions in class antagonisms. In Foucault's analysis of the transition from feudalism to capitalism, if these terms can be applied (since Foucault is also close to Durkheim), this is thrown into question in a number of ways: genealogy, a key dimension of Marx's approach, becomes a crucial form of analysis and detached from a theory of social system reproduction; the very idea of theory changes its nature, for it is not longer the site of a quest for laws, no longer engaged in a search for a system of functions, and no longer a domain in which the patterns of overdetermination are the analytic concern. Indeed the role and importance of system agents (class, class fractions, etc.) lose their centrality and one of the aims of the project is to destabilise terms that have long been taken for granted, either through redefinition (e.g. power) or through re-coinage (e.g. governance and governmentality).

Foucault's objective here was to confront what he saw as the dead-end that theoretical Marxism in particular had reached, and to challenge state theory with the force of a real 'complexity' capable of halting easy or mechanical prophecy or guarantees of truth. What has emerged – and this might be seen as inherent in the logic of Foucault's projects – was that discourse analysis is detached from the problem of 'non-discursive practices', and the analysis of power is abstracted from social struggles or of social institutions.

To gain a clearer picture of Foucault's attempt to deal with the reality of these problems, it is necessary to emphasise that all his projects deal in various ways with the great divide across the Revolution (say the eighteenth/nineteenth century divide). In this he is always close to Comte and to Marx; they are all constructed in a linear manner, and indeed into fairly clear periods (for example the epistemes of *The Order of Things*) yet they all tend to make a critique of the traditional Marxist formulae. For example, in his lecture on Governmentality, Foucault explicitly criticises Althusser's reductive notion of the State to a functioning mechanism (reproducing the relations of production), and the consequence of making the State 'absolutely essential as a target needing to be attacked and occupied.' He adds that 'the State, no more today than at any other time ... does not have this unity, this individuality, this rigorous functionality, nor, frankly, this importance' (in Burchell et al., 1991: 103).

Foucault's analyses construct genealogies. They have the appearance of sequences which typically cross the divide of the French Revolution. They all end well before the present, often in the mid-nineteenth century, and this is reflected in Foucault's methodology. Whereas Comte thought we could know with certainty the future state, and Durkheim was sure that we could know the present one, Foucault holds in *The Archaeology of Knowledge* we can never even know the present, only the past. But does Foucault, in constructing his genealogies, suggest that he is studying a progressive movement in history parallel to Comte and Marx? It is very clear that Foucault's position is no simple endorsement of the progressive claims for these sequences: there is no immanent 'progression' between the states, there is no end point, no imminent higher stage. There are, however, conflictual tendencies: 'disciplinary normalizations come into ever greater conflict with the juridical systems of sovereignty' (in Burchell et al., 1991: 108); it was from the military camp in the mid-eighteenth century that the model of the panopticon arose (*Discipline and Punish* p. 171), and 'by means of such surveillance, disciplinary power became an "integrated" system, linked from the inside to the economy' (p. 176). Not surprisingly, Foucault refers to the Napoleonic period, and I quote at greater length:

> The importance, in historical mythology, of the Napoleonic character probably derives from the fact that it is at the point of the junction of the monarchical, ritual exercise of sovereignty and the hierarchical, permanent exercise of indefinite discipline ... At the moment of its full blossoming, the disciplinary society still assumes with the Emperor the old aspect of the power of the spectacle ... the ultimate figure ... by which the pomp of sovereignty, the necessarily spectacular manifestations of power, were extinguished one by one in the daily exercise of surveillance ... in which the vigilance of intersecting gazes was soon to render useless both the eagle and the sun. (p. 217).

The way out of this new 'society of normalization' is not a return to right and sovereignty, but towards the possibility of a new form of right, 'one which must indeed be anti-disciplinarian, but one at the same time liberated from the principle of sovereignty' (in Burchell et al., 1991: 108).

There remain many basic problems with the legacy of Foucault's intervention, as I discuss in the next chapter. It has not become any clearer what this alternative actually signifies, let alone how it could be realised except at the level of the spiritual government of the self. Since Foucault endorsed their monumental two-volume study *Capitalism and Schizophrenia* (1977, 1988) perhaps Deleuze and Guattari pointed to a solution.

Deleuze and Guattari: segmentarity and fascism

Deleuze wrote an enthusiastic essay on structuralism ('A quoi reconnaît-on le structuralisme?' (1973: 299), in which he concluded that structuralism constituted the crucial locus of theoretical 'productivity of our epoch' (1973: 334). Deleuzian structuralism was to find its way into another important variation of social theory. This variant is curious since it develops its ideas via a return to the sociology of Tarde, and explicitly in a rejection of Durkheim's idea of causation. In Tarde we have the theory of 'imitation' as 'the propagation of a flow' (Deleuze and Guattari, 1988: 219), and an assertion of the principle of segment over organic whole: 'segmentarity is inherent to all the strata composing us' (1988: 208). Deleuze and Guattari realise that this idea implies another version of anthropologisation: 'Why', they ask, 'return to the primitives when it is a question of our own life?' Their answer is that segmentarity is not a prerogative of primitive societies, but modern states are no less segmentary (1988: 209). The question, they insist, is not one of an alternative centralisation. The biological analogy is false as well, since the brain, they say incautiously, is 'itself is a worm' (1988: 210). The political system implies working subsystems, and technology works not through specialisation by through a 'segmentary division of labour'. Thus conceptually, the key distinction is that the primitive system is a 'flexible' segmentary system but the modern one is 'rigid'.

What is curious about the way that this idea is developed is that the theory of the division between spiritual and temporal powers is reintroduced (perhaps under the influence of Virilio's Catholicism) and is combined with the segmentalism not of Tarde but perhaps of Herbert Spencer (who theorised poly-segmentalism in doubly and triply compounded forms). Deleuze and Guattari add to this cocktail the notion of coding and overcoding for different levels in a conception which analyses the relation between abstract and temporal state, and the virulence of the war machine which arises externally to them (Virilio). Thus the tripartite scheme: first, primitive segmentarity of 'territorial and lineal segmentations'; second, the state apparatus which is realised as 'a rigid line, which brings about a dualist organization of segments, a concentricity of circles in resonance of a generalized overcoding'; and third, a war machine 'marked by decoding and deterritorialization' (Deleuze and Guattari, 1988: 222). Totalitarianism is that conservative state in which the abstract machine becomes identical with the State apparatus itself. Fascism, on the other hand, is a 'suicidal' war machine which takes over the State, driving it to 'total war': 'the totalitarian state, which does its utmost to seal all possible lines of flight, fascism is constructed on an intense line of flight' (1988: 230).

For Foucault, in his Preface to the first volume of *Capitalism and Schizophrenia*, Deleuze and Guattari proposed a new ethics 'to the non-fascist life'. At the end of the second volume it is clear that this should have been extended to both the non-fascist and 'to the non-totalitarian life'. And this would have meant surely not a return to the primitive condition of polysegmentalism, as Foucault seemed to imply, to 'develop action, thought, and desires by proliferation ... not by subdivision and pyramidal hierarchization' (Deleuze and Guattari, 1977: xiii), but a strategy that deals with the abstract Machine, the State, and the war machine. This pushes the problem back still further and implies a political and a 'spiritual' project since fascism is not the only form of overcoding. It is in fact only the particular form of what might be termed a neo-Marxist return to the problematic Durkheim, Spencer and Comte: to the question of the relation between institutions, here 'abstract machine' (the spiritual power), the 'State' (the temporal power) and the 'war machine' (it was Spencer who took war out of Comte's evolutionary stages and made it potential State of any stage). But once this institutional problematic re-emerges with a revamped concept of Virilio's 'the war machine', it is clear that Tarde's – at base anthropological – model was a detour, since we return not to a body without organs (i.e. empty or full segmentalism) but to a problem of the specific complexity and functions of organs in the social body (society is not doubly or triply compounded from isomorphic segments). This new theory attempts to indicate ways in which a movement can avoid totalitarianism and fascism as it becomes a revolutionary force.

Deleuze and Guattari, as Marxists, here seem to revive Sorel's notion of 'active minorities' so despised by Mauss. All great innovations, whether left or right, come from proliferation: even 'fascism is inseparable from proliferation focuses in interaction, which skip from point to point' (1988: 101). But this can be read, they say, also to suggest that 'the power of minorities is not measured by their capacity to ... make themselves be felt within the majority system, but to bring to bear the force of the non-denumerable sets ... even if they imply new axioms or, beyond that, a new axiomatic' (1988: 471). This is quite a different perspective from the one that works simply with class power, for 'what is proper to the minority is to assert a power of the denumerable, even if that minority is composed of a single member' (1988: 470). But if revolutionary class power is involved, then they assert that there is another agenda today: that 'of constituting a war machine capable of countering the world war machine by other means' (1988: 472).

This position is not simply a logic of socialism, nor a 'dispersion or fragmentation', but a logic of resistance to 'the peace of generalised terror' by a genuine revolutionary movement, one that situates itself at the base, within multiplicities and in the 'undecidable'. Deleuze has repeated these ideas several times. He insists in clarification, that the idea of the 'war machine' has 'nothing to do with war but to do with a particular way of occupying, taking up, space-time, or inventing a new space-time: revolutionary movements (people don't take enough account, for instance, of how the PLO has had to invent a space-time in the Arab world), but artistic movements too, are war machines in this sense'. Deleuze stresses, again, 'war machines tend much more to be revolutionary, or artistic, rather than military' (Deleuze, 1995: 172, 33).[3]

Conclusions

'Structuralism' was certainly a label, and it is still in use (see Serres, 1995b: 37). Althusser and Foucault dissociated themselves from it, but the label has stuck, as it has to Kristeva. So has the tendency associated with this movement to adopt terms which suggested the 'death of man', 'anti-humanism' in theory, 'process without a subject', the 'death of the author' and so on. This is in keeping with the movement's aims, which were not only to promote a scientific logic in the analysis of the social, whether it be in history, sociology, or in literature or philosophy, but also, as Wernick reminds us, to promote a specific kind of ideological practice, to induce in the coming society a new form of scientific ideology (Wernick, 2001: 231; Althusser and Balibar, 1970: 131). But Foucault, Deleuze and Guattari also managed to fashion an alternative structuralist politics developed at first as an antifascist micropolitics. Yet in later writings it could be seen to presage a general eclectic theory of political and social forms.

There was another outcome of structuralism, which reached its height with the structuralist literary methodology of Barthes (1967, 1985) and Baudrillard ([1968] 1996c). As soon as the structuralist current began to fade, Baudrillard turned against it in a number of sharp critiques. The logic of these critiques, as I discuss in the next chapter, led to another shift into a more anthropological problematic and this involved a radical re-conceptualisation not only of the 'social' but also of 'theory' itself.

Notes

1 He mentions Cavaillés, Bachelard and Hyppolite.

2 This angered Miller, who thought his concept had been 'stolen' – Althusser changed the term to 'structural causality' and passed the concept into general currency. Althusser referred to this as a 'ridiculous incident' in later reflections (1993: 209).

3 Was feminism completely absent from this perspective? Not quite. Woman? 'we all have to become that' (1988: 470, and see discussion of this demand by Braidotti, and Grosz, in Boundas and Olkowski, 1994).

13

Radical Theory and the End of the Social

> What theory can do is to defy the world to be more: more objective ... It has meaning only in terms of this exorcism. The distance theory takes is not that of retreat, but of exorcism. It thus takes on the power of a fatal sign, even more inexorable than reality ... (Baudrillard, 1988: 100)

After existential and then structural Marxism, theory fell for a time under the hegemony of neo-Nietzscheanism. One of the leading thinkers in this current was Baudrillard. Like Bataille, Baudrillard was an outsider, or a latecomer to the scene. In 1966, at the age of 37, he finally got into university teaching 'by an indirect route' (Baudrillard, 1993a: 19). By this time he was known as a brilliant and prolific translator, German to French, translating the major works of Peter Weiss, Brecht, Marx and Engels, and Wilhelm Muhlmann's important study of millenarian movements. He was to forge one of the leading styles of post-Marxist theory.[1]

Baudrillard's trajectory through social theory

Baudrillard's first published essays were written for *Les Temps modernes* in 1962–3 on literary themes. Leaving German literature, Baudrillard moved towards sociology under the teaching first of Henri Lefebvre and then the decisive influence of Roland Barthes. From 1967 Baudrillard was associated with the journal *Utopie* which was close to, though without organisational ties with, the situationist movement. From 1969–73 he taught sociology at Nanterre and was attached to the Centre d'Etudes des Communications de Masse, at this critical time of the confrontation with McLuhan in media theory. From 1975 he worked with Virilio for about fifteen years on the journal *Traverses*. From the same year he began to teach regularly in the USA. The journals he edited were not associated with any political organisation but were engaged in radical and critical cultural theory on the radical left. Later he was to say that the years 'at Nanterre in the sixties and seventies were some of the best years. Once these were over we mourned' (1993a: 20). He presented his doctoral Habilitation at the Sorbonne in February 1986 and retired from the University in 1987.

Baudrillard's formation was therefore decisively influenced by his wide reading of German literature, philosophy and social theory in a meeting of Marxist and Nietzschean traditions, recapitulating many of the themes that had emerged in the work of Bataille a generation before. With the radical emergence of the theory of the system of objects and the consumer society, he then made a radical shift, as Bataille had done, towards an anthropological position against modernism (including Marxism and structuralism). It was from this perspective that he launched his famous confrontations with writers such as Michel Foucault (1987), and cultural critiques such as Baudrillard's famous attack on the architecture of the Pompidou Centre ('Beaubourg Effect' [in Baudrillard, 1994b]), political critiques of the French Socialist and Communist Parties (2001b: 91–119), and in the end an attack on the continued viability of the social sciences themselves with his thesis of the 'end of the social' (1983).

His challenge to modernism led him in this period to be identified as the founder of a theory of postmodernity. Again like Bataille, from his earliest writings it has been evident that he always had time and space to write on politics and political ideas. The collection entitled *La Gauche divine: chronique des années 1977–1984* (in 2001b) contains Baudrillard's analysis of the failure of the Socialist and Communist Parties to confront the problems of the post-1968 political conditions, and *Ecran total* (1997b) collects Baudrillard's writing for the radical newspaper *Libération*, over the decade from 1987, including his provocative analysis of the Gulf War (Baudrillard, 1995). Two theses dominate these political analyses. The first is that proletarian revolutionary transition is no longer on the agenda in Western societies, and second, that this new situation is one of involution within the boundaries of the West with real 'events' occurring only on the fault line (e.g. Bosnia) of this culture (see Cushman and Mestrovic, 1996), or as an 'absolute event' imposed on it from without as with September 11.

Baudrillard's work draws on a large number of sources. He himself has identified Nietzsche as the most profound. It is evident that there is a continuing engagement with and use of modern literature, from Kafka to Ballard, as well as those key theorists he identified in texts of the 1970s: Mauss and Bataille, Saussure, Benjamin and McLuhan. Baudrillard's writings in the 1990s were no longer aimed at providing a 'critical analysis' of modern and postmodern culture. Baudrillard, in an ultimate challenge, tried in various ways to develop 'fatal theory': philosophers have always interpreted a disenchanted world, the point today is to make it even more enigmatic. Some of his interests here have led him to adopt some of the paradoxical formulations of recent science with the result that he has been identified as one of the contemporary 'intellectual impostures' – a description he, with his usual wit, embraced enthusiastically.

Thus Baudrillard, continuing the theoretical tradition's radical rejection of the bourgeois-democratic polity, seems particularly sensitive to alterations of the current cultural and political conjuncture. His writing is reflexive to a high degree, not only with respect to the changing effectiveness of concepts and ideas, but also to the forms of the interventions themselves. Facing the defeat of the May 1968 revolutionary movement, his writing rethinks radical theory in a way that challenges the cultural, technological and political forms of the 'advanced' societies. For many radicals of the 1960s the option has been either to retrench into a fundamentalist Marxism, or to adopt the framework of the consumer society with qualifications (to make it more democratic, more ecologically aware, to promote a postmodern form of multicultural tolerance, etc.). In this context Baudrillard provides an alternative which regards these variations as disastrously involuted forms of a *ressentiment* culture in which a secret *stratégie du pire* holds sway. He is therefore an outsider whose ideas are profoundly at odds with contemporary progressive opinion, be it socialist, liberal, or feminist.

Sign-exchange and the theory of consumer society

It seems clear that there are three or four major themes in Baudrillard's work. The first is a consequence of his early writings on the object and sign-exchange. These ideas, following on from the early lead of Lyotard, have been taken up principally by those, such as Lipovetsky and Maffesoli, who wish to develop a line of Marxism in opposition to structural and particularly Althusserian and Bourdieusian theory (the latter continues to stress the importance of modes of economic production and Marx's theory of capitalism). Baudrillard, along with many others of course, suggested that the evolution of consumer society was a crucial development rendering orthodox Marxism obsolete. Baudrillard's attempt to theorise sign-exchange as an evolution of commodity exchange received considerable critical attention. The notion of hyperreality, especially in relation to American culture, was however bitterly contest by Marxists in particular because it suggested that successful political class struggle and dialectical progression were no longer possible. Baudrillard's second theme – that of the superiority of symbolic exchange as a revolutionary principle – led him into an oppositional stance to virtually all the major critical theorists. His third theme – that of the analysis of seduction, fatal strategies and evil, as secret forms within the semiotic cultures themselves – gave rise to great misunderstanding and further notoriety. He now became the object of praise or vilification as 'high priest of postmodernism'. The theory of the fourth order simulacral forms has fallen on deaf ears.

The first theme, that of the theory of the object system, fuses critical structuralism (Baudrillard's *System of Objects* and Roland Barthes's *The Fashion System* were contemporaneous), with a situationist perspective on the society of the spectacle (Debord). It was nevertheless conceived in a problematic in which Baudrillard could still refer to capitalism and class struggle. His debt to Lukacs and Marcuse is clear in his critique of that form of Althusserian Marxism which had insisted on the universality of the concept of mode of production and the principle of overdetermined contradiction. The most important aspects of Baudrillard's position lay in the fact that it contested the ahistorical analysis of capitalist society and at the same time confronted the economic reductionism of much of orthodox Marxism. Baudrillard's critical discussion of Marxism also highlighted the fact that its major thinkers had already pointed to radical shifts in the nature of capitalist organisation. He pointed particularly to Lenin's notion of the importance of the transition from market to monopoly capitalism. Baudrillard gave this transition an extremely radical interpretation: it initiated the determination of social relation by the semiotic code (Baudrillard, 1975).

But the theory of the object as a relation of sign-exchange pushed his theorising towards aesthetics. At one point (Baudrillard, 1981: 185) he argued that the 'object' emerged specifically with the work of the Bauhaus. In other words, the transition from the commodity form proper towards the object form was essentially a coupling of function (use value) with aesthetic value. This development of the analysis of the commodity evidently departed from the theory of reification and fetishism in important ways. The key development was certainly the attempt to apply semiotics rather than phenomenology to the analysis of exchange. Clearly implicit in Baudrillard's interpretation is a reliance on Saussure's definition of the sign, but Baudrillard was already theorising the sign and sign-exchange as historically associated with a particular stage of the development of capitalism when it was discovered that Saussure had also worked on but not completed a study of anagrams in classical literature of antiquity (Starobinski's book on this was published in 1971 [1979]). With this clear opposition between the anagram and the sign, Baudrillard was able to provide content to his previously somewhat gestural notion of the ambivalence of the symbol.

Certainly the more orthodox Marxists – Bourdieu, but particularly the Althusserians – rejected both the explicitly 'structuralist' methodology of this style of analysis and the general theory of consumer society. Baudrillard's interpretation contributed to a form of analysis which had much wider resonance (parallels are to be found in writers as far apart as Marcuse, Debord, Barthes and Lyotard), suggesting that the moment of proletarian revolution had passed (Gorz) and that with mass consumerism a new form of social integration had evolved within the capitalist order. Althusserian Marxism posed the question in terms of ideological state apparatuses and the new crisis of legitimation in the universities in conditions of a worldwide crisis of capitalism. However it still held to the view that the determinant and revolutionary contradiction was between capital and labour. Baudrillard's reply was to suggest that reinforcing the economic and political organisation of the proletariat in the new conditions of mass consumerism facilitated the neutralisation of the proletariat as a class within late capitalist forms, since the principal site of integration was then not confronted (Baudrillard, 1985).

From social theory to radical theory

Thus Baudrillard's writings are made up of a number of projects which are coherently articulated within the idea of the double spiral (on one side the symbol; on the other the sign). This makes it possible to identify four sets of theoretical writing. The first concerns the quasi-Marxist analysis of the commodity-object, sign-exchange and consumer society. The second concerns the theory of symbolic orders and symbolic exchange and has a strong anthropological character entailing a radicalisation of the notion of the gift and death. The third set comes back to focus on contemporary culture but is no longer framed in a base-superstructure model. The new analysis relies on the concepts of seduction, fate and evil drawn from anthropological perspectives and employed, even methodologically, alongside a surprising survival from French sociology, the concept of pathology (Baudrillard, 1993c). The fourth set concerns the transition of cultures from third to fourth order simulacral forms from a position identified as that of impossible exchange. There is a movement in Baudrillard's work from that of critical structuralism and Marxism, with its desire to expose the alienated workings of the modern social system and its culture, to a theory of the object as pure sign and to a mode of writing that is more poetic, 'fatal', enigmatic, fragmented, embracing the paradoxes produced in the advanced sciences. In Baudrillard's terms, the very evolution of the sign in Western cultures through the genealogy of its various simulacral forms produces its own ironic self-destruction. This situation provides new opportunities and calls for a metamorphosis in the form of radical theory.

The symbolic order

Baudrillard's second thematic, which was a logical development of the theory of the symbol, led to a radicalisation of the notion of the symbolic order embracing directly the ideas of Bataille. For example in his collection *For a Critique of the Political Economy of the Sign*, ([1972] 1981) he argued that '[p]resent theory posits three essential tasks, beginning from and going beyond Marxist analysis'. First it requires 'a radical critique of use value'. Second, because 'Marx offers only a critical theory of exchange value ... [t]he critical theory of use value, signifier, and signified remains to be developed'. Third, there was an urgent need for a 'theory of symbolic exchange' (1981: 128–9). Baudrillard's critique of Marxism was published as *The Mirror of Production* ([1973] 1975), while the theory of symbolic exchange was published as *Symbolic Exchange and Death* ([1976] 1993b).

In the latter Baudrillard wrote a critical assessment of the contribution of Bataille to anthropological theory, emphasising that this contribution was on the threshold of a revolutionary new position in its analysis of 'excess, ambivalence, gift, sacrifice, expenditure, and the paroxysm' (1993b: 155). Although Bataille's position has weaknesses, according to Baudrillard, it provides nevertheless 'the opportunity to disturb every economy' and the 'premonition' of new analytic possibilities. Baudrillard's studies of *Seduction* (1990a), *Fatal Strategies* (1990b) and *The Transparency of Evil* (1993c), evidently attempt to realise these possibilities. Another important general organising principle can be detected from 1976 onwards: namely the schema introduced in *Symbolic Exchange and Death*, charting the genealogy of cultural simulacral forms which run 'parallel to the successive mutations in the law of value since the renaissance' (1993b: 50–86).

It seems that the preparation of this line of analysis was to some extent inspired by the work of Foucault on madness. Baudrillard's genealogy of forms of relations to the dead parallels Foucault's analysis of the role of sequestration and asylums in the genealogy of madness. For Baudrillard, death is a fundamental symbolic form. His analysis follows closely its genealogy as revealed in relation to the body. He charts carefully the movement from early forms in which the dead body is retained in the group to those in which there is a hierarchy of those who pass, under the control of priests, to heaven. His analysis of the cemetery or the necropolis charts the social distance between the living and the dead body. After this period of sequestration the dead, like the mad, are subject to the vicissitudes of civilisation.

When Foucault published his famous *Discipline and Punish*, with its theory of modern forms of power and surveillance, Baudrillard regarded this as a major turning point in Foucault's work. He wrote a stunning review of it published as 'Forget Foucault' in which he argued that Foucault's thought itself had been ensnared in the system of micro power and control which he seemed to be analysing (Baudrillard, 1987). It became evident from this moment on that Baudrillard was to regard structuralism, post-structuralism and deconstructionism as complicit with the code of modern consumer culture and unable to confront it. Baudrillard also lamented Saussure's own failure to develop the opposition to the sign in an adequate theory of the symbol, just as he lamented Freud's and Lacan's universalisation of a particular form of the Oedipal complex, and Lévi-Strauss's failure to develop a symbolic theory of the savage mind (Baudrillard, 1993b). Lyotard retorted that Baudrillard had produced yet another myth of the primitive.

Baudrillard, however, did not stay within the ambit of the theory of symbolic exchange for very long, at least according to the Habilitation presentation. In the three works of the next period, that is *Seduction, Fatal Strategies* and *The Transparency of Evil*, Baudrillard tried to demonstrate the power of fatal over critical theory. The logic of this change of position seems determined by the very loss of revolutionary agency by social forces. No longer aligned with the active alienated subject, Baudrillard concluded that power of agency had passed to the side of the object. What was strikingly effective in Baudrillard's return to the analysis of current cultures in the 1980s was his general proposition that social checks and balances (the ideal of liberal containment of power) and the framework of dialectical progressive development (the ideal of revolutionary sublation) were outmoded logics, and as he himself expressed it, 'our societies have passed beyond this limit point' (Baudrillard, 1988b: 82).

The new situation, he claimed, was not principally one of unremitting mass homogenisation, though this was occurring in the exemplary logic of cloning and replication, and what he identified as the culture of indifference and impatience (homogenisation entailed the disappearance of the historical event: even war could no longer take place [Baudrillard, 1995]). The dominant logic was, however, exponential – a logic driven by the liberation of energies. Baudrillard began to identify the emergence of extreme phenomena against the background of indifference. Two linked propositions were developed at this point. First, the fatal strategy of the object could be seen as a form of intensification: the world was in the grip of the delirious passion of the object. Hyperreal phenomena were just one form of this ecstatic movement of things. More than sexual in the *stratégie du pire*: pornography. More than fat: obesity. But second, with the liberation of energies and the deregulation of balances, Baudrillard also identified the disintegration of boundaries. This led to the emergence of what he called transpolitical phenomena. This process concerned not the intensification of logics, but the intensification of indistinctions. Thus more than sexual: transsexual. More than historical: transhistorical. More than aesthetic: transaesthetic. More than genetic: transgenetic. Baudrillard had already noted that objects were no longer made from traditional materials but new homogenised media like plastics. At this juncture even the boundaries of objects (including those of species) were in the process of dissolution.

The orders of simulacra

A key element of Baudrillard's work has therefore been a crucial contribution to the theory of the symbolic order: exchange, forms, time, etc., and the refusal to make a discipline boundary between anthropology and social theory, indeed to confront sociology with radical anthropology (Genosko, 1998). In Baudrillard's early writing the simple ambivalence of the symbol was contrasted with the univocality of the sign. The radicalisation of his theory became clear in his view that the symbolic order is not simply primordial, but is the superior form, even as it is destroyed by modern rationalities. It is characterised in Baudrillard's view by four significant features. First, as opposed to the sign, it does not organise itself on the reality principle, since the world is apprehended as fable and narrative. Second, the apprehension of time is non-linear, non-accumulative, non-progressive, since the narrative and the gift are both fatal and reversible. Third, other cultures are not apprehended as belonging to a homogeneous world system of differences but to the order of radical otherness, since the symbolic order (based on the rule) is not parallel to the culture of human rights (based on law). Fourth, its relation to the order of things is not possessive, the symbolic order is articulated on metamorphosis in ritual time and space. What is new in Baudrillard's version of the symbolic order is that it is active, dynamic, strategic and based on challenge of radical illusion.

Baudrillard suggests straightaway that the latent idea, the 'anthropological dream' which haunts the modern object, is already apparent as: 'the dream of a sacrificial logic, of gift, expenditure, potlach, "devil's share" consumption, symbolic exchange' (Baudrillard, 1988b: 11). Baudrillard's work gives increasing emphasis to the symbol which becomes the basis of a position which 'generalizes the Marxist critique of capital and commodity in a radical anthropological critique of Marx's postulates' (1988b: 78). Thus in *Symbolic Exchange and Death*, the analysis steps outside of the traditional Marxist frame of political economy, since the radical basis of opposition to capital, and indeed the culture of the sign, is identified as the 'symbolic' and the 'superior authenticity of exchanges' (1988b: 78–9). Baudrillard's strategy aims at the revolutionary subversion of the distinctive oppositions of Western cultures: life and death, masculine and feminine, subject and object, etc. His thesis is organised around the idea that the fundamental term is death, since what happens with death as a form tells us most about the way life itself is conceived.

It is clear that this view of 'primitive culture' reverses many of the assumptions found in the work of sociologists like Max Weber, who sometimes refer to these cultures as superstitious, passive, conservative and traditional. It is one of the many 'banal' illusions of the semiotic cultures that they are progressive, active, accumulative. Baudrillard gives Comte's analysis of rationalisation a radical Nietzschean reading through an analysis of simulacral forms. With the emergence of the idea of the real world, and the ideology of the real (Majastre, 1996: 209), there emerge the cultures of the sign (in the Saussurean manner: signifier/signified/referent-real). This introduces a split in the semiotic cultures between the representation of the meaning, say of death, and the idea of real biological death. This split becomes a generalised premise of the existence of all phenomena subject to objective and scientific investigation. It introduces the dimension of the difference between the true and the false, but also disturbs illusion by introducing the opposition between the real and the simulacrum.

According to Baudrillard's genealogy, a first order of simulacra can be seen in the representations of the body and the world in the renaissance period: the model of the human automaton, in *trompe l'oeil* forms, and represented in media like stucco. With the explosive industrial revolution and the beginnings of mass production, a second order of simulacral forms comes into existence as mass reproduction: the human is represented in crude mechanical robotics, and mass (re)production of commodities in new media like plastic. But this second order is still based on the principle of utility, where production and reproduction arise from an original hand-crafted object. This gives way with the implosive advent of the consumer society to sign-exchange and the emergence of the 'system of objects' – a society dominated by computerised mass media images. Baudrillard's challenging theory is that this affects all domains: relation to the order of things is not only subject to mass media, particularly televisual, mediation (which shifts cultural phenomena into the hyperreal), but also with the matrix revolution (which shifts simulacra into simulational forms). The transition from this third order to fourth order simulacral forms arrives with the full long-term impact of the information revolution which leads to the greatest rupture of all, an apocalpyse which occurs without protagonist or victim, neither explosive nor implosive: the postmodernisation and the virtualisation of the world.

It is important to note that the genealogy of simulacral forms is not a simple historical procession as evidenced by the series of writings which might be termed the notebooks, and which includes the *Cool Memories* series (Baudrillard, 1990c, 1996a, 1997a) and the American notebook called *America* (Baudrillard, 1988a). Baudrillard clearly thinks in terms of variations in the way each culture evolves in relation to his theoretical genealogy. In the case of America, for example, he adopts McLuhan's thesis that American culture is characterised by the absence of second order simulacra; in other words, it has a completely different form of modernity from that of Europe. It is evident from the *Cool Memories* series more generally that even within Europe, Baudrillard's analyses do not homogenise. The cultures of France, Italy, Spain, etc. are all treated as individualities in their own right. Given that Baudrillard has become one of the most travelled theorists, and not only maintains the practice of the journal but also the camera (his photographs also maintain this view of cultural individuality [Baudrillard, 1998c]), any reading of Baudrillard's contribution must come to terms with the great diversity of the forms of his work, which includes a volume of poetry (1978) and the vast range and detail of his analyses.

Radical uncertainty

The final theme in Baudrillard's work is the theory of the fourth order forms. Central to this theory is the continuation of the analysis of the fate of reality, objects and exchange. If the world has indeed escaped the frameworks of regulating balances, then events and phenomena follow a delirious course in a radically new space. Here Baudrillard draws increasingly on the language of the advanced sciences, particularly where the relation of subject and object has become problematic. The structures of time and space are no longer Euclidean; subject and object are no longer independent. It is as if, he suggests, for a period in the history of the sciences, the object was caught unawares by theory (Baudrillard, 1988b: 87). Today the object is no longer content to remain passive in relation to the subject. From a world of rigorous structural determinations, the current situation is one of radical indeterminacy of fundamental principles and knowledge. In this new, 'postmodern' situation, exchange itself becomes increasingly difficult. In consequence, he argues, analysis must be made from a position of 'impossible exchange', recognising the full force of the requirement for a new kind of theory appropriate to a world in radical uncertainty beyond the matrix, one that deals with unique objects, singularities.

Conclusion

It is now becoming clear that Baudrillard has been trying to analyse and theorise the fourth order since the mid 1980s, while most commentaries have remained stubbornly within his concept of hyperreality and the code.

It is also becoming more evident that if Baudrillard does have a concept of postmodernity, it does not have the third order as its object. Indeed it might well be that the break between third and fourth order phenomena is for Baudrillard the most significant one and the one that marks the rupture with hypermodernity. Yet Baudrillard's analysis suggests that this most fundamental transition is not marked by any visible revolutionary event, and as it becomes accomplished it therefore becomes the 'perfect crime'. Unlike Virilio, for example, for whom the apocalypse in the real may arrive with a 'general accident', for Baudrillard of the 'third' order the last judgement had already occurred but the messiah (or the Revolution), missed the appointment (Baudrillard, 1987). However, in the fourth order there is not even an appointment: 'for mutants there can no longer be any Last Judgement … for what body will one resurrect?' (Baudrillard, 1988b: 51).

Note

1 This chapter draws on 'Jean Baudrillard' in A. Elliott and B.S. Turner (2001: 194–204).

14

Fin-de-Cycle: Time of Counter-strategies

> The greatness of a philosophy is measured by the nature of the events to which its concepts summon us or that it enables us to release in concepts. (Deleuze and Guattari, 1994: 34)

In the first cycle Comte coined two essential concepts, sociology and *altruism*; in the second cycle Durkheim added the word *anomie*. The crisis of theory in the 1970s – when the effervescence of May 1968 had subsided – led to a widespread sense of 'logics of disintegration' fully equivalent to that felt at the end of the 1930s, as if things had fallen short of their goals (Dews, 1987). In the *fin-de-cycle* perhaps anomie can occur in another form, that which Baudrillard proposed to call *hypertelia* to denote the movement of things *beyond* their ends. The mature Comte of the 1850s lived the serious but excessive visionary life of a sociocratic priest, writing his last works as if living, posthumously, in 1927. Althusser's own late writings have been described by Derrida as a paradoxical development, one that was 'even more suicidal than the [Communist] Party' (Kaplan et al., 1993: 210). And Derrida himself proposes a form of hypertelic messianic thought in which anticipation supersedes the arrival – the hope is that the messiah will never arrive. Indeed if the messiah is encountered, Derrida's word is to say: 'Don't come' (Caputo, 1997: 245). For Baudrillard, we are beyond the apocalypse, it has already happened, but the messiah missed the appointment.

Today, the widespread shift from the social science idiom to the idiom of neo-fetishism in the sense I have identified can be found in the works of Bataille, Baudrillard, Barthes, Lyotard, Irigaray, Derrida, Serres, Virilio and others. There is a widespread recognition that social sciences should be tolerant of languages that point up and try to go beyond the limitations of secular scientific rationalism whether simple or complex and epistemological progressivism. On the one hand there is fragmentation (Foucault, Lyotard, Baudrillard), and neo-scholasticism (Bourdieu, Berthelot), on the other a shift towards the sacred, indeed an elective *collège sacré virtuel* (Serres, Derrida, Virilio, Irigaray), even the orgy: sacred (Maffesoli, 1993) and profane (Baudrillard, 1993c).

In the introduction to this book I outlined a method of constructing the three cycles examined in this book. At the end it is possible to indicate what kinds of reaction exist to such totalising ideas in a *fin-de-cycle* phase. They are counter-strategies (which involve a multiplicity of complementary methods in effect) which check on the imaginative construction of the such hypothesised cycles, and act as the principal obstacle which any new cycle has to surmount. They demand more: an activity of deconstruction on the principal strategy even as it is being developed, aiming continually to bring to mind the fact that the cycle is a constructed artificiality, both an abstraction drawn from socio-historical texture and projected quasi-compensation for the 'law of rarity' of theory (Foucault, 1972: 118ff.), without any ultimate ground to appeal to, or to guarantee of, solidity. So this is both a constant process of reminding, and recourse to other ways of thinking and unthinking.

The 'release of elements'

Against the implantation of social theory into the framework of a university discipline, there have been other destinies for theory that have been working to extremes. The first are those movements towards fragmentation which are subsumed under the term postmodern: Lyotard (Gane, N., 2002: 89–112), or deconstruction, Derrida, micropolitics and segmentarity, Deleuze and Guattari and what Foucault calls 'effective history' (Foucault, 1977: 139–64). The key thinker of effective history, according to Foucault, is Nietzsche. Its target, as all critiques of 'historicism' emphasise, is the set of metaphysical presuppositions underpinning any abstract linear 'history'. The critique therefore seems to apply directly to Comte, whose work Nietzsche clearly knew well. Durkheim's critique of Comte's 'historical method' follows an identical critical logic, as does Althusser's critique of Sartre's existential 'historicism'. Sometimes Foucault refers to the target as 'traditional history'. Comte refers to his method as the 'historical method' in an attempt to produce 'scientific history' (sociology), but Durkheim regards this as merely a 'traditional history' writ large, which creates a kind of scientific mythology. The critique searches out the illusions, distortions, errors and, deceptions produced, and 'it ceaselessly multiplies the risks, creates dangers in every area; it breaks down illusory defences; it dissolves the unity of the subject; it releases those elements of itself that are devoted to its subversion and destruction' (Foucault, 1977: 163). The linear abstract method appears to offer the route to well-founded knowledge, here to a progressive theoretical logic. The effective method seems to lead to an unregulated attempt to describe the elements of logical violence established by the first. The first is established by the work of a programmed and bureaucratic realist imagination; the second is a radical utopian nominalism. The second can usurp the first only to become prey to rationalisation in its turn. In fact, it is likely that the first is only ever possible as an attempt to control and discipline a nominalistic revolt that has been too successful. Curved immediacy is tamed into linear homogeneous time, perhaps even the 'smooth' time space that is the object of a war machine, according to Deleuze and Guattari, who see creativity associated with 'undisciplined theory' (Genosko, 1998). The opening to creativity is characterised by the weakening of the 'abstract axiomatic', which permits a reinvigoration of segmentarity, flows against 'abstract over-coding', or in the parallel language of Maffesoli (1996), the 'time of the tribes'.

At the end of the twentieth century, the sense of the need to deconstruct the grand narrative of socialism and sociology eventually succumbed to a method which ran out of whole and intact material on which to be effective, but an Epicurean neo-fetishism lives among the fragments of three decaying cycles of social theory. For Barthes, for example, 'it is a moment at once decadent and prophetic, a moment of gentle apocalypse, a historical moment of the greatest possible pleasure' (in Culler, 2002: 109). Thus a second possibility which also keeps a limit on abstract history is the neo-fetishistic method recommended by Barthes at the level of the text: to find the pleasure of the text and the 'return of the author' – but not the author 'identified by our institutions … [and] not even the biographical hero'. This author 'has no unity … he is a mere plural of "charms", the site of a few tenuous details' (Barthes, 1976: 8). This method reduces 'to a few preferences, a few inflections, let us say: to "biographemes" whose distinctions and mobility might go beyond any fate come to touch, like Epicurean atoms, some future body, destined to the same dispersion … like the relief of hiccoughs … the casual eruption of *another* signifier' (1976: 9). The aim of such a method? To release the 'author' that is evoked in the initial analysis from all moral discourse. Barthes writes: 'I unglue the text from its purpose of guarantee: socialism, faith, evil. Whence … I force the displacement (but not to suppress; perhaps even to accentuate) of the text's social responsibility'(1976: 9). Strictly against Sartrean existential ethics, the aim of this method is not to situate the author into his class, period, culture. Barthes suggests perhaps both a return to Proudhon, that 'today [1971 – MG], there is no language site outside bourgeois ideology … The only possible rejoinder is neither confrontation nor destruction, but only theft: fragment the old text of culture, science, literature, and change its features according to formulae of disguise, as one disguises stolen goods' (1976: 10); and to Bataille: the text can be read 'by the violence that enables it to exceed the laws of that a society, an ideology, a philosophy establish for themselves' (1976: 10).

The third release is the form of humour Bataille and Baudrillard counterpose to that form of ridicule ('laughter excretion', cited by Gasché, 2001) which is nonetheless effective *against dignity* – the serious and pretentious which it leaves in ruins) is a form which is non-cumulative, catastrophic, collapses through reversal into nothing. It is only possible on certain conditions of course, notably when it cannot be, though it risks it, overwhelmed by the serious, and is effective *against identity* – 'nonsense is not the hidden hell of meaning, nor the emulsion of all the repressed and contradictory meanings. It is the meticulous reversibility of every term […] only subjects dispossessed of their identity … are devoted to social reciprocity in laughter' (Baudrillard, 1993b: 232–3).

Towards an elective *collège sacré virtuel*: Serres, Virilio, Irigaray

Although Serres wrote a sharply critical introduction to Comte's *Course in Positive Philosophy* when it was reissued in 1975, he was strangely impressed with the late Comte of the subjective method. Serres said in 1990:

> I found Comte to be more profound than his successors, first as the inventor of sociology, and for having been the first to ask the question about the relations between science and society, and more important, between the histories of science and religion. In this he remains unequaled. (Serres and Latour, 1996: 30)

Certainly most readers do not accept the move that Comte made towards the subjective method, for as Pickering notes, at a crucial point in Comte's writing 'he seemed to be getting lost in a useless accumulation of details. He appeared to be playing with his system, rearranging the parts, redefining his terms, and creating schema after schema for no apparent reason.' Pickering is conventional and normative in her judgement that his 'intellectual games suggest that his hold on reality was slipping' (Pickering, 1993: 686). Serres, on the other hand, sees Comte here as witness to the fact that 'there exists something exterior even to the self-sustaining totality, and the second is founded upon the first. He calls the foundation religious, even if it is no more than the immanence of humanity.' (Serres, 1995b: 453). In effect Serres makes the same journey, and has paid the price of exclusion, for he has attacked at the root, and against Comte, the idea of the progressive and accumulative nature of the sciences – and societies. Paradoxically, Serres is against fragmentation, which is for him 'a by-product of war but equally a technique of conservation. Museums are stuffed with bits and pieces, with disparate members … synthesis requires courage – the audacity of the frail.' Thus it is the large and not the small which is fragile. The ideal is not the system which aims at solidity and permanence, but a synthesis or what Serres calls a *syrrhèse* – 'a confluence … a mobile confluence of fluxes … Clouds of angels passing' (Serres, and Latour, 1996: 122). The aim is other than a ponderous positivism, or theoretical labour and heaviness – invention 'requires rapid intuition and being as light as weightlessness' (1996: 37).

Michel Serres refers without hesitation to the miracle at Lourdes. So does Paul Virilio in his book *The Aesthetics of Disappearance* ([1980] 1991) which mourns the loss of apparitions (Armitage, 2000). Virilio notes that

> for more than a century now children have seen the Virgin *appear*, and the police and religious authorities have had to take down their testimony … [there is] a sort of background against which another designation of meaning suddenly emerges, a background which would be already a kind of *dissolving view*, reminding us of … Paul of Tarsus … all is calm, and yet: *this world as we see it is passing away*. (Virilio, 1991: 37)

He has no hesitation in claiming that the testimony of such a witness is as valuable as any work of the German romantics and idealist philosophers. Indeed he sees a profound unity between the 'simple story' of a young seer, and the 'elaborate tales of the transcendental poets' (1991: 42). One finds here, he says, a 'sort of para-optic aesthetics of the real world, an unusual activity of the senses, usurping their function by chance' (1991: 42). Bernadette's visionary experience is cited as primary evidence of the experience of time:

> I saw poplars beside the torrent and brambles in front of the cave quiver as if the wind was shaking them, but all around nothing moved and suddenly I saw

> something white ... a white girl no bigger than me. She greeted me, bowing. (1991: 38)

Virilio is bitterly critical of the way children are now deprived of their apparitions. Bernadette said of her experience that 'for that moment you'd give a whole lifetime'; Virilio records 'this is exactly what she does by hiding in a convent at Nevers where she dies at age 35' (1991: 39). Nevers is now marked by Virilio's Bunker church. Virilio has subsequently noted the similarity of the experience of being in the grotto at Lourdes and being in a bunker (Virilio and Brausch, 1997: 35).

Virilio muses on the mystery of the bunker. 'As a young man I wondered about the aesthetics of war machines ... I found myself often contemplating a bunker or the silhouette of some submarine seen at a distance, wondering why their polished forms were so inscrutable', he writes. His first reflections related these forms to

> zoomorphism, to metamorphism, but all of that was comparison, imitation and could not satisfy me. Then I believed these forms were inscrutable because they all related to speeds that were different, excessive ... But the over-production of movement implied by war changed the way things looked; the motor, since it relates directly to the state of paradoxical wakefulness replaced the causal idea – that was its revolution; the motor proceeds from the soul. (Virilio, 1991: 103)

The deepest threat is the systematic elimination of genuine religious consciousness (Virilio and Lotringer, 1997: 124). In his *L'Horizon négatif* Virilio specifies the nature of this threat and the military as a false priesthood. It is a struggle between two temporalities: the 'instant' is the warrior, the 'eternal' the priest (Virilio, 1984: 291). The condition of nuclear pure war sees the emergence of the cult of military-scientistic objects, a millenarianism founded as a cargo cult of the arsenal. It is the evocation of a mystical apocalypse through the 'adoration of vehicles'. It is 'the nuclear faith' (1984: 305), a pure parody of religion. Virilio is fighting the war of a new virtual Christian priesthood. Here we do not need the 'charms' of the author in the way Barthes has suggested. The point is that in the modern world, says Virilio, 'children will be as a rule deprived of their apparitions' (Virilio, 1991: 39).

Irigaray's feminism is fought significantly in the symbolic. Modern monotheisms deprived women of their goddesses as the single all-powerful God was enthroned. So 'in seizing hold of the oracle, of truth, the gods-men severed them from their earthly and corporeal roots ... A new logical order was established, censuring women's speech and gradually making it inaudible ... [p]atriarchal traditions have wiped out traces of the mother–daughter genealogies.' This absence is linked to the meaning of virginity. The real significance of virginity is not in its signification as

> defensive or prudish virginity, as some of our profane contemporaries might take it to mean, nor does it signify an allegiance to patriarchal culture and its definition of virginity as an exchange value between men; it signifies the woman's fidelity to her identity and female genealogy. Respect for these female filiations and qualities attests to the sacred character of the home. (Irigaray, 1993: 18–19).

Virginity and motherhood are the spiritual identities which patriarchy has withdrawn from women. Irigaray advocates then a link here between virginity, motherhood and the spiritual:

> Women must develop a double identity: virgins and mothers. At every stage of their lives. Since virginity, no more than female identity, isn't simply given at birth. There's no doubt that we are born virgins. But we also have to become virgins ... For me, becoming a virgin is synonymous with a woman's conquest of the spiritual. (1993: 117)

Foucault: spiritual governance and the rehabilitation of the flesh

Foucault's work on government and 'governmentality' developed out of his courses (which still had an Althusserian 'repressive apparatuses' tone) on 'apparatuses of security'. He notes at the beginning of his 1978 lecture that the modern problem of government arose at what he called

> the crossroads of two processes: the one which, shattering the structures of feudalism, leads to the establishment of the great territorial administrative and colonial states; and that totally different movement which, with the Reformation and Counter-Reformation, raises the issue of how one must be spiritually ruled and led on this earth to achieve eternal salvation. (Foucault, 1991: 87–8)

Very quickly Foucault (who in 1983, a year before his death, remarked that 'Yes I have a very strong Christian, Catholic background' [in Foucault, 1999: xvi]) became interested in that form of early Christianity in which effacement of self was essential for self-understanding and care of the self. What interested him was 'what might be called the "arts of existence" ... those intentional and voluntary actions by which men ... seek to transform themselves, to change themselves in their singular being, and to make their life into an oeuvre that carries certain aesthetic values'. He continues that these arts 'were assimilated into the exercise of priestly power in early Christianity, and later into educative, medical, and psychological types of practices' which might be called 'techniques of the self' (1985: 10–11). Thus Foucault came to study the 'practices of the self' through ethical problematisations rather than through moral codes and their sanctions. That is, there may be moral rules, but there are also ways of conducting oneself as a moral agent (1985: 13, 26).

Foucault builds up a long historical analysis which follows the ethical problematisations of the governance of the self from the Greek and Roman world, through Catholic Middle Ages, to the rise of Protestantism and up to the present. His thesis finishes with a picture of the transition to an aesthetic discourse, but one with a notorious conclusion: the S&M practices of Californian gay culture in the 1970s. Here the forms of personal experimentation are freed from the constraints of earlier times. Foucault described the change as follows:

> When sexual encounters become extremely easy and numerous, as is the case with homosexuality nowadays [1982–3], complications are introduced only

> after the fact. In this type of casual encounter, it is only after making love that one becomes curious about the other person ... all the energy and imagination, which in the heterosexual relation were channeled into courtship, now become devoted to intensifying the act of sex itself ... You find emerging in places like San Francisco and New York what might be called laboratories of sexual experimentation ... the counterpart of the medieval courts where strict rules of proprietary courtship were defined. (Foucault, 1997: 151)

Towards the idea of virtual Communist International: Derrida

At the level of the political movement itself, Derrida commends the resurrection of Marxism in the form of a new virtual International (Derrida, 1994: 84). This corresponds to the change in Derrida's philosophy since the 1970s. In an interview in 1971 he said that what he wanted to deconstruct was 'logocentrism' and a simultaneous 'deconstitution of idealism or spiritualism in all their variants' (1981: 51) and to struggle against the metaphysical closure of concepts such as history. He specified: 'the metaphysical character of the concept of history is not only linked to linearity, but to an entire system of implications (teleology, eschatology, elevating and interiorizing accumulation of meaning, certain type of traditionality, a certain concept of continuity, of truth etc.).' The considerable changes in Derrida's position can be seen in relation to the idea of eschatology. In the 1990s Derrida supported

> the transformation and opening up of Marxism ... in conformity with the ... the spirit of Marxism [...] [w]e will not claim that this messianic eschatology common both to the religions it criticizes and to the Marxist critique must be simply deconstructed. While it is common to both of them, with the exception of content [...] it is also the case that its formal structure of promise exceeds them or precedes them (1994: 59).

Derrida then marks the terrain of the new position: 'what remains irreducible to any deconstruction, what remains as undeconstructible as the possibility itself of deconstruction is, perhaps, a certain experience of the emancipatory promise; it is perhaps even the formality of a structural messianism, a messianism without religion, even a messianism without messianism' (1994: 75). What Derrida works towards is a rethinking of historicity, this time 'to open up access to an affirmative thinking of the messianic and emancipatory promise as promise: as *promise* and not as ontotheological or teleo-eschatological programme or design.' So today, Derrida writes no longer in negative but affirmative mode, 'Not only must one not renounce the emancipatory desire, it is necessary to insist on it more than ever, it seems, and insist on it, moreover, as the very indestructibility of the "it is necessary". This is the condition of a re-politicization' (1994: 75).

In this perspective it might be possible to regroup the later ideas of Althusser, Foucault, Baudrillard and Derrida (and others) to see Marx not as a founder of a new science, having achieved decisive discoveries and established the laws of movement of capitalist society, but as having established a new kind of critique of bourgeois culture: a 'critique of political economy' but within the frame of a promise not a programme. Indeed the most radical of Derrida's ideas on this suggests that it is essential for an emancipatory politics that this promise never become a programme, that the messiah never arrive. Or in other terms, 'we propose to speak of a democracy *to come*, not a *future* democracy in the future present, not even of a regulating idea, in the Kantian sense, or of a utopia' (1994: 64–5). The proposal for a new International is therefore carefully phrased: it is

> what calls to the friendship of an alliance without institution among those who … continue to be inspired by at least one of the spirits of Marx … [in] a kind of counter-conjuration, in the [theoretical and practical] critique of the state of international law, the concepts of State and nation … in order to renew this critique, and especially to radicalize it' (1994: 84–5; see also *Parallax*, no. 20, 2001)

Canguilhem's epistemology falls into uncertainity

Some authors previously secure in their knowledge and judgements become prone to uncertainty. The problem is evident in the way that a recent collection of extracts from Canguilhem's writings called *A Vital Rationalist* (1994) have been edited (by F. Delaporte) and introduced (by P. Rabinow). This collection could have attempted to display the development of Canguilhem's thought and method. It chooses however to present Canguilhem's thought topic by topic, placing side by side extracts from five or six different decades. Paul Rabinow, with unintended irony, calls it the "book" Canguilhem never wrote (1994: 15). And François Delaporte in his introductory remarks stresses that in making the selection of extracts;

> importance was given to questions of methodology in the history of science. This in itself was necessary because the object of historical discourse is not scientific discourse as such but the historicity of scientific discourse insofar as it represents the implementation of an epistemological project [*projet de savoir*]. If the history of science is the history of a discourse subject to the norm of critical rectification, then clearly it is a branch of epistemology.

Delaporte makes things more complicated by adding 'Taking the macroscopic view of the history of science, Canguilhem undertook to study the emergence of three disciplines: biology, physiology and medicine' (1994: 9–10). The question is thus posed right at the beginning of the collection: what does Canguilhem study – the emergence of sciences or disciplines, disciplines to sciences, or the 'historicity' of these transitions? What does Canguilhem mean by the terms 'history of science' or 'philosophical epistemology' (Canguilhem, 1983: 23)?

Paul Rabinow's introduction to the collection however leads the reader away from these questions. After noting Althusser's remarks on Canguilhem's respect for real science, he turns to Latour's project of the 'dismantling of the very idea of science' and remarks that his currently popular position is 'a position as far from Canguilhem's as one could imagine' (Canguilhem, 1994: 13). Rabinow suggests that there is an immanent logic in modern epistemology that moves from Bachelard, through Canguilhem to Latour. He also notes that Canguilhem's position now appears out of date, to run 'counter to much of contemporary *doxa* in the social studies of science' (1994: 15). In order to bring Canguilhem back towards this *doxa*, to bring him up to date, Rabinow presents Canguilhem as a kind of wayward existentialist: 'one easily hears echoes of Sartre and Merleau-Ponty's early themes, transposed to a different register' (1994: 20). The later Canguilhem is presented as the philosopher of existential error, a philosopher of the 'theme of normality as situated action, not as pre-given condition' (1994: 20), and on the search for knowledge 'as "an anxious quest" for the right information' (1994: 21). Rabinow states his own point of view as follows: 'The rise and ephemeral glory of structuralism and Althusserianism have shown that removing the humanist subject in the social sciences by itself guarantees neither an epistemological jump from ideology to science nor more effective political action' (1994: 22). The importance of Canguilhem's work today, says Rabinow, is that it reveals '[l]iving beings are capable of correcting their errors, and Canguilhem's work offers us tools to begin, once again, the process of doing so' (1994: 22). This judgement overlooks the important fact that it was under the influence of Canguilhem that the Althusserians introduced the idea of a practice of rectification into their Marxism, and began, to general astonishment at the time, to undertake systematic rectifications of their own works in a wave of self-criticisms (Althusser, 1976).

Thus in reading the recent contributions of Delaporte, Rabinow and French commentators on Canguilhem, Renard and Dagognet, it is not altogether clear whether Canguilhem is or is not afflicted by a claim to have studied the emergence of sciences, to have or not have rectified his own work, to have contributed or not to the study of intellectual progress. This new but quite ambivalent consensus is then the exact opposite of the one that intrigued philosophers like Lecourt, Balibar, Macherey and other Althusserians in the 1960s, for whom Canguilhem seemed important for a consistent and rational critique of subjectivism, psychologism and relativism. These Althusserian responses were not unreciprocated, for Canguilhem embraced Althusserian ideas and concepts in return in a fundamental realignment of his own position. Instead of a simple continuity, the more closely we look, the more we tend to find discontinuities, shifts, and indeed some radical paradoxes in positions Canguilhem was able to graft onto his fundamental notions.

Bourdieu's scholastic Marxist continuation

Bourdieu (1930–2002) studied at the ENS. After a spell in Algeria (1956–60), he returned to Paris and studied with Lévi-Strauss and Aron. He worked in Lille (1961–4), and then returned to the Ecole Pratique des

Hautes Etudes at Paris (founding a Bourdieu network which included Passeron and Boltanski, and by reputation has demanded a high degree of loyalty). Having arrived at the Collège de France in 1981, he became France's leading sociologist. His own position he described as a reaction to both existential and structural methods, 'to bring real-life actors back in who had vanished at the hands of Lévi-Strauss and other structuralists, especially Althusser … I do mean "actors" not "subjects"' (in Honneth, 1986: 41). It is clear that Bourdieu reacted quickly to what he saw as the weaknesses of structural methods, the ones he himself used in his early essays. He moved through what he called 'epistemological experiments to try to remedy these shortcomings which in effect try to reverse Lévi-Strauss's inversion of Durkheim' (Jenkins, 1992: 37, 45–65).

Bourdieu's main concepts are habitus, field, practice. After his anthropological works, his major studies turned to analyses of education and culture: *Reproduction in Education, Society and Culture* ([1970], 1990); *Homo Academicus* ([1984] 1988); *The State Nobility, Elite Schools in the Field of Power* ([1989] 1996); *The Inheritors: French Students and their Culture* ([1964] 1979); and *Distinction* ([1979] 1984). His writings also include major works on the theory of practice: *Outline of a Theory of Practice* ([1972] 1977) and *The Logic of Practice* ([1980] 1990). Compared with Althusser's brief essays and interventions, Bourdieu has furnished an immense oeuvre aimed to solve the principal methodological problems of sociology and to provide it with exemplary studies equal to those of the Durkheim school brought up to date.

Bourdieu's study *Distinction* ([1979] 1984) is a good example of his social theory at work. The study concerns the distribution of cultural taste by social class, and is based on large-scale social surveys and a questionnaire (1984; 512–17) and an observation schedule (1984: 517–18) carried out in 1963 (692 subjects) and 1967–8 (grand total 1,217). The subjects are classified by a number of factors and then arranged in social class hierarchy (bourgeoisie, petite-bourgeoisie, proletarian) by conversion of terms such as employer, teacher, manual worker. The study contains a formidable introduction on methodology which defines how the terms 'social space', 'habitus', 'dynamics of fields' and 'distinction' are to be employed. In the main analysis the results of the survey are used principally to analyse class tastes, and Bourdieu uses the Althusserian term 'class fractions', the 'variants of petite-bourgeois tastes', that is the 'declining', the 'executant' and the 'new petite-bourgeoisie', before looking at the relation of class cultures to politics. This study is then a 'sociology of taste' in the sense an investigation into the correlation between forms of cultural consumption and class (with further factors of education and gender added). The analysis is formal, general, and draws on a familiar range of stereotypical evaluations. The language is replete with structuralist idioms, from 'structural causation' to 'cultural apparatus'; from 'structuring structures' to 'systems of schemes generating classifiable practices, i.e. Distinctive signs (tastes)'; the class fractions are the 'bearers' of culture.

The overwhelming critical reaction to the text has been negative (see Frow, 1987; Robbins, 1991: 127–31; Jenkins, 1992: 137–49; Alexander 1995), read as failing to live up to the promise of its ambitions. Certainly the text is an ambitious attempt to reveal the changing class nature of cultural consumption. In a sense it represents a direct attempt to verify the Marxist claim that culture is not only a hierarchical structure reflecting a given class formation in a capitalist society, but also a means by which class positions are reproduced through distinctions of cultural taste, and that cultural change is associated with change of class structures. The work is certainly not an existential study, since no individuals are examined to show through their actions as actors how they come to form cultural evaluations. Bourdieu uses educational attainment, and 'cultural capital' as an intermediary structure to examine how a complex system of judgements is produced yet is class related ('economic capital'). Much of the value of this thesis depends on the precise identification and definition of the fractions of the petite-bourgeoisie (1984: 339–71):

- *The declining petite-bourgeoisie*: craftsmen and shopkeepers. Their tastes are found to be reactions to 'modernism or comfort'. Their taste in music is for the 'déclassé works of bourgeois culture' such as Bizet, and the most 'old fashioned singers'. They live neat and tidy lifestyles.
- *The rising petite-bourgeoisie*: junior executives and office workers with modest educational attainment. They are aspiring and have probably met with obstacles in their careers. They tend to like music like the Sabre Dance and Petula Clarke, and are 'interested in photography and the cinema'. Their political ideals are 'ambiguous'.
- *The new petite-bourgeoisie*: They work in sales, marketing, advertising, fashion, therapeutics, cultural production and other new middle-class occupations. Some of this group have high educational attainment but have not found a way into the bourgeoisie proper. They tend to like composers such as Stravinsky and Vivaldi. They also like symbolic 'defiance' music such as jazz. A larger percentage of women are found in this group than in others, which brings a new aesthetic demand for 'self-presentation' services.

What Bourdieu has achieved here is a synthesis of the French sociological methodological tradition and a basic Marxist social scheme shorn of all subtlety, and of course its 'proletariat' as revolutionary agency, but not its virulent contempt for the *petite-bourgeoisie*. The survey produces raw material which is classified first by occupations, educational attainment, cultural consumption items. Bourdieu then converts these into hierarchies through his Marxist classifications. The last process is a general interpretation with selected examples to indicate preferences and modalities by which 'lifestyles' are realised (this is entirely reminiscent of Durkheim's attempt to interpret modes of suicide). In effect the reader has to complete the task of analysis, for Bourdieu has indeed discovered something in his survey which is only registered vaguely and imprecisely.

As has been suggested, Bourdieu here identifies postmodern sensibility in the ambiance of the new petite bourgeoisie (Lash, 1990). But Bourdieu does not take the opportunity to link these phenomena together. He remains content to write simply on a shift 'from duty to the fun ethic' and of a

> new ethic espoused by the vanguard of the bourgeoisie and petite bourgeoisie ... [which is] perfectly compatible with a form of enlightened conservatism ... and process of supplying the economy with the perfect consumer ... The most important contribution of the new ethic may well be that it produces consumers who are isolated ... in short freed from the temporal structures imposed by domestic units. (Bourdieu 1989: 371)

In other words, Bourdieu remains trapped within the framework of a theory of modes of production, what he calls 'conditions of existence', so missed theoretically the transition to a new form of social integration (lifestyle as determined by modes of consumption and the disappearance of 'class' identity). He also missed the opportunity to link his analysis to cultural institutions and so to link new forms of consumption (and leisure) to the theory of the State, and therefore social reproduction (see Lash, 1990: 250–4).

Berthelot: the meticulous mapping of sociologies

One of the features of present French social thought is a rebuilding of all the main aspects of sociology since Durkheim and Weber. Conspicuously this reconstruction omits Comte and Marx, and abandons the aim for the moment of constructing a general overarching theory for the social sciences, indeed any overall definition of the nature of French or Western society. There is a significant shift from an eschatological Marxism to a Marxist sociology for example in the later works of Althusser. He describes in his autobiography that just before the onset of the illness which was to lead to such catastrophic consequences for the Althussers, that he had entered on a 'very creative phase'. It was a project which was intended to draw out the 'practical conclusions of' his 'anti-theoreticist self-criticism' (Althusser, 1993: 245; trans. modified). The theme of the research proposed was the study of the links between the practical and theoretical sides of social movements in a new centre: Centre for the Study of Popular Movements their Ideologies and Theoretical Doctrines (CEMPIT). A meeting was held at the ENS in 1980, and Althusser gained the co-operation of 'over a hundred' experts from different disciplines, 'to achieve, if possible, comparative results' (1993: 245-6). Althusser more than once refers to his 'friend' Alain Touraine, a Marxist sociologist who had been studying, with Wieviorka and Dubet, the 'workers' movement' in France and who had 'valuable things to say' on popular movements (1993: 238). It seems that Althusser in re-evaluating the relationship between theory and practice had become a sociologist.

One of the key writers in the effort to redefine sociology in this period is Jean-Michel Berthelot, who has been active in assembling detailed accounts of the different sub-fields of sociology in France, working through each of its branches, checking and learning from the knowledge already in place in the discipline. Berthelot was a student at the ENS under Althusser and converted to sociology. His *L'Intelligence du social* maps out in a detailed logical form the argumentative modes adopted by causal, functional, structural, hermeneutic, action and dialectical analysis (1990: 89) and how exchanges occur between them (1990: 103). Berthelot draws on Gerald Holton's notion of themata, to form a concept of 'schemes of intelligibility' (1990: 152). After a long analytic examination of the forms of argument and modes of demonstration and proof in sociology, Berthelot's conclusion is that the 'specificity of the social sciences resides in the last analysis not so much in the production of positive knowledge, than in this incessant exploration of modes of intelligibility and cognisance/reconnaissance [*intelligence*] of their object' and their themata in two registers, analytic and symbolic (1990: 243). Against the 'positivist illusion' this intelligibility is now realised in a plurality of disciplines and sub-disciplines, paradigms, epistemologies and methods.

In his recent collection *La Sociologie Française Contemporaine* (Berthelot, 2000), Berthelot has included two overviews of French sociology today, seven accounts of the main approaches in sociology, and eleven accounts of '*grands domains*', here meaning topic areas such as education, culture, health, religion. Berthelot's chapter is on 'the epistemological constitution of French sociology' and begins with an account of Durkheim's rules of sociological method and the empirical study *Suicide* (2000: 30). Post 1945, Berthelot tries to draw up a careful balance sheet. After the Collège de Sociologie and the contributions of Aron, the discussion focusses on two streams. The first is phenomenology, principally Merleau-Ponty and Marxism. The second is the institutional sociology of Gurvitch, reflecting the influence of Durkheim in a dialectical and dynamic sociology out of which two programmes developed. One is connected to the endurance of the empirical tradition from Durkheim and which is represented currently in the work of Raymond Boudon, who has attempted to find a continuation of positivism in what he has described as 'the crisis of sociology' (1980). The other comes again from Durkheim via Mauss into the work of Lévi-Strauss. After the war these traditions led to two lines of research: one leading to an emphasis on structure and history and including the work of Althusser; the other represented by Bourdieu et al. in *Métier de Sociologie* (1968), which sought a common element in Marx, Durkheim and Weber from a Bachelardian point of view (epistemological break, construction of the object). In the last thirty years, there has been a gradual awakening in studies of the history of sociology, and a new interest in a range of different methodologies from quantitative to interpretative (including ethnomethodology). Berthelot's own account of the history of sociology had already outlined a definition of the *plural* nature of sociology and he defined its object in a new way: it is the (conflictual) articulation of all the programmes within the discipline constituting its 'disciplinary matrix' (Berthelot, 1991: 124).

Conclusion

The age of the law has passed, and with it that of the socius and the social contract. (Baudrillard, 1990a: 155)

Conclusion

> The philosophical concept does not refer to the lived, by way of compensation, but consists, through its own creation, in setting up an event. (Deleuze and Guattari, 1994: 33)

If the 'positive polity' did not succeed in establishing itself in France, either in its Comtean or Marxist form, what polity did establish itself? The answer to this question is clearly a form of what might be called, after Comte's grand narrative, the 'metaphysical polity' and the sequence of the sub-phases of the metaphysical state can now read perhaps as 1500–1685: *Protestant* period; 1686–1799, *deist* period; and, I suggest, 1800–2000 could be baptised the *Saint-Simonian* period. Certainly at moments in this period, the positive tradition (including neo-Marxism), became a major challenge to the French metaphysical polity, while at others it became a major pillar of it. The lineage of the 'positive' series could be sub-divided into three phases representing the three parts of this book: 1800–79 Comtean; 1880–1939 Durkheimian; and 1940–2000, neo-Marxist phase. The metaphysical Republican polity clearly was not stabilised in France until the Third Republic, with massive support from the 'positivist' tradition. Stabilised again in the Fifth, after the turbulence of the Fourth Republic: its form of compromise between the church and social democracy having successfully resisted the various extreme forces levelled against it.

An assessment which applied Comte's analytic techniques today would attempt to draw up a balance sheet for the ways in which the negative and positive series characteristic of the metaphysical period have been continued up to the present time, and this would require a radically new vision of the form of the future state as a theoretical fiction. In retrospect, Comte's vision of a positive polity seems very much of its time; its value as an ideal could hardly be assessed by its efficacy as a guide to action. And this raises the question of the relation of social theory to 'historical reality'. For it is clear that theory in the French tradition has never been a tool developed in order simply to grasp and possess a current reality. If the French tradition has attempted to find ways of addressing ideals, it has also struggled to identify abnormalities, pathologies, deviations. It has held fast to the view that the French experience has been exceptional both in terms of the problems it has had to confront, and in terms of the ideals it has generated in facing up to them. It is thus an experience of universal significance, arising not just from the fact that radical social theory has never been satisfied with the limited compromises of the metaphysical (bourgeois-democratic) society and has always wanted to go beyond its confines, but from the conviction that this society is a transitional form. To investigate this thesis it has always resorted to systematic methodological reflection.

Methodologies

Method throughout has occupied a central place in French thought and in many cases has turned out, strangely, to be an Achilles' heal for key thinkers. It has also been on the ground of methodology that some of the key dramas have been played out. There is often an ambivalent relation on the part of French thinkers themselves to the Cartesian tradition with its demands for methodological clarity and conceptual rigour. None of the key thinkers in social theory from the nineteenth century on was content with this tradition, regarding it as simplistic. But all the major theorists, including those who officially denied any interest in method, expressed rules of method and tried to work with consistent definitions and procedures. There seems to be a general and elemental acceptance of the view that method is not simply important, but lies at the heart of understanding theory and knowledge itself. Characteristic of the French style of social theory has been the insistence that these rules of method be made as conscious and rigorous as possible. Method has a much wider significance in French practice than that accorded to social sciences in other traditions. In the English-speaking cultures method tends to refer to techniques of empirical investigation and to the gathering of information. In French social thought it concerns the whole range of problems from the initial definition of the status of the object of investigation, the classification of subject matter, through to the role of theory in forms of conjecture and administration of procedures of verification. This has been true of existential as well as structural, post-structural and postmodern methodologies.

But there are some crucial differences of opinion within the French tradition about how theoretical fictions are introduced into social theory, which implies that different kinds of reading are necessary. Certainly it is tempting to suggest that the two periods of Comte's intellectual life should be read differently. In the first, that dominated by objective method, an appropriate mode of reading would be that developed by Althusser. This would be particularly sensitive to the epistemological novelty of Comte's new positive idiom, yet not be bound by the manifest order of the surface of these texts. Althusser has written of the way that a science 'can only pose problems on the terrain and within the horizon of a definite theoretical structure, its problematic, which constitutes its absolute and definite condition of possibility, and hence the absolute determination of the forms in which all problems must be posed, at any given moment in the science'. Althusser adds: 'Comte often came very close to this idea.' Here there is no longer an individual subject with a vision, and vision 'loses the religious privileges of divine reading' (Althusser and Balibar, 1970: 25). Elsewhere Althusser acknowledged the importance of Comte's distinction between the historical order of a science's formation and the order of its doctrine (see Macherey, 1964: 52). Comte also theorised the idea of the order of exposition of a scientific doctrine, and came close to formulating the principles of structural causation so central to Althusserian epistemology. And this should not be surprising since

Althusser was decisively influenced by the work of Gaston Bachelard, described by Serres as 'Comte among us' (in Comte, 1975, vol. i: 4). The central idea of the 'epistemological break', that is the thesis that all sciences are formed in a break with ideological knowledge, an idea central to the French tradition of historical epistemology (Heilbron, 1995: 262–6), is essentially a reading of Comte's law of the three states as a law of all scientific revolution. Comte gave great importance to the transitional role of biology, but Althusser tended to reduce the system of the sciences to three 'great scientific continents': those of mathematics, physics and history. Nevertheless, the ambition was the same, to discover the law of the social as a fundamental law of a domain. Such a law would define a unique order of phenomena. Comte and Durkheim called it sociology; Althusser called it history.

Althusser applied the theory of social evolution to Marx, and all the problems which had haunted French theory now came to haunt this parallel theory of the transition to the final state. The theory now emphasised the material basis of production and class struggle as the driving force of history, thus picking up on the ideas of the Saint-Simonian matrix which focused on the transition from feudal to industrial society and the claim for real not formal distributive justice. Althusser's critique of the notion of *praxis* was based on Comte's distinction between metaphysical and scientific ideas. In fact Comte's historical epistemology was probably more subtle than that of Althusser, since all the notions of fetishism, theologism and metaphysics were levelled by Althusser to one concept of pre-scientific ideology (which has therefore no history). The key levels of the social (base and superstructure) were evident in Althusser as they were in Comte, as were ideas of scientific revolution (a radical break to a new problematic organised on a new epistemological framework) and social revolution (transition from capitalism to communism), as were key elements of theoretical analysis (for static and dynamic analysis Althusser used the terms synchronic and diachronic, etc.). In fact, Althusser found many of these ideas already expressed in Marx's own methodological writings of the 1850–60s, but they had been developed by Comte in writings decades earlier, as Althusser admitted.

Today it is important to reflect on Althusser's relation to his own tradition. For example, his analysis of historicism as a problematic led him to suggest that when Sartre, who used the historicist method, came into contact with Marxism, he 'immediately gave an historicist reading of it' just as Gramsci had done (but from another tradition) (Althusser and Balibar, 1970: 135). Althusser derived his critique from the French structural tradition and this was one of the major points of latent disagreement between Derrida and Althusser. Derrida held that the leading critique of historicism had been made paradoxically by Sartre's mentor, Husserl, against Dilthey at the beginning of the century. Althusser's refusal to acknowledge this, says Derrida, 'irritated me even if I understood, without approving of it, the political strategy involved' (Kaplan and Sprinker, 1993: 192). Reading Althusser against himself here (but in a different direction for the moment to that of Derrida),

I suggest that French structural Marxism deliberately aligned its method with the matrix that used the same materials as Comte and Durkheim (which I call Saint-Simonianism). When Althusser encountered Marx's version of the Saint-Simonian matrix, he produced a structuralist reading of it, just as Comte had done. Now it was not a 'bourgeois' reading, for as we know Comte associated the bourgeoisie intimately with, and as a social support for, metaphysical philosophy and its polity (parliamentary democracy). Comte's own position, which reflects his new version of masculinity, was essentially one that advocated the anti-bourgeois patriarchal bloc: patrician, proletarian, neo-papacy (not fascism which is Caesaro-patrician-proletarian). Althusser's own ideal is certainly anti-bourgeois and proletarian, but its precise political form always remained undefined (see Elliot, 1987). Wernick's recent insightful reading, which parallels the discussion of Debray (1983) and Serres (1995b), suggests that Althusser was led 'to think Lenin's 'vanguard party' – the locus of fusion between intellectuals and militants, theory and practice, science and politics – into the space of Comte's revamped *pouvoir spirituel*' (Wernick, 2001: 235, emphasis in original). Latent here is the social polity of a papal-patrician-proletarian social form which is common to all the Saint-Simonian variations left and right. This form and its terminology, to my knowledge, have never been carefully examined, yet the French tradition clearly suggests that it is this social structure which is the real basis of bourgeois Western democracies and will come to replace them in a final social transition. Social science discipline will play a crucial part in this, and as Comte often said scientific 'method from every point of view has a higher value than doctrine' (Comte, 1968, vol. iv: 155).

Durkheim reconstructed Comtean sociology through a radical critique of its method, and by providing key new studies which would guide social reconstruction (but as I have shown, his own method failed and he was forced to return to Comte's). For Althusser the crucial task was how to read Marx in order to demonstrate that the scientific breakthrough Marx achieved involved a theoretical and a political revolution. Rather than show the science and its laws in practice however, Althusser was essentially interested in showing how Marx's theory embodied all the abstract characteristics and prerequisites of scientificity, and how this differed from pre-scientific knowledge. An Althusserian interpretation of the development of social theory would argue that in its Comtean and Durkheimian form, the sociology is developed primarily within the orbit of a bourgeois class culture which had decisively influenced its development. Marx's aim was to develop social science politically, that is from a proletarian class position and from within the experience of struggle itself. The Althusser of the 1960s held that Marx had founded the new science which discovered that all social formations were 'determined in the last instance' by the economic mode of production (a thesis which Derrida noted was perhaps the 'metaphysical anchoring' of the whole theoretical edifice [in Kaplan et al., 1993: 204]). By the late 1970s Althusser had changed his view to one closer to that of Foucault, which held that Marx's theory had only provided a first critique of 'political economy', a science which belonged to a nineteenth-century *episteme;* and so 'Althusserianism' came to an end.

Theory

This book has examined method as changing modes of theoretical discipline. This must be understood as concerning 'theory' disciplined in two senses. The first is the discipline imposed by method, the rationalist internal forms which discipline the flight of theory: rules, constraints. The scientific gaze is trained, evidence is produced in a certain way, scientific logic is subject to a particular rigour as is the 'administration' of proof, in order to reach a verification, a truth. Foucault was not interested (at least in the 1960s) in the 'speaking subject' and strictly excluded an examination of 'communal opinion' in favour of what is said as it is caught in the 'play of an exteriority' (1972: 123). This book has examined the way Saint-Simonian thought has had *epistemic* organisation and how other knowledges are produced in relation to it, but with the following caveat. Foucault was careful not to limit his studies to the formed and established sciences but also to examine what he called studies of bodies of knowledge at the 'threshold of epistemologisation', that is at the point where knowledge formations are 'defined by their positivity' but where their 'epistemological figures... are not necessarily all sciences' (and which may never, in fact, succeed in becoming sciences). Here 'one is trying to reveal between positivities, knowledge, epistemological figures, and sciences, a whole set of differences, relations, gaps, shifts, independencies, autonomies, and the way in which they articulate their own historicities on one another' (1972: 190–1). I have added to the analysis Bazard's idea that such knowledge has a cyclic impulsion.

This book has also encountered, in the manner discussed by the later Foucault, the importance of biography, even auto-hagiography, the effects of group solidarity, group projects and organisation, political experience, reflection and reaction to political events as also affecting territorial 'intersection' and 'exteriority'. The second sense of an investigation into theory's discipline, follows what Foucault in later works suggested could be considered 'modes of subjection [*assujettissement*]', that is 'the way in which the individual establishes his relation to the rule and recognizes himself as obliged to put it into practice' (Foucault, 1985: 27). This is also evidently social, and includes the study of the elaboration of rules of membership, bylaws of practice of members, hierarchies of authority, processes of regulation of social bodies, and forms of exclusion. This embraces that field Althusser called truth 'in the practical state' and asks what are the sanctions, other than exclusion and excommunication, open to cults, sects, scientific societies and political parties? And how do these relate to the projects of such groups? The aim of these groups is purported to be speaking the truth (*veridiction*), or practising the truth in the cause of social justice – against power, or against *idola, simulacra*. Mauss, for instance, describes the 'self-sacrifice' necessary for the formation of the 'workshop atmosphere' created by the Durkheimians (1983: 140). In order to achieve this, the group operates collective discipline, perhaps a discipline of 'disciples' in relation to a sacred college (Bazard, Bataille).

Thus it is possible and indeed necessary to turn the later against the early Foucault. The early Foucault, criticising Marx and Comte, called 'anthropologisation' that situation where well-founded knowledge (language, life, production), when subject to 'the slightest deviation from ... rigorously defined planes sends thought tumbling over into the domain occupied by the human sciences ... "Anthropologisation" is the great internal *threat* to knowledge in our day' (1970: 348, my emphasis). The impression of 'haziness, inexactitude, and imprecision left by almost all the human sciences is merely a surface effect of what makes it possible to define them in their positivity' (1970: 355). In other words, unlike all the other sciences, the 'human sciences' do not have their own true objects but are simulacra, 'sciences of duplication, in a "meta-epistemological" position' in respect to existing sciences (1970: 355). Foucault during the period of high rationalism defined this space negatively and with contempt. He came to reverse this judgement however and to see that it is precisely in that zone, once called 'metaphysics', in which new kinds of problems concerning the transformation of human values (including human freedom) are encountered and assessed.

I have examined one such theoretical space: the questions which Saint-Simonianism and the intellectual traditions which sprang from it posed and tried to answer. This book has been a discussion of that thought in France, from Comte to Baudrillard, which sought to find solutions to human problems beyond the confines of *bourgeois* and *mass* society. But these solutions have not been realised. An unusually violent outburst by Bourdieu against Sollers revealed deep resentments associated with its defeat and betrayal of this project: Sollers, says Bourdieu, 'the ideal-typical incarnation of the individual and collective history of a whole generation of writers of ambition, of all those who, having moved, in less than thirty years, from Maoist or Trotskyist terrorism to positions of power in banks, insurance companies, politics or journalism, will readily grant him their indulgence' (Bourdieu, [1995] 1998: 13).

The question which emerges here is even more serious. It may be asked whether the basic Saint-Simonian matrix which can be analysed in its greater complexity today, has always been in a fundamental complicity with the political structures of modernisation and progressivity in France – as Foucault and others suggest part of the vast ideological complex of the new post-revolutionary 'disciplinary' society in France – or whether it has been, as Althusser's main works argue, in contestation with it? The former would mean that all the various types of interpretative problematics, from historicist and humanist at one end of the spectrum to structuralist and post-structuralist at the other end did not escape the culture of the new society, even though its ambitions were to transcend it. They would simply lend legitimacy to a new form of 'social science'. Of course the ideological structures of the demand for human rights, equality of the sexes and formal liberal democratic institutions now appear to be at the heart of the project of the bourgeois 'society of individuals', the bourgeois enlightenment project with its new sense of 'modernity'. But the Saint-Simonian matrix which has played such a large part in the intellectual and philosophical sphere has played a dynamic role in claiming the necessity of transcending the limits of such purely bourgeois forms through new forms of knowledge and religious belief on the one hand and new ideals of social justice on the other. The central question now is: was this ideology of opposition and transcendence based on an independent reality, or was this matrix and its promises simply a part of the dynamic of the society itself, its old function of pseudo-alterity now redundant? Do the positions of the later writings of Althusser (see Elliot, 1987: 313–23), Foucault, Lyotard and Baudrillard in particular simply bear witness to the last episode of a declining cycle of thought, or do they provide the beginnings of a critique of its matrix role and function as prop and supplementary social control within the very structure of power they denounce, a critique which parallels but far exceeds the critique made by Nizan of the role of the professors of the Third Republic?

In the end, as Bourdieu rightly points out, a discusion of the work of major intellectuals can only be of interest if there is a problem that is confronted. Gary Gutting (2001) has argued that the central problem is that of individual freedom; Dominique Lecourt sees the end of Marxism leading on to issues of 'original ways of forming relations of love, kinship, friendship, or labour' (2001: 138). Expressing the problem in these very trite ways suggests that French social theory has indeed reached the end point of this cycle. But both of these recent accounts radically misconceive the present state of social theory because both authors work with a corpus that is too narrow and with little sympathy for an 'end-of-cycle' condition; a condition, it is clear, has its own necessity and cannot be ended by fiat. It is therefore instructive to turn to Comte's own end-of-cycle ideas on reading and writing theory, as they are rich and radical. Comte argues that our own system of writing, derived from the theistic stage, will be replaced in the positive polity by a new form of algebraic writing. This would be a writing in space, not on a material substance, and could be imagined as a green text on a white ground (1856: 11–13). John Stuart Mill's reaction to these postmodern ideas was scathing, calling them 'deplorable', 'strange conceits', a 'melancholy decadence' and 'ridiculous' (1961: 194f.). But had Mill really taken on board the full force of Comte's critique of pure rationalism? Mill seemed to think that the combination of positive science with a neo-fetishism was an extension of positivism into decadence (rather in the same way that Comte in his earlier work (1974b: 727) himself ridiculed the 'vagaries' of the reflections of Newton in old age).

These notions could, charitably, be viewed as theoretical devices, ideal types, whose main purposes were/are to provide means of analysing current, present problems, particularly where the individual theorist has immense difficulty in living within them. These are essentially *hypertelic* forms. More than one such theorist, Nietzsche being the best known, has said following Auguste Comte, 'I live posthumously'. The modality is quite different from the dilemmas later opened by Foucault: we find here in his work a complete refusal to indulge in utopian thought and general programmes, but at the same time there is an engagement in radical sexual experimentation, a desire to make unambiguous discoveries within the sexual experience (Halperin, 1995). In the messianic frames there is however an ambivalence, even tension, between the future as the terminus of a current trend or tendency, and the future seen as a leap into a new condition. French theory today is increasingly taken up with Walter Benjamin's distinction between future as programmed utopia, and future as explosive or implosive catastrophic shifts (Benjamin, 1970: 255–66). Derrida's position holds that the messianic frame is essential to the Western historical experience of justice, but what must never happen is the arrival of the messiah, a parody of the 'wait' for the female messiah inaugurated by the Saint-Simonians in the 1830s. This complex trans-theoretical form is a combination of positive and negative relations: a negative positivity. The ultimate anti-metaphysical position, refuting Derrida's view that the messianic is not deconstructible, is that of Baudrillard, who suggests that the day of judgement (the essential moment harmony of the messianic) came, but the messiah missed the appointment. We find in the variations of Derrida and Baudrillard the Judaeo and Catholic patriarchal forms under threat, retrenched, partially reconstructed in a Nietzschean direction. And it is the thematic of the liberation of energies, libidinal among them, which, according to Baudrillard, specifically differentiates theory today from the crises at the end of the first and second cycles.

Patriarchal social theory

Baudrillard's thematic is somewhat more complex than the disillusioned formula of messianic procrastination might suggest.[1] In a recent text, he argues that the history of masculinity could be formulated as follows. At the beginning of the nineteenth century – what I have identified here as the opening of the crisis of masculinity – there was a replacement of aristocratic forms of seduction by a new (bourgeois) form of romantic love. This new configuration projected a specific ideal model of femininity onto women, or one might say the femininity of the new woman was 'called' into existence by men experiencing a crisis in their masculinity, their own sexual ambivalence. Politically, feminism also answered a call from men for a new woman as citizen. Second wave feminism is the more recent product of the male demand for a sexual woman who is also citizen and intellectual. But all of these progressive changes have had the effect of breaking down the symbolic structures of radical otherness in the culture between men and women. This is a demand for a sex 'removed from artifice, illusion and seduction', and created in a structure of sexual (in)difference. It is at this point that the initiative has passed to women:

> We have here the problem of a woman, having once become the subject of desire, no longer finding the other she could desire as such ... For the secret never lies in the equivalent exchange of desires, under the sign of egalitarian difference; it lies in inventing the other who will be able to play on – and make sport of – my own desire, defer it, and thus arouse it indefinitely. Is the female gender capable today of producing – since it no longer wishes to personify it – this same seductive otherness? Is the female gender still hysterical enough to invent the other? (Baudrillard, 1996b: 120)

Not only is there a general scenario in which the (male) messiah missed his appointment with the day of judgement. There is another moment: the day of the historic reversal of power within gender relations: did this day ever come, will it ever come, and will there be a female messiah present at the appointed rendezvous?

Baudrillard's view here is that this appointment was not missed by parapraxis, but that the dominant invention was here born of resentment: the new male is produced only as agent of sexual harassment. For Baudrillard in a sense this is also to miss the appointment, for 'it marks the arrival on the scene of an impotent, victim's sexuality, a sexuality impotent to constitute itself either as object or as subject of desire in its paranoid wish for identity and difference' (1996b: 122). It is not that the female messiah did not arrive. The call for her to appear was answered – but in a way that failed to produce either a new masculinity or a new femininity. Baudrillard's analysis of Madonna provides a picture of the female messiah, and by implication the future of gender relations:

> Madonna is 'desperately' fighting in a world where there is no response – the world of sexual indifference. Hence the urgent need for hypersexual sex, the signs of which are exacerbated precisely because they are no longer addressed to anyone ... For want of some other who would deliver her from herself, she is unrelentingly forced to provide her own sexual enticement, to build up for herself a panoply of accessories – in the event a sadistic panoply, from which she tries to wrench herself away. Harassment of the body by sex, harassment of the body by signs. (1996b: 126)

Not only is the scene dominated by the sexual politics of harassment and resentment, but, since there is no radical other for her identity, the messiah becomes a woman who harasses her own body 'in a cycle or closed circuit'. Madonna can 'play all the roles' and 'all the versions of sex' so as to 'exploit this fantastic absence of identity'.

Baudrillard's position inevitably follows Comte by rejecting feminism as a phenomenon of contemporary resentment and metaphysics. It also stigmatises modern feminism as falling under a masculine form of gender identification where femininity becomes a mode of production, this time of the eroticised material body requiring sexual pleasure as an obligatory end (cf. Grace, 2000: 122f.). Thus sexual 'liberation' leads not to a reconstruction of the social contract, a new dialectic, or religious bond as envisaged by the Saint-Simonians, but to a logic of excess. This logic is one that attacks and breaks down the traditional polarities of ritual exchange, and produces new hypertelic forms, be it transgenetic, transaesthetic, or transsexual (Baudrillard,

1993c: 20f.). One of the crucial sites of such a process is the culture of male–female symbolic exchanges. The modern crisis is not one simply of the female role and identity (as was widely believed in the sociology of the 1950s and in the 1990s). The cultural movement of liberation attacks traditional forms of masculinity as well, while transforming the modalities of seduction (they are complicit products of masculine desire: positive and judged by performance).

Because Comtean sociology fell into ridicule when Comte began to devote his life to the worship of Clotilde de Vaux, emblem of Humanity in his new cult in the 1840s, Durkheim and Mauss later built up modern French sociology on a quite different terrain. Baudrillard, once a sociologist, has deserted the discipline and few mainstream French sociologists have regretted his departure. It seems clear that both Comte, who instituted a programme of 'cerebral hygiene', and Baudrillard, who now writes only to make the world more enigmatic, have found it difficult to come to terms with liberal democracy. Comte sought a way out of his defeat in a sentimental and optimistic world of sociological theory-fiction. Baudrillard's way out is to chase fetishistic perversities in their downward 'spiral of the worst' and intends never to make a naïve judgement. However, this strange variation points to a radical future for gender relations: the culture of resentment (in all its transpolitical variants) is but a form of (dis)illusion in which, paradoxically, a logic of hysterical excess is unleashed. Instead of moving to a consensus, events either shoot off with great energy, hysterically, to extremes, or become increasingly and paradoxically homogeneous. Baudrillard's position refuses to admit the adequacy of a critical sociology of this situation. The role of fatal messianic theory-fiction is to challenge a new and different world into existence. Whereas Comte sought to challenge the world into the good by offering the fantasy of a matriarchal asexual utopia and a papal model of masculinity, Baudrillard challenges it into a fantastic spiral of excess and the hell of the same.

The fate of the social

It was Durkheim who most clearly saw the relation between Saint-Simonianism and the birth of the 'social'. His lectures on socialism suggest that eighteenth-century thought was obsessed with communal utopias; only after the collapse of the Empire in 1815 was this line of thought challenged by a genuine socialist thought, particularly that of Saint-Simon. It was not the emergence of new issues around a new social agency, the proletariat, that was the signal for these ideas. Durkheim's first conclusion is that

> what was lacking in the eighteenth century was not that the Revolution be once and for all a *fait accompli*, but, in order for these factors to produce their social or socialist consequences, they had first to produce their political consequences ... Could it be that the changes wrought in the organisation of society, once realised, demanded others which moreover stemmed from the same causes which had engendered them? (Durkheim, 1962: 105).

Durkheim argues that it was quite logical for Saint-Simon himself to attack the reduction of economic activity to purely individual interests for,

> having established that henceforth the only normal manifestation of social activity is economic activity, [he] concludes that the latter is a social thing, or rather that it is *the social thing* ... Society cannot become an industrial unless industry is socialised. This is how industrialism logically ends in socialism. (1962: 180–1, emphasis in original)

It was Baudrillard who identified the moment of the 'end of the social'. The general theory developed in Baudrillard's work is articulated around the opposition between symbolic and semiotic cultures. These orders, in principle, unlikely as it may seem, mirror the Comtean three states:

> Relative to the dangers of seduction that haunt the universe of games and rituals, our own sociality and the forms of communication and exchange it institutes, appear in direct proportion to their secularisation under the sign of the Law, as extremely impoverished, banal and abstract. But this is still only an intermediary state, for the age of the law has passed, and with it that of the socius and the social contract. (Baudrillard, 1990a: 155)

More specifically, the semiotic orders and Baudrillard's 'orders of simulacra' follow a trajectory which provides an ironic continuation of Comte's account of the rise of positivism and reason in Western Christian cultures. If in Comte's later work fetishism reappears as a necessary and irreducible fundamental force in the new social cult called the Religion of Humanity, in Baudrillard this role is more complex. First, there is a fundamental role for the fatal which is conceived actively in terms of strategies that lie at the basis of all human cultures. In modernity they become the driving force of technology fetishised in new forms of alienation. Baudrillard, following Nietzsche, stigmatises the modern state, its democratic ideologies and human rights movements, as essentially metaphysical and self-contradictory forms of resentment (fatal strategies turned against themselves). Second, whereas Comte after 1848 conceived of the future as a long, linear and programmable procession in which he wanted to see 'order and progress', Baudrillard's vision maintains the primacy of apocalyptic messianism over historical time. The paradox, he argues, is that the time of the world today as we encounter it seems to want to hurry, seems to have a 'secret millenarianism about it'. Historical time, Baudrillard says, entails the belief that there is a 'succession of non-meaningless facts, each engendering the other by cause and effect, but doing so without any absolute necessity and all standing open to the future, unevenly poised' (Baudrillard, 1994a: 7). In effect this modern experience did not arise spontaneously nor was it easily adopted, for 'this model of linearity must have seemed entirely fictitious, wholly absurd and abstract to cultures which had no sense of a deferred day of reckoning ... it was, indeed, a scenario which had some difficulty in establishing itself ... was not achieved without violence' (1994a: 7).

In this sense Baudrillard's strategy provides something of an updated inversion of the law of the three states in which fetishism (as a structure and as a force) comes to dominate consumer society, even science, since scientific research 'follows' its objects as its own destiny subject to fashion. In this context a further extreme shift can occur, such that the subject becomes the fetish of the object. The three stages are again but three logics: rituality, sociality and digitality. Whereas Comte saw the triumph of science as marking the transition to a higher form of truth and thereby a new form of legitimation of the social, Baudrillard suggests that

> Not only are we no longer living in an era of rules and rituals, we are no longer living in an era of laws and contracts. We live today according to Norms and Models, and we do not even have a term to designate that which is replacing sociality and the social. (Baudrillard, 1990a: 155)

Futures

In this book I have reconstructed the main discursive formations that have developed out of the Saint-Simonian matrix. I have projected them into a single, if complex and unstable, abstract space in the manner of Comte's historical method. Whereas this space for Comte was planar, the complexity of this space arises here in the intersection of scientificity and the surrounding platforms that are its supporting and disseminating environment. Beginning at the fall of Napoleon I (end of a precursor political cycle of the Revolution itself) and ending with the fall of Napoleon III (and the defeat of the Paris Commune), was a cycle dominated by the works of Comte and Littré. In this first cycle there is the field of debate and argument within the Saint-Simonian milieux: the Saint-Simonian church (Bazard, Enfantin, feminism), the positivist society (Comte and Littré), The Religion of Humanity (Comte, Laffitte), the Sociological Society (Littré and Wybrouboff).

The period of the Third Republic, 1880–1940 (from the Commune to the fall of France) is dominated by the work of Durkheim and Mauss and, at the end of the 1930s, Bataille. With Durkheim, in this second cycle, the main focus of work is within the academy, with the formation of the 'French school' of sociology which itself in the 1890s again turned from a political to a religious problematic, continued after the 1914–18 war by Mauss in a more and more socialist direction. At the end of the cycle there was a last turn to the extra-mural, 'sacred college' and its 'sacred sociology' (Bataille).

The third cycle sees the reign of Marxism through three recent phases: Sartre's existential version 1945–60, structural Marxism, 1960–75, and then the 'crisis of Marxism', and postmodernism, 1975–2000. There were some key thinkers of the third cycle who themselves had a trajectory that carried them through the main stages of the entire period, through existential, then structural (with the important struggle of Althusser within the French Communist Party) and finally post-structural theory (most notably Baudrillard). In this last of the three cycles there are some writers who could be predominantly structural throughout (Lévi-Strauss), or those who refused to accept the dominance of structuralism (Sartre himself). The cycle itself witnessed a massive shift in the dominant idiom of Marxist thinking in the early 1960s: the displacement of humanist existential Marxism by structural Marxism (sometimes referred to as the '*linguistic turn*', since the heuristic model for structuralism was the structure of codes). But the 'crisis of Marxism' which arrived in the 1970s affected both idioms and led to a final displacement (sometimes called the '*cultural turn*') since there was a shift to the analysis of symbolic systems appropriate to a new scene – 'the death of the social'. In effect this was a partly conscious and partly unconscious rendezvous of the Marxist and Durkheimian (even Comtean) modes of social theory, probably most clearly visible is the 'paroxyst' (i.e. penultimate) 'radical theory' of Baudrillard.

In this perspective I examined the principal methods and theories developed at each cycle as key variations drawn from a basic matrix of Saint-Simonian ideas. Each new period has a forceful dynamic of theoretical reconfiguration and reconstruction. There is no direct continuity of thinkers between each period – no direct lineage between the Comteans still working in the 1880s and the emerging school of Durkheimian sociology; there is no direct continuity between Mauss, or the curious religiosity of the Collège de Sociologie around Bataille and Caillois, and the rising school of existential Marxism headed by Sartre and de Beauvoir which led the shift to new methods and theory in the 1940s. Within each of the three periods there is considerable continuity despite the significant shifts which are noticeable within them. Each describes a cycle of an initial period of intellectual creativity around a new programme of work. Existential Marxism was anticipated in earlier thinkers such as Lefebvre and Bataille. Comte's religious ideas were prefigured by Bazard. Durkheim's ideas were prefigured in the later sociology of Littré. But it would be wrong to say that these anticipations were simple precursors. Each of the new programmes as they got underway seemed to have great new creative momentum and sparked off new urgent debates and oppositions. Then, as obstacles are encountered and defeats to the project are experienced, new idioms of writing emerge – religious, scholastic, defensive and fragmented idioms – as utopian thought degenerates.

One way of reflecting on the current crisis of social theory is to suggest that theory will be regenerated because its basic problems are not resolved through formal bourgeois forms:

> modern, postrevolutionary suspicion founded sociology as an attempt by Auguste Comte, and by Marx, to remake otherwise (but how?) what political economy could only demolish. This remaking has not ended. Marcel Mauss, describing the gift in primitive societies as a total social phenomenon, or Georges Bataille meditating on sacrifice, both of them unreservedly opposed to calculable reciprocity, plainly continue the same concern, and each time it is sociology that assumes Penelope's impossible task: to remake, to reweave what political economy ... destroys and isolates by the cleavage that it introduces and the autonomization that it installs. (Goux and Wood, 1998: 40)

This implies the struggle to realise the demand for social justice and solidarity cannot be achieved, within a single metaphysical frame of the Enlightenment's grand narrative for bourgeois society.

French social theory from Comte and Baudrillard attempted to think the present from the point of view of a radical future. The hypertelic violence in Comte was visible to all those who wanted to construct a rational and liberal secular elite, after the death of God (Serres, 1995b: 449). Comte is not just a post-theological logothete who says in effect that the loss of the metaphysical world is a loss that 'must be ordered in order to become unconditional' (Barthes, 1976: 5). Rather, he is a logothete who transgresses the metaphysical revolution itself by closing 'the ethical circle, answering by a final vision of values ... the initial revolutionary choice' (Barthes, 1977: 77). Comte presented a social vision that was both a perfect scientific structuration and a sentimental reactionary synthesis, which opened the door to the radical and extreme right.

The radical view today is expressed by Baudrillard: 'You can always fight the global in the name of the universal. I prefer the direct confrontation between globalization and all the antagonistic singularities ... what happens may run against history, against politics' (Baudrillard, [1997] 1998a: 23). Singularity against history. The challenge to theory here asks whether a problematic, such as the Saint-Simonian, based as it is on the struggle against poverty, exploitation and anomie, can still address issues that arise in a post-industrial society dominated by hypertelic forms: problems of obesity, saturation, fetishistic individualism and extreme phenomena?

These issues threaten to take theory beyond end-of-cycle postmodernism.

Note

1 In this conclusion I have drawn from Mike Gane, 'Reading gender futures, from Comte to Baudrillard', *Social Epistemology*, (2001), vol. 14, no. 2: 77–89.

References

Alexander, J. (1995) *Fin de Siècle Social Theory*. London: Verso.

Allen, N.J. (2000) *Categories and Classifications: Maussian Reflections on the Social*. Oxford: Berghahn Books.

Allen, N., Pickering, W.S.F., and Watts Miller, W. (eds) (1998) *On Durkheim's Elementary Forms of Religious Life*. London: Routledge.

Althusser, L. (1971) *Lenin and Philosophy*. London: New Left Books.

Althusser, L. (1972) *Montesquieu, Rousseau, Marx*. London: Verso.

Althusser, L. (1976) *Essays in Self-Criticism*. London: New Left Books.

Althusser, L. (1983) 'Note on the ISAs' in Gane (1983, 455–66).

Althusser, L. (1990) *Philosophy and the Spontaneous Philosophy of the Scientists*. London: Verso.

Althusser, L. (1993) *The Future Lasts a Long Time*. London: Chatto & Windus.

Althusser, L. (1997) *The Spectre of Hegel: Early Writings*. London: Verso.

Althusser, L. and Balibar, E. (1970) *Reading Capital*. London: New Left Books.

Anderson, P. (1983) *In the Tracks of Historical Materialism*. London: Verso.

Aquarone, S. (1958) *The Life and Works of Emile Littré*. Leyden: Sythoff.

Armitage, J. (ed.) (2000) *Paul Virilio: From Modernism to Postmodernism and Beyond*. London: Sage.

Aron, R. (1964) *German Sociology*. New York: Free Press.

Aron, R. (1975) *History and the Dialectic of Violence*. Oxford: Basil Blackwell.

Atkinson, J.M. (1978) *Discovering Suicide: Studies in the Organisation of Sudden Death*. London: Macmillan.

Baehr, P. (1998) *Caesar and the Fading of the Roman World*. London: Transaction.

Bair, D. (1991) *Simone de Beauvoir: A Biography*. London: Vintage.

Barthes, R. (1967) *Elements of Semiology*. London: Cape.

Barthes, R. (1973) *Mythologies*. London: Paladin.

Barthes, R. (1976) *Sade, Loyola, Fourier*. New York: Hill & Wang.

Barthes, R. (1977) *Barthes by Barthes*. New York: Farrat, Strauss & Giroux.

Barthes, R. (1985) *The Fashion System*. London: Cape.

Bataille, G. (1985) *Visions of Excess: Selected Writings, 1929–1939*. Manchester: Manchester University Press.

Bataille, G. (1990) *Literature and Evil*. London: Marion Boyars.

Baudelot, C. and Establet, R. (1984) *Durkheim et le Suicide*. Paris: Presses Universitaires de France.

Baudrillard, J. (1975) *The Mirror of Production*. St Louis: Telos.

Baudrillard, J. (1978) *L' Ange de stuc*. Paris: Galilée.

Baudrillard, J. (1981) *For a Critique of the Political Economy of the Sign*. St Louis: Telos.

Baudrillard, J. (1983) *In the Shadow of the Silent Majorities*. New York: Semiotext(e).

Baudrillard, J (1985) *La Gauche divine*. Paris: Grasset.

Baudrillard, J. (1987) *Forget Foucault*. New York: Semiotext(e).

Baudrillard, J. (1988a) *America*. London: Verso.

Baudrillard, J (1988b) *The Ecstasy of Communication*. New York: Semiotext(e).

Baudrillard, J. (1990a) *Seduction*. London: Macmillan.

Baudrillard, J. (1990b) *Fatal Strategies*. London: Pluto.

Baudrillard, J. (1990c) *Cool Memories*. London: Verso.

Baudrillard, J. (1993a) *Baudrillard Live: Selected Interviews*. London: Routledge.

Baudrillard, J. (1993b) *Symbolic Exchange and Death*. London: Sage.
Baudrillard, J. (1993c) *The Transparency of Evil*. London: Verso.
Baudrillard, J. (1994a) *The Illusion of the End*. Cambridge: Polity.
Baudrillard, J. (1994b) *Simulacra and Simulation*. Ann Arbor: University of Michigan Press.
Baudrillard, J. (1995) *The Gulf War Did Not Take Place*. Sydney: Power.
Baudrillard, J. (1996a) *Cool Memories II*. Cambridge: Polity.
Baudrillard, J. (1996b) *The Perfect Crime*. London: Verso.
Baudrillard, J (1996c) *The System of Objects*. London: Verso.
Baudrillard, J. (1997a) *Fragments. Cool Memories III*. London: Verso.
Baudrillard, J. (1997b) *Ecran total*. Paris: Galilée.
Baudrillard, J. (1998a) *Paroxysm: Interviews with Philippe Petit*. London: Verso.
Baudrillard, J. (1998b) *The Consumer Society: Myths and Structures*. London: Sage.
Baudrillard, J. (1998c) *Car l'illusion ne s'oppose pas à la réalité*. Paris: Descartes.
Baudrillard, J. (1999) *L'Echange impossible*. Paris: Galilée.
Baudrillard, J. (2001b) *The Uncollected Baudrillard*, (ed.) G. Genosko. London: Sage.
Bauman, Z. (1992) *Intimations of Postmodernism*. London: Routledge.
Beauvoir, S. de (1948) *Ethics of Ambiguity*. New York: Citadel.
Beauvoir, S. de (1972) *The Second Sex*. London: Penguin.
Beauvoir, S. de (1977) *Old Age*. London: Penguin.
Beauvoir, S. de (1991) *Letters to Sartre*. London: Radius.
Benjamin, W. (1970) *Illuminations*. London: Cape.
Berenson, E. (1989) 'A New Religion of the Left: Christianity and Social Radicalism in France, 1815–48' in *The French Revolution and the Creation of Modern Political Culture*. F. Furet and M. Ozouf (eds), Oxford: Pergamon, vol. 3, ch. 29.
Berthelot, J-M. (1988) 'Les règles de la méthode sociologique ou l'instauration du raisonnement expérimental en sociologie' in: E. Durkheim, *Les règles de la méthode sociologique*, Paris: Flammarion.
Berthelot, J-M. (1990) *l'Intelligence du social*. Paris: Presses Universitaires de France.
Berthelot, J-M. (1991) *La construction de la sociologie*. Paris: Presses Universitaires de France.
Berthelot, J-M. (1995) *1895: Durkheim: l'avenement de la sociologie scientifique*. Toulouse: Presses Universitaires du Mirail.
Berthelot, J-M. (ed.) (2000) *La sociologie Française contemporaine*. Paris: Presses Universitaires de France.
Besnard, Philippe (ed.) (1983) *The Sociological Domain: The Durkheimians and the Founding of French Sociology*. Cambridge: Cambridge University Press.
Besnard, P. (1993) 'Les pathologies des sociétés modernes', in Besnard, P. et al., *Division du travail et lien social*. Paris: PUF, pp. 197–211.
Besnard, P., Borlandi, M., and Vogt, P. (eds) (1993) *Division du travail et lien social*. Paris: Presses Universitaires de France.
Bolt-Irons, L.A. (ed.) (1995) *On Bataille: Critical Essays*. Albany, NY: State University of New York Press.
Boudon, R. (1980) *The Crisis in Sociology: Problems of Sociological Epistemology*. London: Macmillan.
Boudon, R. (1995) 'Weber and Durkheim: beyond the differences. A common important paradigm?' in: *Revue internationale de Philosophie*, 192: 221–39.
Bouglé, C. (1904) *La démocratie devant la science*. Paris: Alcan.
Boundas, C.V. and Olkowski, D. (eds) (1993) *Gilles Deleuze and the Theater of Philosophy*. London: Routledge.
Bourdieu, P. (1958) *Sociologie de l'Algérie*. Paris: Presses Universitaires de France.
Bourdieu, P. (1977) *Outline of a Theory of Practice*. Cambridge: Cambridge University Press.
Bourdieu, P. (1979) *The Inheritors. French Students and their Relation to Culture*. London/Chicago: University of Chicago Press.
Bourdieu, P. (1984) *Distinction: A Social Critique of the Judgement of Taste*. London: Routledge & Kegan Paul.
Bourdieu, P. (1988) *Homo Academicus*. Cambridge: Polity Press.

Bourdieu, P. (1990a) *The Logic of Practice*. Cambridge: Polity Press.

Bourdieu, P. (1990b) *Reproduction in Education, Society and Culture*. London: Sage.

Bourdieu, P. (1996) *The State Nobility. Elite Schools in the Field of Power*. Cambridge: Polity.

Bourdieu, P. (1998) *Acts of Resistance*. Cambridge: Polity Press.

Bourdieu, P. (2001) *Masculine Domination*. Cambridge: Polity Press.

Bourdieu, P. et al. (1991) *The Craft of Sociology: Epistemological Preliminaries*. New York: de Gruyter.

Brooks, J. (1998) *The Eclectic Legacy: Academic Philosophy and the Human Sciences in Nineteenth Century France*. London: Associated University Presses.

Burchell, G., Gordon, C. and Miller, P. (eds) (1991) *The Foucault Effect*. London: Harvester Wheatsheaf.

Canguilhem, G. (1975) *La connaissance de la vie*. Paris: Vrin.

Canguilhem, G. (1983) *Etudes d'histoire et de la philosophie des sciences*. Paris: Vrin.

Canguilhem, G. (1988) *Ideology and Rationality in the History of the Life Sciences*. Cambridge, Mass: MIT Press.

Canguilhem, G. (1989) *The Normal and the Pathological*. New York: Zone Books.

Canguilhem, G. (1994) *A Vital Rationalist. Selected Writings from Georges Canguilhem*. New York: Zone Books.

Canguilhem, H. (1998) 'The Decline of the Idea of Progress', *Economy and Society* 27 (2&3): 313–29.

Caputo, J. (1997) *The Prayers and Tears of Jacques Derrida: Religion without Religion*. Bloomington, Indiana: Indiana University Press.

Carlisle, R.B. (1987) *The Proffered Crown: Saint-Simonianism and the Doctrine of Hope*. Baltimore: Johns Hopkins University Press.

Charlton, D.G. (1959) *Positivist Thought in France during the Second Empire*. Westport, Co: Greenwood Press.

Charlton, D.G. (1974) 'French thought in the nineteenth and twentieth centuries' in D.C. Potts and D.G. Charlton, *French Thought since 1600*, London: Methuen, pp. 41–86.

Chatelet, F. (ed.) (1973) *Histoire de la philosophie: le xxe siècle*. Paris: Hachette.

Clarke, T. (1973) *Prophets and Patrons: The French University and the Emergence of the Social Sciences*. Cambridge, Mass.: Harvard University Press.

Clément, C. and Kristeva, K. (2001) *The Feminine and the Sacred*. London: Palgrave.

Cohen, D. (1965) 'Comte's changing sociology', *American Journal of Sociology* lxxi: 168–77.

Cohen-Solal, A. (1988) *Sartre: A Life*. London: Heinemann.

Comte, A. (1891) *The Catechism of Positivism*. London.

Comte A. [1844] (1903) *A Discourse on the Positive Spirit*. London: William Reeves.

Comte, A. (1856) *Synthése Subjective*. Paris: Dalmont.

Comte A. (1878) *The Religion of Humanity*, ed. R. Congreve. London: Kegan Paul.

Comte, A. (1889) *Appeal to Conservatives*. London: Trübner & Sons.

Comte, A. (1910) *Confessions and Testament of Auguste Comte and his Correspondence with Clotilde de Vaux*, ed. A. Crompton. Liverpool: Henry Young & Sons, pp. 349–57.

Comte, A. (1968) [1875–7] *A System of Positive Polity*, 4 vols. First edn London: Longmans [1875–7]. Reprinted in New York (1968): B. Franklin.

Comte, A. (1974a) *Crisis of Industrial Civilization*. London: Heinemann.

Comte, A. (1974b) *The Positive Philosophy*. New York: AMS Press.

Comte, A. (1975) *Cours de philosophie positive*, 2 vols. Paris: Hermann.

Comte, A. (1998) *Early Political Writings*, ed. H.S. Jones. Cambridge.

Cuin, Charles-Henri (ed.) (1997) *Durkheim d'un siècle a l'autre*. Paris: Presses Universitaires de France.

Culler, J. (1975) *Structuralist Poetics*. London: Routledge & Kegan Paul.

Culler, J. (2002) *Barthes: a Very Short Introduction*. Oxford: Oxford University Press.

Cunliffe, J. and Reeve, A. (1996) 'Exploitation: the Original Saint-Simonian Account', *Capital and Class* 59: 61–80.

Cushman, T. and Mestrovic, S. (eds) (1996) *This Time We Knew*. New York: Columbia University Press.

Dagognet, F. (1997) *Georges Canguilhem: philosophie de la vie*. Le Plessis-Robinson: Synthélabo pour la progrès de la connaissance.

Debray, R. (1983) *Critique of Political Reason*. London: Verso.

Deleuze, G. (1973) 'A quoi reconnaît-on le structuralisme?' in F. Chatelet, *Histoire de la philosophie*. Paris: Hachetle, pp. 299–343.

Deleuze, G. (1995) *Negotiations 1972–1990*. New York: Columbia University Press.

Deleuze, G. and Guattari, F. (1977) *Anti-Oedipus: Capitalism and Schizophrenia*. New York: Viking.

Deleuze, G. and Guattari, F. (1988) *A Thousand Plateaus: Capitalism and Schizophrenia*. London: Athlone Press.

Deleuze, G. and Guattari, F. (1994) *What is Philosophy*? Cambridge: Cambridge University Press.

Derrida, J. (1981) *Positions*. Chicago: Chicago University Press.

Derrida, J. (1994) *Specters of Marx*. London: Routledge.

Derrida, J. (2001) *The Work of Mourning*. Chicago: University of Chicago Press.

Descombes, V. (1980) *Modern French Philosophy*. Cambridge: Cambridge University Press.

Deutscher, P. (1999) 'Bodies, lost and found: Simone de Beauvoir from the second sex to old age', *Radical Philosophy*, 96: 6–16.

Dews, P. (1987) *Logics of Disintegration*. London: Verso.

Dillon, W. (1968) *Gifts and Nations*. The Hague: Mouton.

Douglas, J. (1967) *The Social Meanings of Suicide*. Princeton, NJ: Princeton University Press.

Dubar, C. (1969) 'La méthode de Marcel Mauss', *Revue Française de Sociologie*, x: 515–21.

Dunn, J. (ed.) (1995) *Contemporary Crisis of the Nation State*? Oxford: Blackwell.

Durkheim, Emile (1915) *'Germany Above All': German Mentality and War*. Paris: Armand Colin.

Durkheim, E. et al. (1960) *Essays on Sociology and Philosophy*. New York: Harper.

Durkheim, E. (1953) *Sociology and Philosophy*. London: Cohen & West.

Durkheim, E. (1962) *Socialism and Saint-Simon*. New York: Collier.

Durkheim, E. (1964) *The Division of Labour in Society*. London: Collier.

Durkheim, E. (1970) *Suicide*. London: Routledge.

Durkheim, E. (1973) *Moral Education*. London: Collier.

Durkheim, E. (1975a) *Textes*, ed. V. Karady. Paris: Editions de Minuit.

Durkheim, E. (1975b) *Durkheim on Religion*, ed. W.S.F. Pickering. London: Routledge.

Durkheim, E. (1977) *The Evolution of Educational Thought in France*. London: Routledge & Kegan Paul.

Durkheim, E. (1978) *Durkheim on Institutional Analysis*, ed. M. Traugott. Chicago: University of Chicago Press.

Durkheim, E. (1980) *Emile Durkheim: Contributions to L'Année Sociologique*, ed. Y. Nandan. New York: Free Press.

Durkheim, E. (1982) *The Rules of Sociological Method*. London: Macmillan.

Durkheim, E. (1983) *Durkheim and the Law*. Edited and introduced by S. Lukes and A. Scull. Oxford: Martin Robertson.

Durkheim, Emile (1988) Les règles de la méthode sociologique, ed. J-M. Berthelot. Paris: Flammarion.

Durkheim, Emile (1992) *Professional Ethics and Civic Morals*. London: Routledge.

Durkheim, Emile (1995) *The Elementary Forms of the Religious life*. Oxford: Oxford University Press.

Durkheim, Emile (1996) 'Cours de philosophie fait au Lycée de Sens en 1883–84' in: *Durkheimian Studies* vol. 2, ns.: pp. 5–30.

Durkheim, Emile (1997) 'French rebut Germany's bad faith', in: *Durkheimian Studies*, vol. 3, ns., pp. 3–10.

Elbow, M. (1953) *French Corporative Theory*. New York: Columbia University Press.

Elias, N. (1978) *What is Sociology*? London: Hutchinson.

Elliot, G. (1987) *Althusser: The Detour of Theory*. London: Verso.

Elliot, A. and Turner, B. (eds) (2001) *Profiles in Contemporary Social Theory*. London: Sage.

Engels, F. (1943) *Anti-Dürhing*. London: Lawrence & Wishart.

Fanon, F. (1967) *The Wretched of the Earth*. Harmondsworth: Penguin.

Fanon, F. (1970) *Toward the African Revolution*. Harmondsworth: Penguin.
Ffrench, P. (1995) *The Time of Theory: a History of Tel Quel (1960–1983)*. Oxford: Clarendon Press.
Foucault, M. (1970) *The Order of Things*. London: Tavistock.
Foucault, M. (1972) *The Archaeology of Knowledge*. London: Tavistock.
Foucault, M. (1977) *Language, Counter-Memory, Practice*. New York: Cornell University Press.
Foucault, M. (1985) *The Use of Pleasure*. London: Penguin.
Foucault, M. (1991) *The Birth of the Clinic*. London: Routledge.
Foucault, M. (1997) *Essential Works of Foucault. vol 1. Ethics*. London: Penguin.
Foucault, M. (1999) *Religion and Culture*. Manchester: Manchester University Press.
Fournier, M. (1994) *Marcel Mauss*. Paris: Fayard.
Fraser, C.G. (1990) 'Lagrange's analytical mathematics, its Cartesian origins and reception in Comte's positive philosophy', *Studies in History and Philosophy of Science*, 21 (June): 243–56.
Frick, J-P. (1988) 'Le problème du pouvoir chez A. Comte et la signification de sa philosophie politique', *Revue Philosophique* 3: 271–301.
Frow, J. (1987) 'Accounting for tastes: some problems in Bourdieu's sociology of culture', *Cultural Studies*, 1 (1): 59–73.
Fullbrook, K. and Fullbrook, E. (1993) *Simone de Beauvoir and Jean-Paul Sartre. The Remaking of a Twentieth-Century Legend*. London and New York: Harvester Wheatsheaf.
Furedi, F. (1992) *Mythical Past, Elusive Future*. London: Pluto.
Furet, F. (1992) *Revolutionary France: 1770–1880*. Oxford: Blackwell.
Gane, M. (1983) 'On the ISAs Episode', *Economy and Society*, 12(4): 431–67.
Gane, M. (1988) *On Durkheim's Rules of Sociological Method*. London: Routledge.
Gane, M. (ed.) (1992) *The Radical Sociology of Durkheim and Mauss*. London: Routledge.
Gane, M. (1993) *Harmless Lovers? Gender, Theory and Personal Relationships*. London: Routledge.
Gane, M. (1995a) 'Unresolved Comte', *Economy and Society*, 24(1): 138–49.
Gane, M. (1995b) 'La Distinction du Normal et du Pathologique' in Borlandi et al. (eds) *Les règles de la méthode sociologique*. Paris: L'Harmattan, pp. 185–205.
Gane, M. (1997) 'Durkheim contre Comte' in H. Cuin (ed.), *La méthode Durkheimienne d'un siècle à l'autre*. Paris: Presses Universitaires de France, pp. 31–8.
Gane, M. (1999) 'In and out of (Messianic) Time', *Parallax* 5(1): 13–20.
Gane, M. (2000a) *Jean Baudrillard: In Radical Uncertainty*. London: Pluto.
Gane, M. (1991a) *Baudrillard: Critical and Fatal Theory*. London: Routledge.
Gane, M. (1991b) *Baudrillard's Bestiary: Baudrillard and Culture*. London: Routledge.
Gane, N. (2002) *Max Weber and Postmodern Theory: Rationalization versus Re-enchantment*. London Palgrave.
Gasché, R. (1995) *The Heterological Almanac*, in Boldt-Irons (ed.) On Bataille pp. 157–208.
Gellner, E. (1985) *Relativism and the Social Sciences*. Cambridge: Cambridge University Press.
Genosko, G. (1994) *Baudrillard and Signs: Signification Ablaze*. London: Routledge.
Genosko, G. (1998) *Undisciplined Theory*. London: Sage.
Genosko, G. (1999) *McLuhan and Baudrillard: The Masters of Implosion*. London: Routledge.
Gérard, A. (1970) *La révolution Française; mythes et interprétations (1789–1970)*. Paris: Flammarion.
Gorz, A. (1982) *Farewell to the Working Class*. London: Pluto.
Goux, J-J. and Wood, P. (1998) *Terror and Consensus: Vicissitudes of French Thought*. Stanford: Stanford University Press.
Grace, V. (2000) *Baudrillard's Challenge*. London: Routledge.
Grange, J. (1996) *La Philosophie d'Auguste Comte: science, politique, religion*. Paris: PUF.
Gross, N. (1996) 'A note on the sociological eye and the discovery of a new Durkheim text', *Journal of the History of the Behavioural Sciences*, 32(2): pp. 408–23.
Grosz, E. (1990) *Jacques Lacan: A Feminist Introduction*. London: Routledge.
Gutting, G. (ed.) (1994) *The Cambridge Companion to Foucault*. Cambridge: Cambridge University Press.
Gutting, G. (2001) *French Philosophy in the Twentieth Century*. Cambridge: Cambridge University Press.
Hacking, I. (1990) *The Taming of Chance*. Cambridge: Cambridge University Press.

Haines, B. (1978) 'The inter-relations between social, biological, and medical thought, 1750–1850: Saint-Simon and Comte', *British Journal for the History of Science*, 11 (March): 19–35.

Halperin, D. (1995) *Saint Foucault: A Gay Hagiography*. Oxford: Oxford University Press.

Hamilton, P. (1996) *Historicism*. London: Routledge.

Hawkins, M. (1979) 'Comte, Durkheim and the sociology of religion', *Sociological Review*, 27: 429–46.

Hawkins, M. (1981) 'Democracy and absolutism in Durkheim's political theory', *History of Political Thought*, 2: 369–90.

Hawkins, M. (1984) 'Reason and sense perception in Comte's theory of mind', *History of European Ideas*, 5: 149–63.

Hawkins, M. (1994) 'Durkheim and occupational corporations: an exegesis and interpretation', *Journal of the History of Ideas*, 55: 461–81.

Hawkins, M (1995) 'Durkheim and Republican citizenship' in: K. Thompson (ed.), *Durkheim, Europe and Democracy*, Occasional Papers 3, Oxford: British Centre for Durkheimian Studies.

Hayek, F.A. (1952) *The Counter-Revolution of Science: Studies in the Abuse of Reason*. Glencoe, Illinois: Free Press.

Hayward, J. (1960) 'Solidaristic syndicalism: Durkheim and Duguit', *Sociological Review*, 8: 17–36.

Hayward, J. (1991) *After the French Revolution: Six Critics of Democracy and Nationalism*. New York: New York University Press.

Hegarty, P. (2000) *Georges Bataille*. London: Sage.

Hegel, W. (1952) *Philosophy of Right*. Oxford: Clarendon Press.

Heilbron, J. (1990) 'Auguste Comte and modern epistemology', *Sociological Theory*, 8 (Fall): 153–62.

Heilbron, J. (1995) *The Rise of Social Theory*. Cambridge: Polity Press.

Hollier, D. (ed.) (1988) *The College of Sociology*. Minneapolis: University of Minnesota Press.

Hollier, D. (1992) *Against Architecture: The Writings of Georges Bataille*. Cambridge, Mass.: MIT Press.

Honneth, A. (1986) 'The fragmented world of symbolic forms', *Theory Culture and Society*, 3: 55–66.

Iggers, G. (ed.) (1972) *The Doctrine of Saint-Simon: An Exposition*. New York: Schocken.

Irigaray, L. (1993) *Je, tu, nous. Toward a Culture of Difference*. London: Routledge.

Jenkins, R. (1992) *Pierre Bourdieu*. London: Routledge.

Joly, D. (1991) *The French Communist Party and the Algerian War*. London: MacMillan.

Jones, R.A. and Anservitz, R.M. (1975) 'Saint-Simon and Saint-Simonism: A Weberian View', *American Journal of Sociology*, 80 (5): 1095–123.

Kaplan, E. and Sprinker, M. (eds) (1993) *The Althusserian Legacy*. London: Verso.

Kaplan, R. (1995) *Forgotten Crisis: The Fin-de-Siècle Crisis of Democracy in France*. Oxford: Berg.

Knights, B. (1978) *The Idea of the Clerisy in the Nineteenth Century*. Cambridge: Cambridge University Press.

Kofman, S. (1978) *Aberrations: Le devenir-femme d'Auguste Comte*. Paris: Flammarion.

Kofman (1996) *Edgar Morin*. London: Pluto.

Kolakowski, L. (1972) *Positivist Philosophy*. London: Penguin.

Kremer-Marietti, A. (1982) *Entre le signe et l'histoire: l'anthropologie d'Auguste Comte*. Paris: Klincksieck.

Kristeva, J. (1977) *About Chinese Women*. London: Marion Boyars.

Kristeva, J. (1982) *The Powers of Horror: an Essay on Abjection*. New York: Columbia University Press.

Kristeva, J. (1986) *The Kristeva Reader*, (ed.) T. Moi. Oxford: Blackwell.

Kristeva, J. (1992) 'Julia Kristeva' in: D. Jones and R. Stoneman, (eds) Talking Liberties. London: Channel Four Books, pp. 15–20.

Kroker, A. (1992) *The Possessed Individual: Technology and Postmodernism*. London: Macmillan.

Kumar, K. (1978) *Prophecy and Progress*. Harmondsworth: Penguin.

Lacroix, B. (1981) *Durkheim et le politique*. Quebec: Presses de Université de Montréal.

Lash, S. (1990) *Sociology of Postmodernism*. London: Routledge.

Latour, B. (1987) 'The Enlightenment without critique: a word on Michel Serres' philosophy' in P. Griffiths (ed.) *Contemporary French Philosophy*. Cambridge: Cambridge University Press, pp. 83–97.

Latour, B. (1999) *Pandora's Hope*. London: Harvard University Press.

Laudan, L. (1971) 'Towards a reassessment of Comte's "méthode positive"', *Philosophy of Science*, 38 (March): 35–53.

Leclercle, J-J. (2001) 'Pragmatists of the world unite!', *Radical Philosophy*, 109: 36–38.

Lecourt, D. (1977) *Proletarian Science? The Case of Lysenko*. London: Verso.

Lecourt, D. (2001) *The Mediocracy: French Philosophy since the Mid-1970s*. London: Verso.

Lepenies, W. (1988) *Between Literature and Science: The Rise of Sociology*. Cambridge: Cambridge University Press.

Lévi-Strauss, C. (1967) *The Scope of Anthropology*. London: Cape.

Lévi-Strauss, C. (1969) *Totemism*. Harmondsworth: Penguin.

Lévi-Strauss, C. (1987) *Introduction to the Work of Marcel Mauss*. London: Routledge.

Lewisholm, D. (1972) 'Mill and Comte on the methods of social science', *Journal of the History of Ideas*, 33: 315–24.

Littré, E. (1864a) 'Préface d'un disciple' in: *Auguste Comte et la philosophie positive*, 2nd edition, Paris: Hachette.

Littré, E. (1864b) *Auguste Comte et la philosophie positive*. Paris: Hachette.

Littré. E. (1879) *Conservation, révolution et positivisme*. 2nd edition. Paris: Ladrange.

Lukes, S. (1969) 'Durkheim's "Individualism and the Intellectuals"', *Political Studies*, xvii: 14–30.

Lukes, S. (1973) *Emile Durkheim*. London: Allen Lane.

Lyotard, J-F. (1957) 'Note sur le Marxisme' in A. Weber and D. Huissman (eds) *Tableaux de la Philosophie Contemperaine de 1850 à 1957*. Paris: Fischbacher.

Lyotard, J-F. (1984) *The Postmodern Condition*. Manchester: Manchester University Press.

Lyotard, J-F. (1986) 'Complexity and the sublime' in *Postmodernism*. ed. L. Appignanesi. London: ICA, pp. 10–12.

Lyotard, J-F. (1988) *Peregrinations*. New York: Columbia Press.

Lyotard, J-F. (1989a) *The Lyotard Reader*, Oxford: Blackwells.

Lyotard, J-F. (1989b) *La Guerre des Algeriens*, Paris: Galilée.

Lyotard, J-F. (1991) *Phenomenology*, New York: State University of New York Press.

Lyotard, J-F. (1993a) *Libinal Economy*. London: Athlone Press.

Lyotard, J-F. (1993b) *Political Writings*. London: UCL Press.

Macciocchi, M. (1973) *Letters from Inside the Italian Communist Party to Louis Althusser*. London: New Left Books.

Macherey, P. (1964) La Philosophie de la Science de George Canguilhem. In *La Pensée*, no. 113: 50–4.

Macherey, P. (1989) *Comte: La philosophie et les sciences*. Paris: Presses Universitaires de France.

Macksey, R. and Donato, E. (1972) *The Structuralist Controversy*. Baltimore: Johns Hopkins University Press.

Maffesoli, M. (1993) *The Shadow of Dionysus: A Contribution to the Sociology of the Orgy*. New York: State University of New York Press.

Maffesoli, M. (1996) *The Time of the Tribes*. London: Sage.

Majastre, J.O. (ed.) (1996) *Sans oublier Baudrillard*. Brussels: La Lettre Volée.

Marcel, J.C. (2001) *Le Durkheimism dans l'entre-deux-guerres*. Paris: Presses Universitaires de France.

Marx-Scouras, D. (1996) *The Cultural Politics of Tel Quel*. Pennsylvannia: Pennsylvania State University Press.

Mauss, M. (1966) *The Gift*. London: Cohen & West.

Mauss, M. (1983) 'An intellectual portrait' in: P. Besnard et al. (eds) *The Sociological Domain*. Cambridge University Press: Cambridge. pp. 139–51.

Mauss, M. (1992) 'A sociological assessment of Bolshevism (1924–5)', in M. Gane (ed.), *The Radical Sociology of durkheim and Mauss*. London: Routledge, pp. 165–225.

Mauss, M. (1997) *Écrits Politiques*, ed. M. Fournier. Paris: Fayard.

Mauss, M. (2001) *A General Theory of Magic*. London: Routledge.
Merleau-Ponty, M. (1974) *Adventures of the Dialectic*. London: Heinemann.
Merquior, J.G. (1986) *From Prague to Paris*. London: Verso.
Michel, J. (ed.) (1991) *La Nécessité de Claude Bernard*. Paris: Klincksieck.
Milbank, J. (1993) *Theology and Social Theory*. Oxford: Blackwell.
Mill, J.S. (1961) *Auguste Comte and Positivism*. Ann Arbor: University of Michigan Press.
Mill, J.S. (1973) *A System of Logic*, 2 vols. Toronto: University of Toronto Press.
Moses, C.G. (1982) 'Saint-Simonian men/Saint-Simonian women'. *Journal of Modern History*, 54 (June) 240–67.
Moses, C.G. and Rabine, L.W. (1993) *Feminism, Socialism and French Romanticism*. Bloomington: Indiana University Press.
Mucchielli, L. (1998) *La découverte du social: naissance de la sociologie en France*. Paris: La Découverte.
Muglioni, J. (1995) *Auguste Comte*. Paris: Kime.
Nandan, Y. (1977) *The Durkheimian School*. London: Greenwood Press.
Nietzsche, F. (1982) *Daybreak*. Cambridge: Cambridge University Press.
Nye, R. (1982) 'Heredity, pathology and psychoneurosis in Durkheim's early work', *Knowledge and Society*, 4: 103–42.
Pankhurst, R.K.P. (1957) *The Saint Simonians, Mill and Carlyle*. London: Sidgwick & Jackson.
Pefanis, J. (1991) *Heterology and the Postmodern: Bataille, Baudrillard and Lyotard*. Durham, North Carolina: Duka University Press.
Petit, A. (1991) 'La révolution occidental selon Auguste Comte: Entre l'histoire et l'utopie', *Revue de Synthèse*, (Jan–March): 21–40.
Pickering, M. (1993) *Auguste Comte: An Intellectual Biography*, vol. I. Cambridge: Cambridge University Press.
Pickering, M. (1997) 'Rhetorical strategies in the works of Auguste Comte', *Historical Reflections/Réflexions Historiques*, 23(2): 151–7.
Pickering, W.F,S. (1984) *Durkheim's Sociology of Religion: Themes and Theories*. London: Routledge & Kegan Paul.
Pickering, W.S.F. and Martins, Herminio (1994) *Debating Durkheim*. London: Routledge.
Pickering, W.S.F. and Walford, G. (eds) *Durkheim's Suicide: A Century of Research and Debate*. London: Routledge.
Pope, W. (1976) *Durkheim's Suicide: A Classic Analysed*. Chicago: University of Chicago Press.
Popper, R. (1960) *Poverty of Historicism*. London: Routledge and Kegan Paul.
Poster, M. (1975) *Existential Marxism in Postwar France: From Sartre to Althusser*. Princeton, NJ: Princeton University Press.
Ray, L. (1999) *Theorizing Classical Sociology*. Buckingham: Open University Press.
Renard, G. (1996) l'Epistémologie chez Georges Canguilhem. Paris: Nathan.
Rey, A. (1970) *Littré: l'humaniste et les mots*. Paris: Gallimard.
Richter, M. (1995) *The History of Political and Social Concepts*. Oxford: Oxford University Press.
Ritzer, G. (1997) *Postmodern Social Theory*. New York: McGraw-Hill.
Ritzer, G. and Smart, B. (eds) (2001) *Handbook of Social Theory*. London: Sage.
Robbins, D. (1991) *The Work of Pierre Bourdieu*. Milton Keynes: Open University Press.
Rojek, C. and Turner, B. (eds) (1993) *Forget Baudrillard*? London: Routledge.
Rojek, C. and Turner, B. (eds) (1998) *The Politics of Jean-Francois Lyotard*. London: Routledge.
Rousseau, J-J. (1968) *The Social Contract*. Harmondsworth: Penguin.
Saint-Simon, H. (1964) *Social Organisation, the Science of Man and Other Writings*. ed. F. Markham. New York: Harper.
Saint-Simon, H. (1975) *Henri Saint-Simon (1750–1825)*. ed. K. Taylor. London: Croom Helm.
Sartre, J.P. (1947) *Situations, I*. Paris: Gallimard.
Sartre, J.P. (1957a) *Being and Nothingness*. London: Methuen.
Sartre, J.P. (1957b) *Transcendence of the Ego*. New York: Farrar.
Sartre, J.P. (1963) *The Problem of Method*. London: Methuen.
Sartre, J.P. (1971) 'Replies to structuralism', *Telos*, 9: 110–6.
Sartre, J.P. (1973) [1948] *Existentialism and Humanism*. London: Methuen.

Sartre, J.P. (1978) *Critique of Dialectical Reason I. Theory of Practical Ensembles*. London: New Left Books.
Sartre, J.P. (1991) *Critique of Dialectical Reason II: The Intelligibility of History*. London: Verso.
Sartre, J.P. (2001) *Colonialism and Neocolonialism*. London: Routledge.
Scharff, R. (1995) *Comte after Positivism*. Cambridge: Cambridge University Press.
Schmaus, W. (1982) 'A reappraisal of Comte's three-state law', *History and Theory*, 21(2): 248–66.
Schmaus, W. (1985) 'Hypotheses and historical analysis in Durkheim's sociological methodology: A Comtean tradition', *Studies in History and Philosophy of Science*, 6 (March): 1–30.
Schmaus, W. (1994) *Durkheim's Philosophy of Science and the Sociology of Knowledge*. Chicago: University of Chicago Press.
Schwarzer, A. (1984) *Simone de Beauvoir Today*. London: Chatto & Windus.
Sernin, A. (1985) *Alain: un sage dans la cité*. Paris: Laffont.
Serres, M. (1995a) *The Natural Contract*. Ann Arbor, Michigan: Michigan University Press.
Serres, M. (ed.) (1995b) A *History of Scientific Thought*. Oxford: Blackwell.
Serres, M. (1997) *The Troubadour of Knowledge*. Ann Arbor, Michigan: University of Michigan Press.
Serres, M. and Latour B. (1996) *Conversations on Science, Culture and Time*. Ann Arbor, Michigan: Michigan University Press.
Shields, R. (1999) *Lefevre, Love and Struggles: Spatial Dialectics*. London: Routledge.
Shilling, C. and Mellor, P. (2001) *The Sociological Ambition*. London: Sage.
Simon, W.M. (1963) *European Positivism in the Nineteenth Century*. Ithaca, New York: Cornell University Press.
Sokal, A. and Bricmont, J. (1998) *Intellectual Impostures*. London: Profile Books.
Stanton, D. (ed.) (1984) *The Female Autograph*. Chicago: University of Chicago Press.
Stanton, D. (1987) *The Female Autograph*. Chicago: Chicago University Press.
Starobinski, J. (1979): *Words upon Words: The Anagrams of Ferdinand Saussure*. New Haven, Colorado: Yale University Press.
Stearns, W. and Chaloupka, W. (eds) (1992) *Jean Baudrillard: The Disappearance of Art and Politics*. London: Macmillan.
Stone, G. and Farberman, H. (1967) 'On the edge of rapprochement: was Durkheim moving towards the perspective of symbolic interaction?', *Sociological Quarterly*, 8: 149–64.
Strenski, I. (1997) *Durkheim and the Jews of France*. Chicago: University of Chicago Press.
Surya, M. (1987) *Georges Bataille: la mort à l'oeuvre*. Paris: Séguier.
Tarot, C. (1999) *De Durkheim à Mauss: l'invention du symbolique*. Paris: La Découverte.
Thomas à Kempis (1997) *The Imitation of Christ*. Oxford: Oxford University Press.
Thody, P. (1989) *French Caesarism from Napoleon I to Charles de Gaulle*. London: Macmillan.
Traugott, M. (ed.) (1978) *Durkheim on Institutional Analysis*. Chicago: University of Chicago Press.
Turner, S. (ed.) (1993) *Emile Durkheim: Sociologist and Moralist*. London: Routledge.
Vernon, R. (1984) 'Auguste Comte and the withering-away of the state', *Journal of the History of Ideas*, 45: 549–66.
Vernon, R. (1986) 'The political self: Auguste Comte and phrenology', *History of European Ideas*, 7: 271–86.
Virilio, P. (1984) *l'Horizon négatif*. Paris: Galilée.
Virilio, P. (1991) *The Aesthetics of Disappearance*. New York: Semiotext(e).
Virilio, P. and Brausch, M. (1997) Voyage d'hiver: entretiens. Paris: Parentheses.
Virilio, P. and Lotringer, S. (1997) [1983] *Pure War*. New York: Semiotext(e).
Wallerstein, E. (1991) *Unthinking Social Science*. Cambridge: Polity Press.
Wallwork, E. (1984) 'Religion and social structure in *The Division of Labor, American Anthropologist*, 86(1): 43–64.
Warnock, G.J. (1969) *English Philosophy since 1900*. London: Oxford University Press.
Wernick, A. (2001) *Auguste Comte and the Religion of Humanity*. Cambridge: Cambridge University Press.
Yamamoto, T. (ed.) (1998) *Philosophical Designs for a Socio-Cultural Transformation*. Boulder, Colorado: Rowman & Littlefield.
Zizek, S. (1999) *The Ticklish Subject: the Absent Centre of Political Ontology*. London: Verso.
Zizek, S. (2001) *Did Somebody Say Totalitarianism? Five Interventions in the (Mis)Use of a Notion*. London: Verso.

Name Index

Subject Index